AF599147

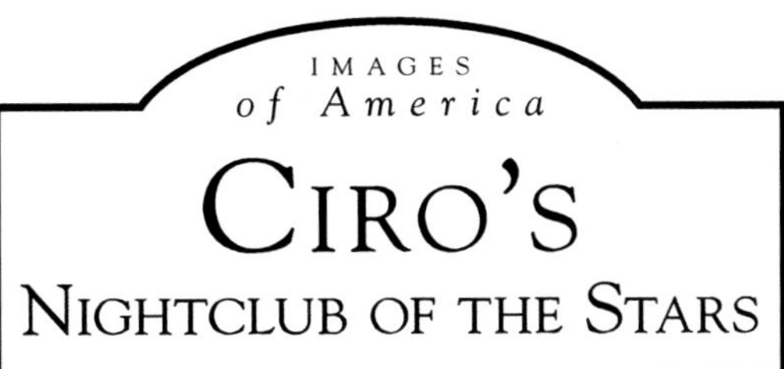
IMAGES
of America
CIRO'S
NIGHTCLUB OF THE STARS

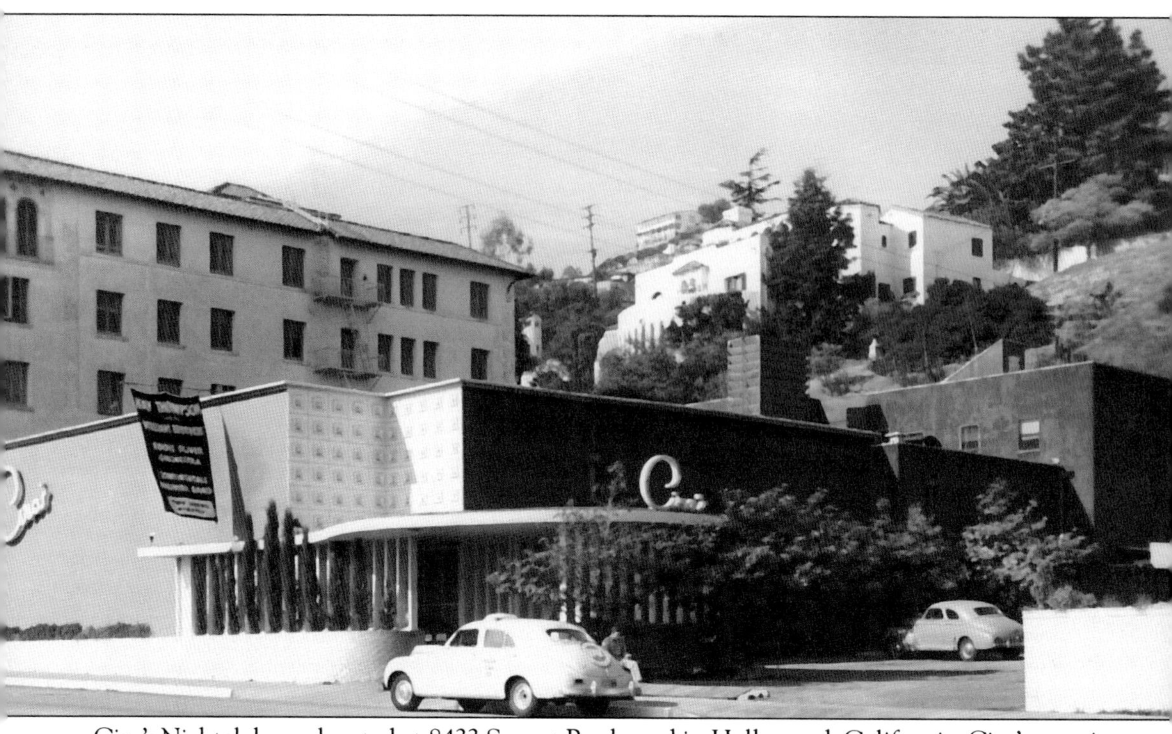

Ciro's Nightclub was located at 8433 Sunset Boulevard in Hollywood, California. Ciro's exterior, as seen here, was unassuming, but the baroque interior created a luxurious atmosphere for its patrons. Originally, Ciro's was owned and operated by W.R. Wilkerson. Herman Hover took over management and later purchased Ciro's. The nightclub was wildly popular during the 1940s–1950s. In 1972, it became the home to the Comedy Store nightclub. (Courtesy of Regina Denton-Drew.)

On the Cover: Many stars frequented Ciro's Nightclub, where they dined with friends, family, and other actors. Pictured on the front cover is Peter Lawford (third from the left), who was a popular actor of film and television from the 1940s through the 1960s. Iconic comedic actress Lucille Ball (front right) was the first female studio executive, best known for her hit television series *I Love Lucy*, which aired for six seasons. (Courtesy of Regina Denton-Drew.)

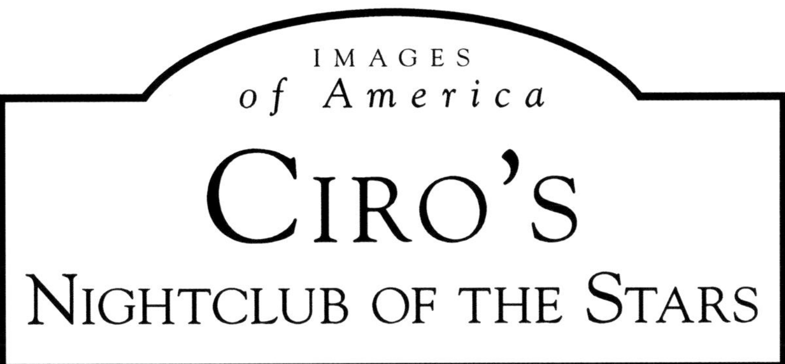

Andra D. Clarke and Regina Denton-Drew

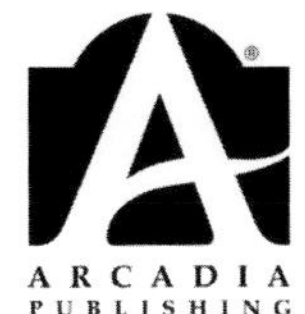

ISBN 978-1-4671-3379-1

Published by Arcadia Publishing
Charleston, South Carolina

Printed in the United States of America

Library of Congress Control Number: 2015951449

For all general information, please contact Arcadia Publishing:
Telephone 843-853-2070
Fax 843-853-0044
E-mail sales@arcadiapublishing.com
For customer service and orders:
Toll-Free 1-888-313-2665

Visit us on the Internet at www.arcadiapublishing.com

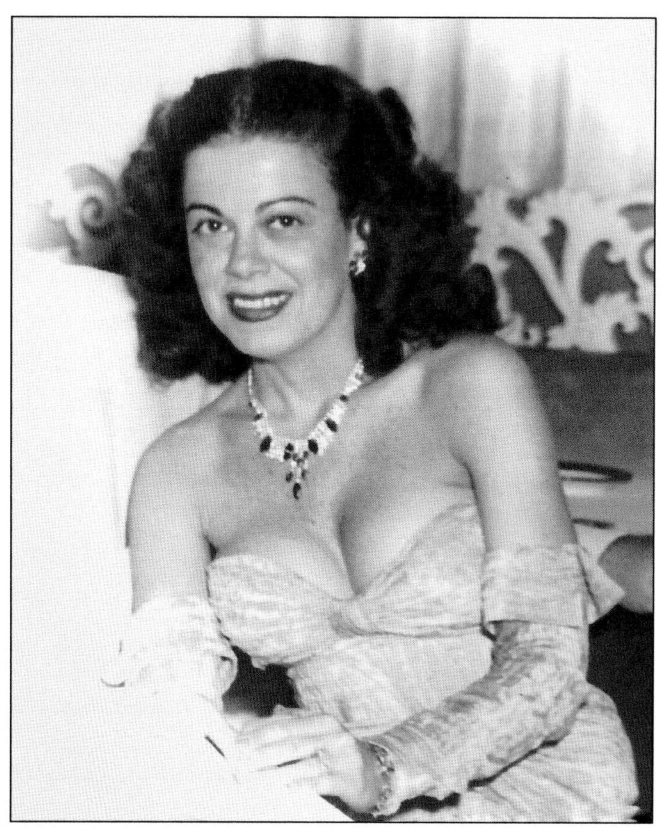

This book is dedicated to the memory of Nancy Caporal (pictured), a happy, beautiful friend who always had a sweet smile for everyone.

Contents

Acknowledgments

This book is the brainchild of my mother, Regina Denton, now deceased. It was her dream to create a book highlighting Ciro's, which was her favorite place of employment during a favorite time in her life.

Many people believed in this project from its inception over a decade ago and have helped contribute along the way. The format has changed and the person spearheading the project has changed, but the heart of the project and content have never wavered.

I have a heart full of gratitude for the support I have received from the following people: Charlie Numark, a dear family friend who helped my mom begin this project; Sukwan Myers, who spent countless hours with me scanning pictures and creating an e-book; April Dammann, who assisted me in navigating the world of authoring and pointed me in the direction of Arcadia Publishing; Hillary Kane, who provided legal advice; Barbara Neuberg, who offered accounting advice; my kids, Riley and Cailey, and my sweet friend Jill Stephens for making a trek with me to Little Rock to help record an interview with my mom for the book. I thank also my many longtime friends, friends from church, work friends, family, and neighbors who helped edit or look over the book in its infancy and encouraged me with the project. My gratitude is owed also to Pam, Jil, Ronda, Debbie, Rebecca, and Vikki for their ongoing emotional support every step of the way. I thank my stepmom, Jennifer Denton, for her keen editing skills, and my dad; half sisters, Sam and Kim; and in-laws for their encouragement. To the well-connected Jim Gleason and the knowledgeable librarians at the Academy of Motion Picture Arts and Sciences—Kristine Krueger, Stacey Behlmer, and Elizabeth Eiben—I give thanks. I am grateful for the amazing group at Hollywood Heritage, who helped identify many stars and connected me to others who could help further. A thank-you is owed to Marc Wannamaker for his generosity, wisdom, and expertise in the golden era of Hollywood; his assistance was invaluable. I am thankful for my wonderful husband, Chauncey, who understood from the beginning how important this project was in order for me to fulfill my mom's dream, and for my brother Randy and sister Karen, as well as my mother's good friends, who will always be connected to this book through my mother. And a special thanks goes to the people at Arcadia Publishing who believed in this project and who specialize in working with novice authors who desire to remind others of magical bygone eras. Thank you all!

The images that appear in this book are, unless otherwise noted, courtesy of the personal collection of Regina Denton-Drew.

INTRODUCTION

The 1940s and 1950s were known as the golden age of Hollywood. Sunset Boulevard, referred to as the Strip, had grown from a simple road to the beach into a glittering mecca for movie stars and millionaires, with flourishing nightclubs like Cafe Trocadero, Cocoanut Grove, Mocambo, and the subject of this book, Ciro's.

Billy Wilkerson opened Ciro's in 1940 at 8433 Sunset Boulevard, on the corner of Sunset and Kings Roads. Wilkerson had enjoyed a great deal of success with the first nightclub on the Strip, Cafe Trocadero, which he opened in 1934. Wilkerson also owned and ran a very active Hollywood trade paper called the *Hollywood Reporter*. By November 1942, Wilkerson had hired Herman D. Hover to operate Ciro's and, in 1945, sold the club to Hover. The day after Christmas in 1942, Hover had a grand opening that featured Xavier Cugat's band playing to an audience that included Lana Turner, Cary Grant, Lucille Ball, Desi Arnaz, Mickey Rooney, Joe E. Lewis, Carmen Miranda, and Tony Martin, just to name a few.

Hover had the interior remodeled and added a unique 3,000-square-foot dome of soft, peach light, created to cast a flattering glow over everyone in the room. Hover purposely designed an unusually small dance floor so that his patrons would have the pleasure of rubbing shoulders with movie stars. Later, he added a second story to the building where the television talk show *Table at Ciro's* was filmed; Paul Coates hosted, interviewing celebrities. Ciro's soon became a place where celebrities came to relax, be entertained, be pampered, and be seen. It was truly the "Nightclub of the Stars" and has been called as much a part of Hollywood as the movie studios and the stars themselves.

The biggest names in the entertainment industry were featured on Ciro's neon marquee, with headliners like Sammy Davis Jr., Danny Kaye, Patti Page, Martha Raye, Billy Daniels, Mae West, Sophie Tucker, Danny Thomas, and newcomers Dean Martin and Jerry Lewis. Bleachers were set up after the Academy Awards or a major premiere so that fans could get a good look at their favorite stars as they stepped out of their limousines and were ushered into Ciro's while press cameras flashed and reporters vied for a spontaneous interview.

At 8:00 p.m., the main room, which seated 500 people, began to fill for those who wanted to see the 10:00 p.m. show. Attendees enjoyed a leisurely, full course dinner costing between $3.75 and $5, with most drinks at $1. The main room had a $1.50 cover charge, while the lounge carried no cover charge. Often, the banquet room would have to be opened to seat an additional 150 guests, who could still enjoy a good view of the dance floor and stage. By 9:30 p.m., most of the celebrities had made their grand entrances and were seated at ringside. The show would last about one hour and 45 minutes and would finish only a few minutes before a new group of celebrities, rising stars, socialites, and average folks moved in for the midnight show. Men wore shirts, ties, and jackets, and women dressed in formal wear. The very wealthy would go to Ciro's for their birthdays and anniversaries; private parties could be reserved in the main room.

In 1945, and for three years thereafter, Hover devoted every other Sunday to treating wounded veterans to dinner and a show, free of charge. This became known as "Hero's at Ciro's." Many well-known entertainers volunteered to perform. Occasionally, Saturday afternoons would be devoted to children; they would be entertained, eat sandwiches, and enjoy soda.

Ciro's and the Strip peaked by the mid-1950s, before big-money and big-name entertainers moved on in order to work in various venues in Las Vegas. The Vegas casinos were paying higher wages for entertainers, more than Hover could afford. By December 1957, almost 15 years to the day the club was opened, Hover locked the latch on Ciro's nightclub forever. Hover passed away in April 1996 at the age of 88.

A Cigarette Girl's Memories

My first night at Ciro's, in 1949, was the opening night for Dean Martin and Jerry Lewis. It was an exciting evening with a star-filled audience; the new duo "brought down the house." Dick Stabile, a great saxophonist, was their bandleader and also the house band for Ciro's.

Another night, I recall the Will Mastin Trio, starring Sammy Davis Jr., opening at Ciro's for the first time. The audience would not let him off the stage. Although Sammy had been in showbiz for years, Ciro's was his big break. I remember when Sammy returned to Ciro's, after losing an eye in an automobile accident, to a packed audience of friends and fans. He was, without a doubt, the greatest performer I had ever seen.

I remember the night the shah of Iran came in with his entourage. The shah told Mr. Hover he would like to meet me and another cigarette girl, Gloria. After the Secret Service interviewed us, we met him. It was an honor.

I also remember the night the audience was filled with stars. Many of them got up and performed impromptu, Al Jolson and Judy Garland among them. What a show!

In 1953, the nominations for *From Here to Eternity* were held at Ciro's. I took pictures of the nominated stars that night, and the movie won an Oscar that year.

I remember the night Barbara Eden was discovered in the chorus line by an executive from 20th Century Fox. Barbara went on to act in the television hit *I Dream of Jeannie* and many movies.

I remember the night Ciro's owner Herman Hover took me to hear singer Frankie Laine, who was appearing at the Pasadena Auditorium. Hover decided to book him at Ciro's.

There was the memorable night Alan Young brought a huge lion into Ciro's. Jackie the Lion was the star in the movie *Androcles and the Lion*. I stood face-to-face with him for a photo shoot.

Working in a posh, world-famous club, seeing the world's greatest performers and shows, and meeting so many stars and fascinating people were memorable years for me. I will always treasure these memories and the special time when I worked at Ciro's.

—Reggie Denton

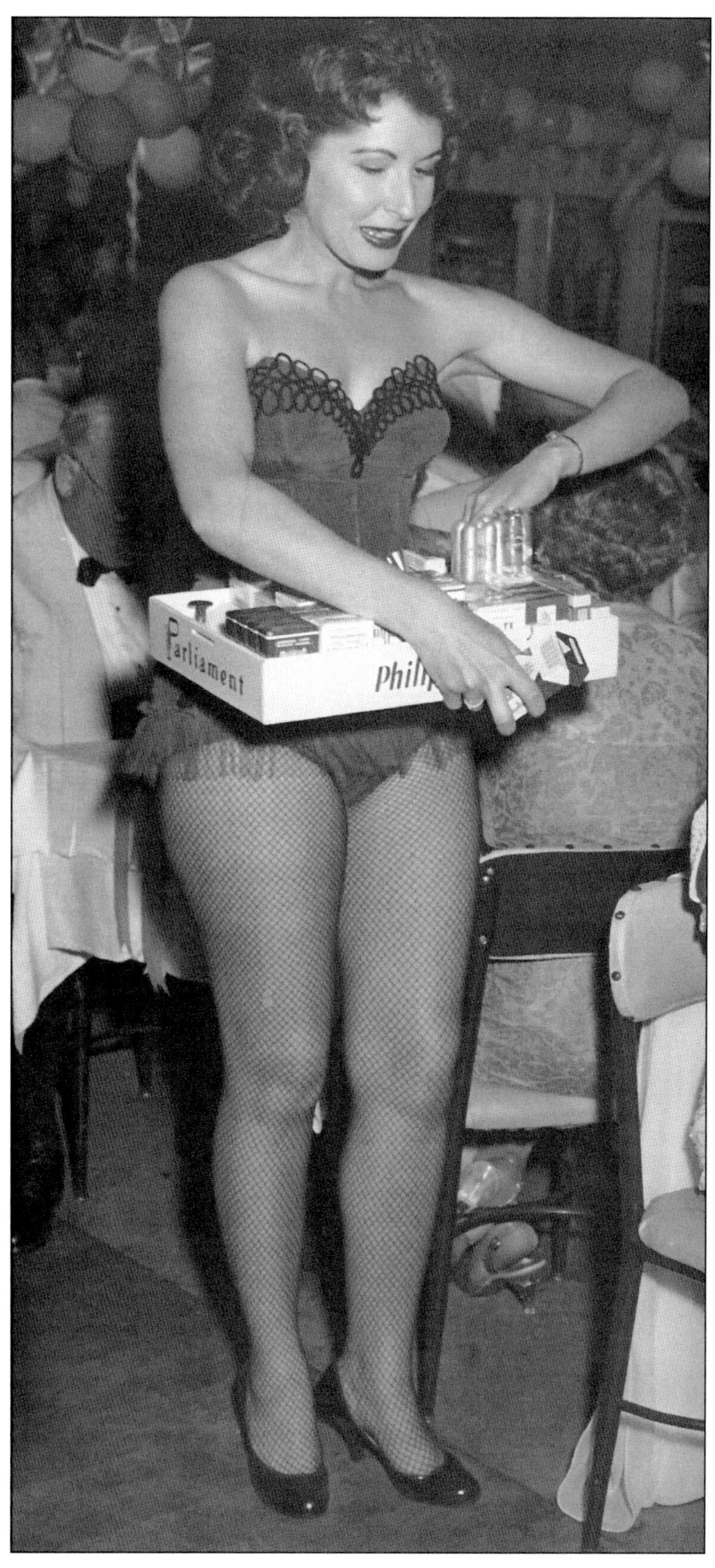

Regina "Reggie" Drew worked at Ciro's from 1949 to 1956, first as a cigarette girl. She took publicity photos of the stars and did television commercials for Phillip Morris and the Paul Coates show *Table at Ciro's*, which aired from Ciro's. She was a showgirl at Earl Carroll's in Hollywood and later owned cigarette and hatcheck concessions at other popular Hollywood nightspots such as Kings, Garden of Allah, and Club Seville.

One

Well-Known Couples and Noteworthy Dates

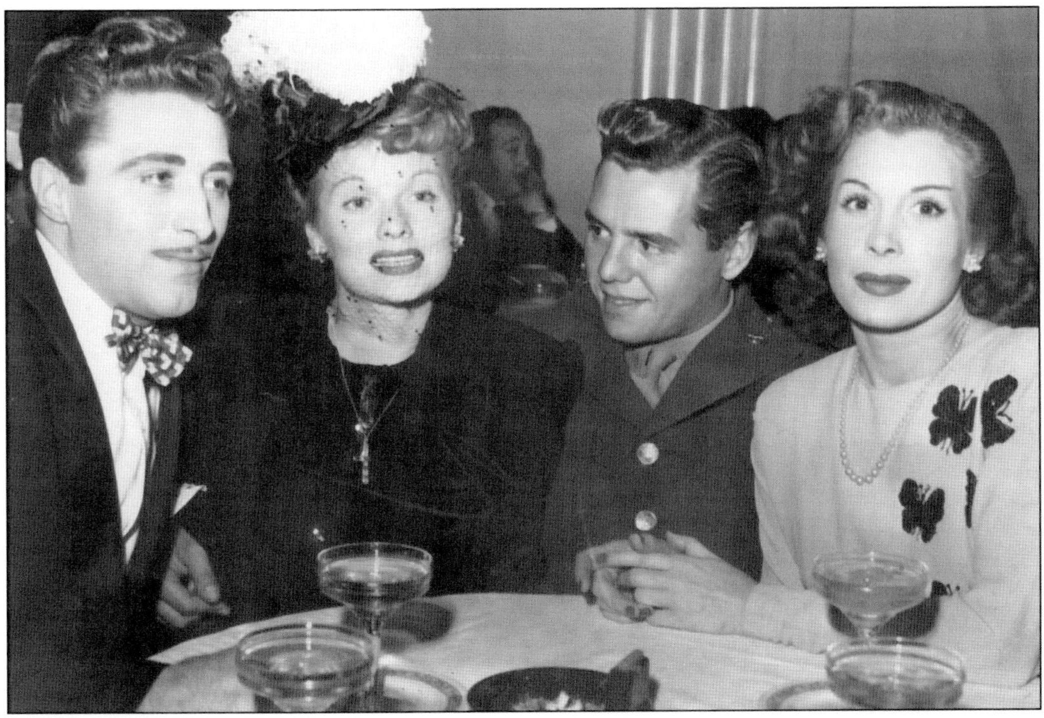

Lucille Ball (second from left) was an iconic sitcom star of the *I Love Lucy* show. Desi Arnaz (second from right), Ball's husband and costar, was also an accomplished musician and bandleader. Ball and Arnaz were married from 1940 to 1960. The *I Love Lucy* show, in its original format, aired from 1951 to 1957. More than 60 years since its inception, *I Love Lucy* continues in syndication today. Helen Grayco (far right) was a singer, actress, and the wife of musician and bandleader Spike Jones.

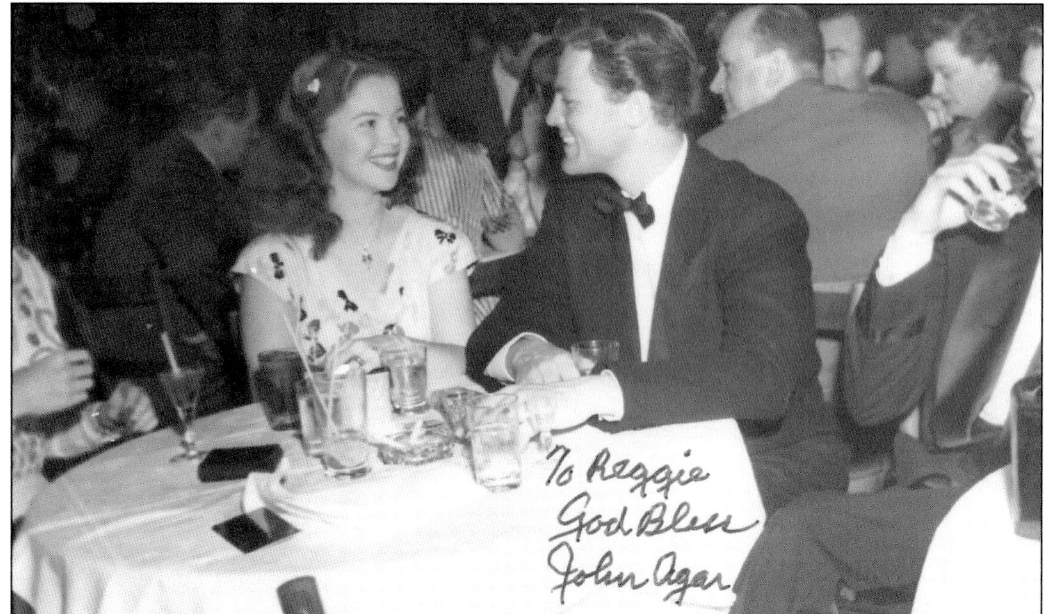

Shirley Temple and John Agar were married from 1945 to 1950. Temple began her film and television career by singing, acting, and dancing her way into the hearts of her admirers at age three. Temple was the top box-office draw from 1935 to 1938, but her popularity waned during adolescence. Temple was later ambassador to Ghana and Czechoslovakia. Agar was a film and television actor who appears in six John Wayne movies and numerous B movies.

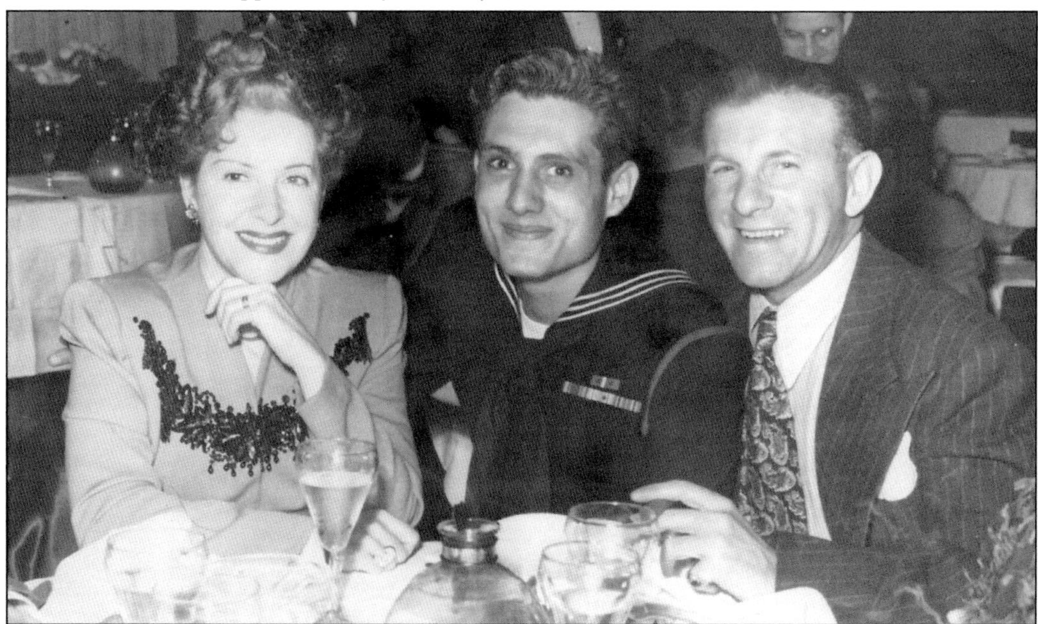

Comedy duo Gracie Allen and George Burns (far right) were married from 1926 until Allen's death in 1964. Allen and Burns enjoyed a successful joint career in vaudeville, radio, television, and film for four decades. Burns wrote much of the material and played the straight man while Allen played his silly, confused counterpart. Burns continued working in show business up until his death in 1996 at 100 years old.

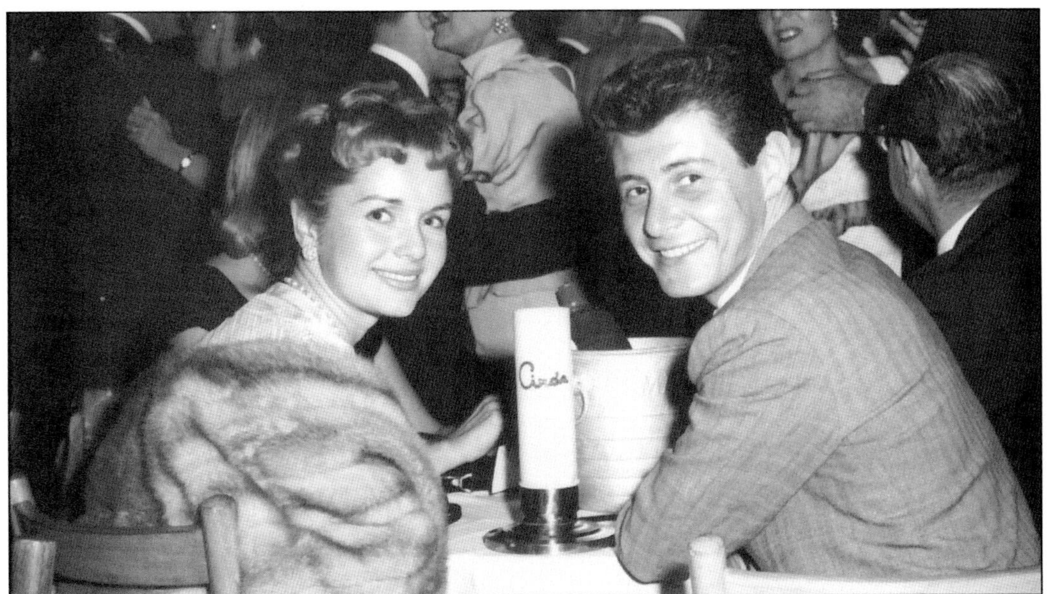

Popular entertainers Debbie Reynolds and Eddie Fisher enjoy a pre-marriage date night at Ciro's. Reynolds, an actress, singer, and dancer, began her career at age 16. At 19, she was the lead in the well-known musical *Singin' in the Rain*, and by the 1950s, she was considered a major star. Reynolds has received numerous nominations and awards over the years and, in 2014, she received the Screen Actors Guild Life Achievement Award. Her career spans over seven decades. Eddie Fisher, a traditional pop singer, had numerous hit songs and sold millions of records. He was a television star as well. Reynolds and Fisher were married from 1955 to 1959. They had two children, both in the entertainment industry. Fisher married his second wife, Reynolds's friend Elizabeth Taylor, in 1959. Fisher died in 2010 at age 82.

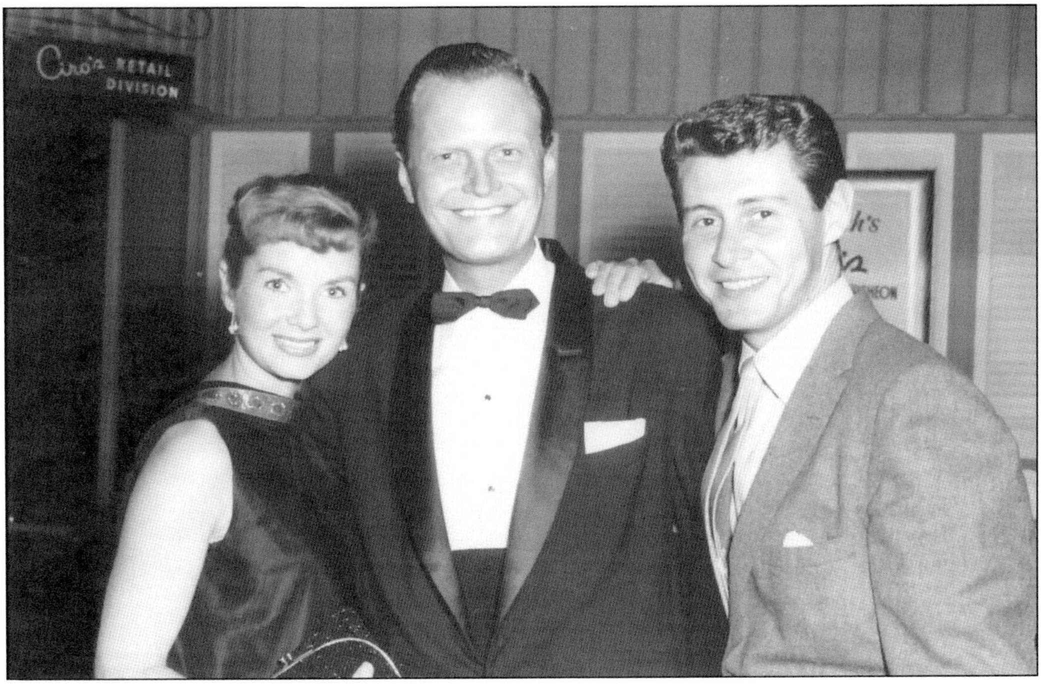

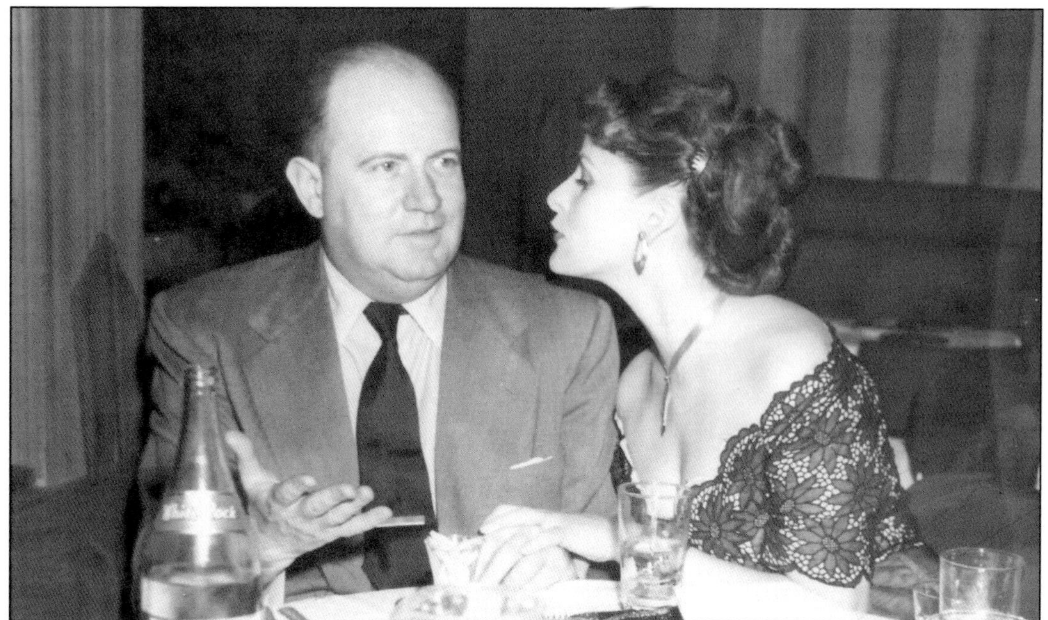

Johnny Meier dated many beautiful actresses and was press agent to Howard Hughes. Rhonda Fleming, a glamorous redheaded actress, appeared in over 40 films during the 1940s and 1950s. In 1991, in memory of her sister, Fleming and her fifth husband created the Rhonda Fleming Mann Clinic for Women's Comprehensive Care at the UCLA Medical Center, which focuses on integrative care for women going through cancer treatment.

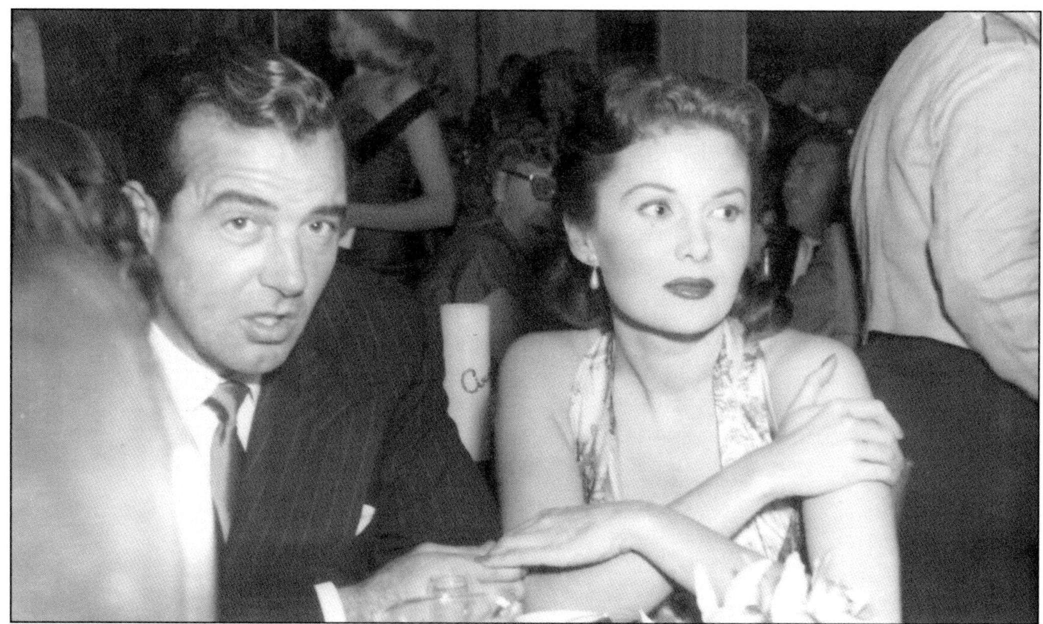

Rhonda Fleming was one of the most famous actresses of her day. Fleming has been a tireless humanitarian and philanthropist for many years, volunteering on various boards that range from helping cancer patients to the homeless. John Payne, an actor and singer in numerous crime dramas and musicals, is best remembered as the lead in the 1947 film that airs each Christmas, *Miracle on 34th Street*.

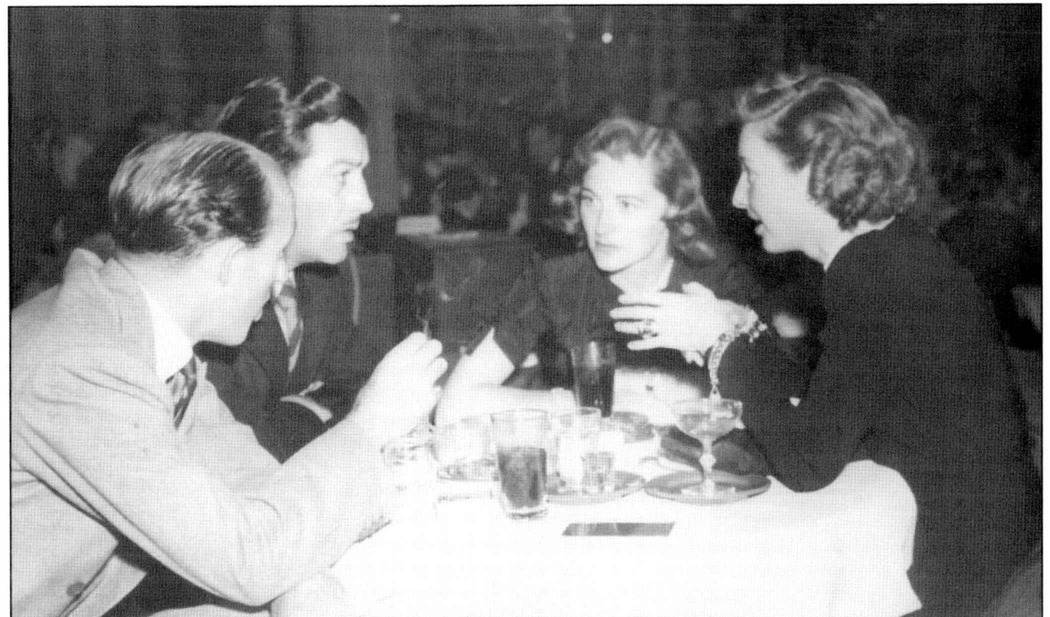

Robert Taylor (second from left) and Barbara Stanwyck (far right) were married from 1939 to 1951. Stanwyck was a versatile actress of stage, film, and television. She was active for over 60 years. Prior to acting in television, she was in 85 films. She was nominated four times for the Academy Award for Best Actress, won three Emmys, and won one Golden Globe for *The Thorn Birds*. She received an Honorary Oscar in 1982 and a Golden Globe Cecil B. DeMille Award.

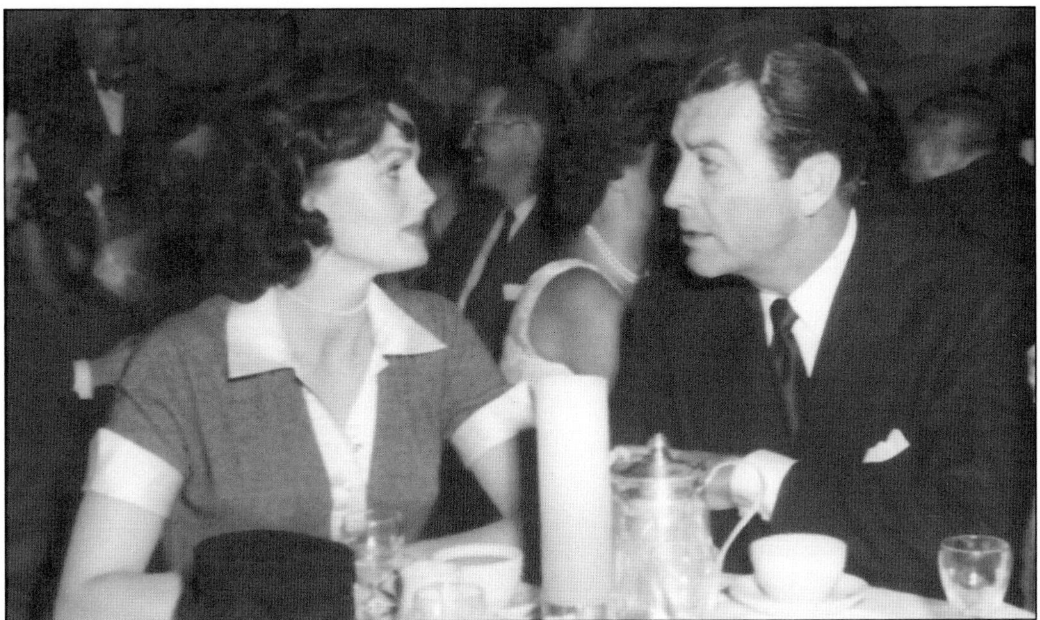

Actress Ursula Thiess is shown above with her second husband, Robert Taylor, who was a film and television actor. They were married from 1954 to 1969. Thiess left acting to focus on being a homemaker. Taylor, a popular leading man, began his career in 1934 and was active until 1968. He starred in many movies and in the television show *The Detectives* that aired from 1959 to 1962. Taylor was a heavy smoker and died at age 57 of lung cancer.

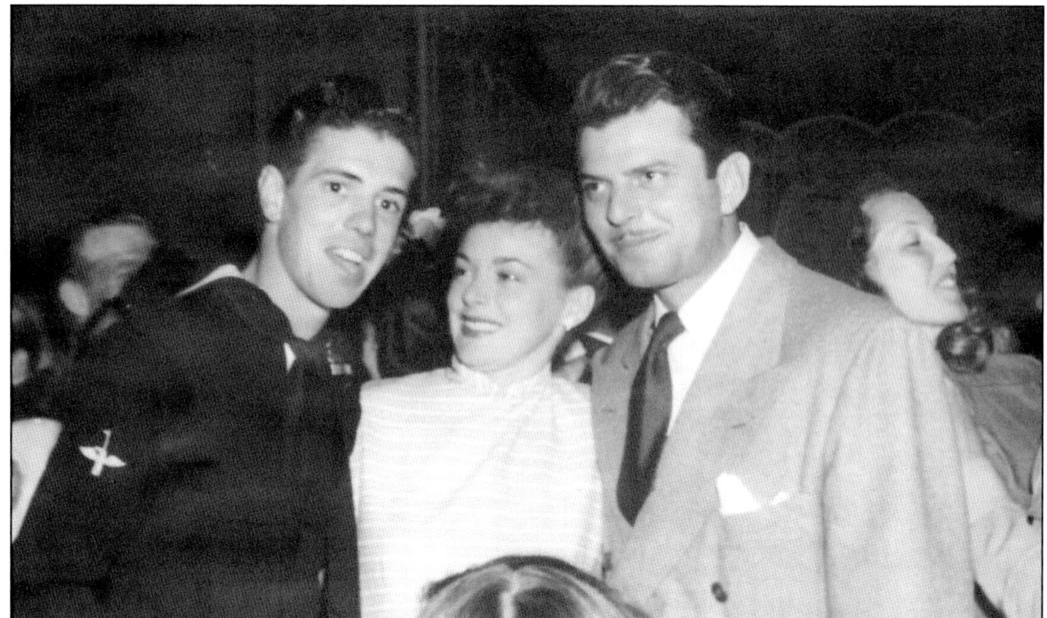

Actor John Carroll (right) was in several Western films and is possibly best remembered in *Flying Tigers* with John Wayne. He appears in other well-known movies from the 1940s, such as *Only Angels Have Wings* and *Go West*. Beginning in the 1940s, Marguerite Chapman (center) played the lead in the adventure film series *Spy Smasher*. In the 1950s, she played primarily secondary roles, like Miss Morris in *The Seven Year Itch* with Marilyn Monroe.

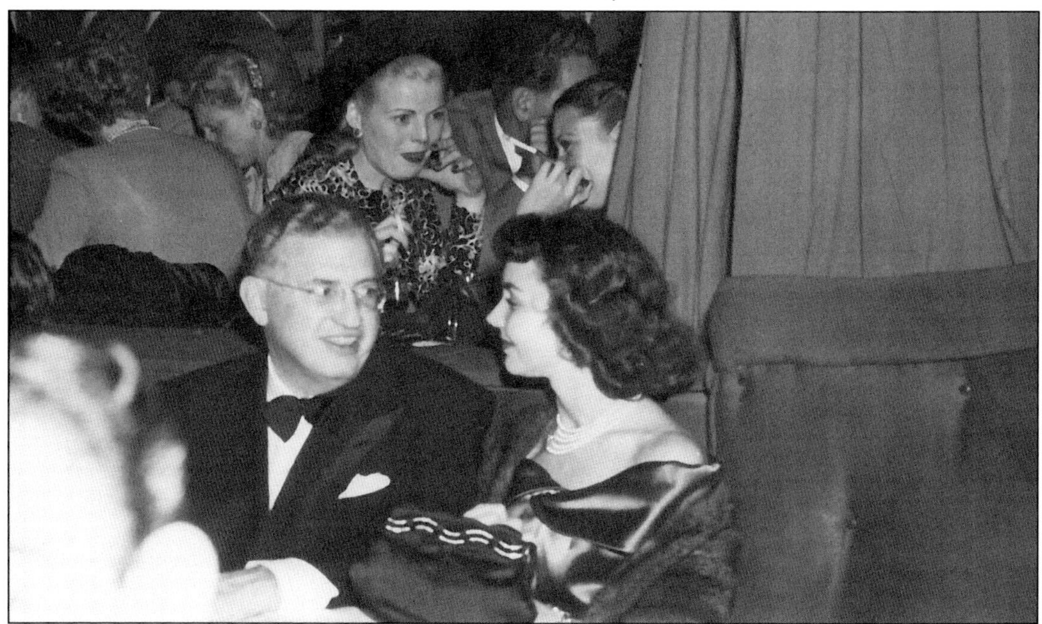

David Selznick was a leading producer and studio film executive. He is best known for the epic 1939 production *Gone with the Wind*, which won an Academy Award for Best Picture. He also won an Academy Award for *Rebecca* in 1940. Jennifer Jones was an Academy Award–winning actress who received an Oscar for Best Actress for *The Song of Bernadette*. Selznick and Jones were married from 1949 until Selznick's death in 1969.

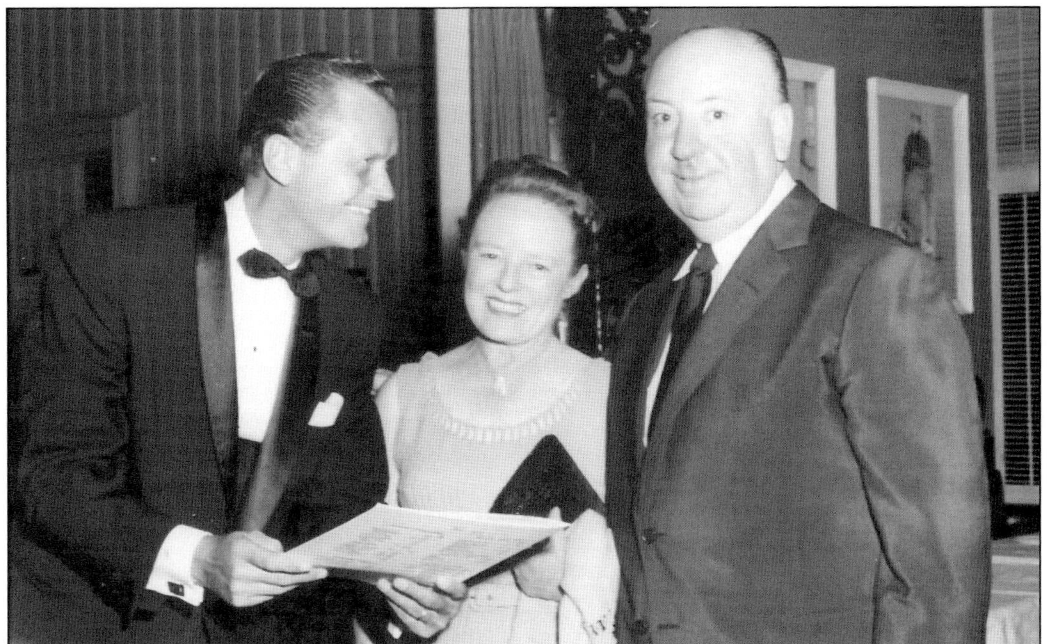

English film pioneer, director, and producer Alfred Hitchcock (right) is pictured with his wife, Alma Reville, and Ciro's captain. Hitchcock's career spanned over six decades, and he directed over 50 feature films. He was often referred to as the "Master of Suspense." A few of his best-known films include classics *Vertigo*, *Notorious*, *The Birds*, *Psycho*, *North by Northwest*, and *Rear Window*.

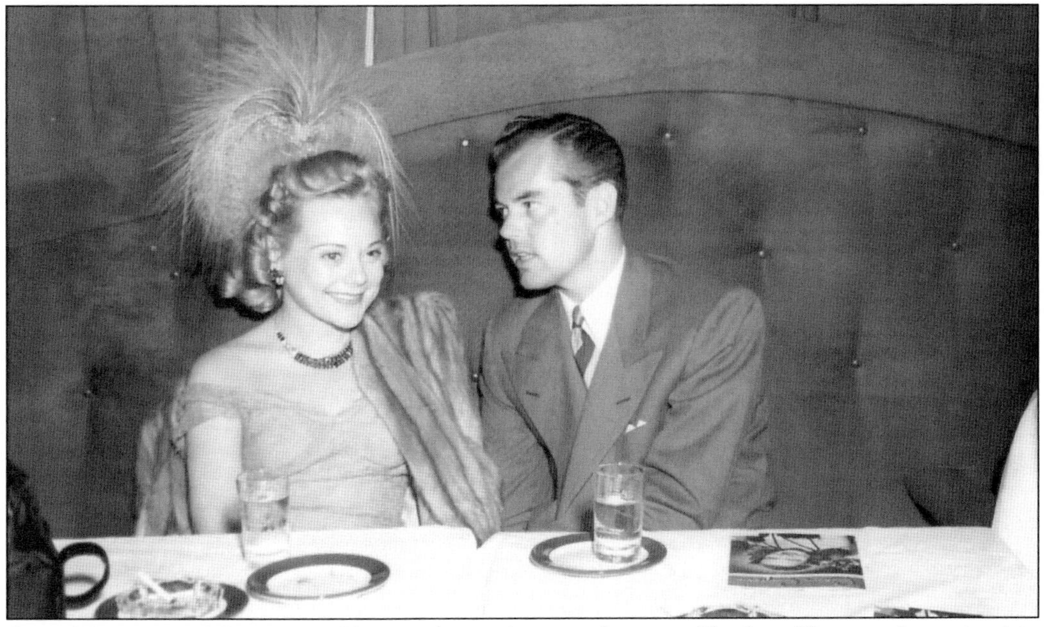

Sonja Henie was a Norwegian Olympic figure skater and actress. Her first Olympic championship was won at age 15 in 1928. She won again in 1932 and 1936. She is recorded as being the Ladies' Singles World Champion ten times and European Champion six times. At the height of her acting career, Henie was one of the top-paid actresses of that time, earning $400,000 for her role in the 1936 film *One in a Million*.

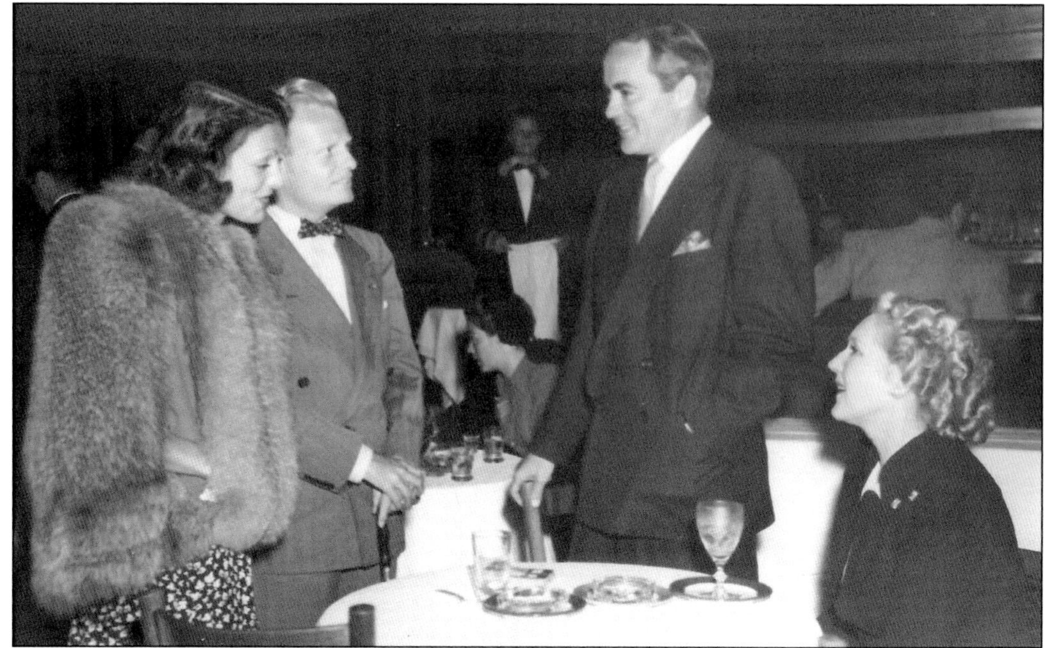

Buddy Rogers (second from right) and his wife, Mary Pickford (right), greet friends at the club. Rogers was an actor, jazz musician, and singer. Pickford was a silent film actress, cofounder of United Artists, and one of the founders of the Academy of Motion Picture Arts and Sciences. Rogers and Pickford were married from 1937 until Pickford's death in 1979.

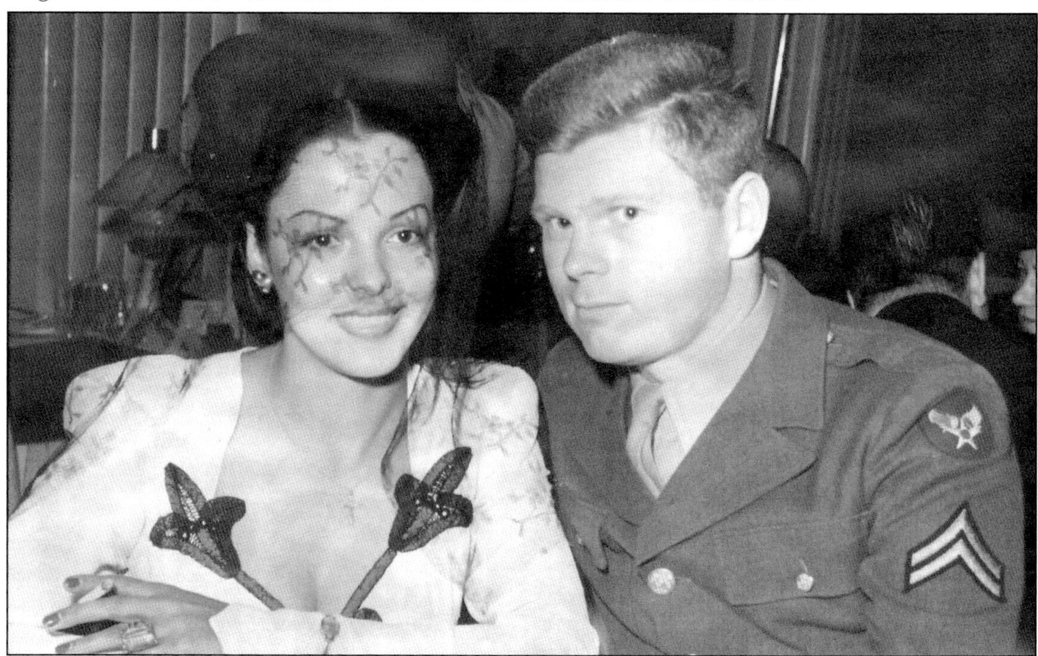

Barry Nelson is pictured with his first wife, Teresa Celli. They were married from 1951 to 1965. Nelson, a likeable and well-respected actor, was the first to play the role of secret agent James Bond. Nelson remained active in film and television for about 50 years. Celli was an actress best known for her role in *The Asphalt Jungle*.

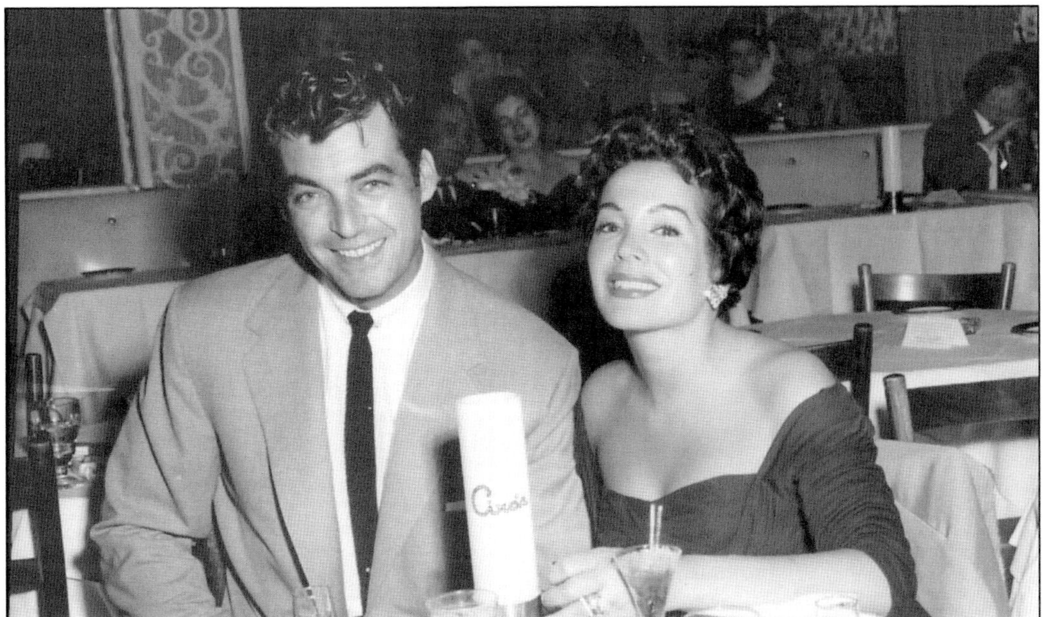

Rory Calhoun and his wife, Lita Baron, were married from 1948 to 1970. Calhoun was an actor, producer, and screenwriter, remembered for the movies *How to Marry a Millionaire* and *River of No Return*. In the late 1950s, he found success in a Western television show called *The Texan*. Beautiful actress Baron filed for divorce, citing Calhoun's 79 affairs; Calhoun admitted to significantly more.

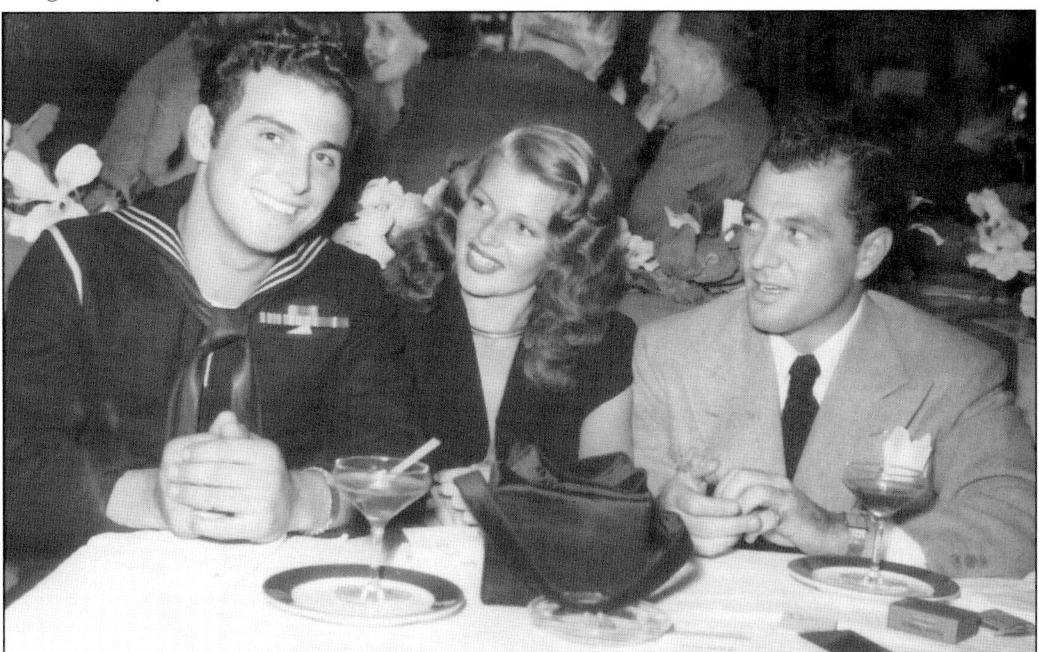

Rita Hayworth was one of the top stars in the 1940s. She was one of six actresses to have danced on-screen with both Gene Kelly and Fred Astaire. She appeared in 61 films and is considered one of the 100 greatest stars of all time. Possibly her most memorable performance is in the film *Gilda*. Tony Martin (right) was an actor and a traditional and big band singer with numerous hit records.

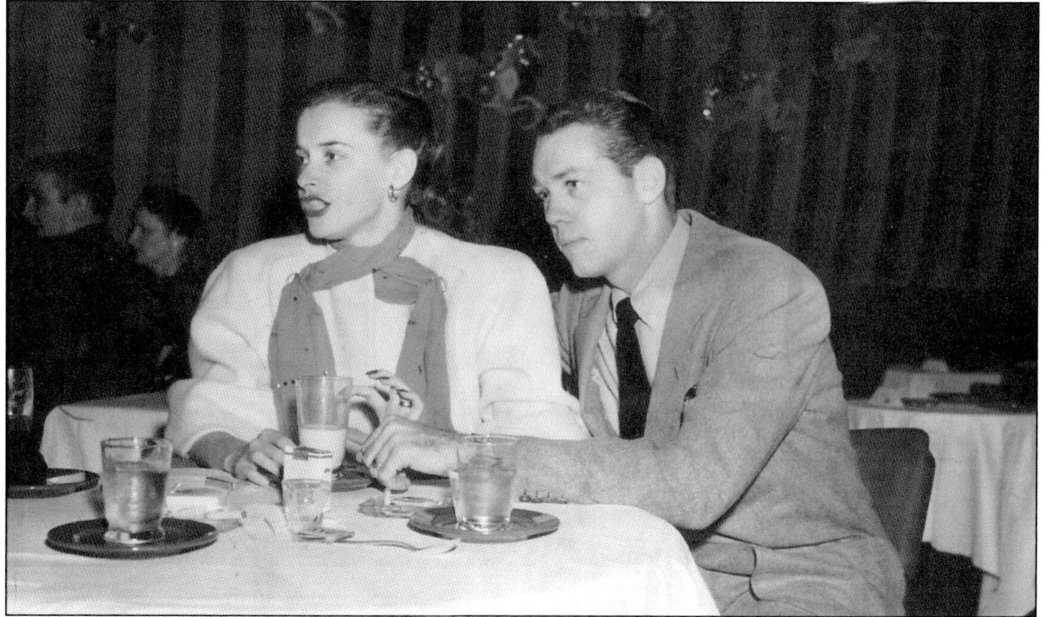

The above photograph shows actress Susan Peters with her husband, actor Richard Quine. Peters was contracted by Metro-Goldwyn-Mayer (MGM) and groomed for starring roles but suffered a hunting accident in 1945 that cut short her career. Quine acted in many films, including *Babes on Broadway*, *Little Men*, and *No Sad Song for Me*, prior to switching to directing. In his later years, he suffered from depression and ill health and consequently committed suicide in 1989.

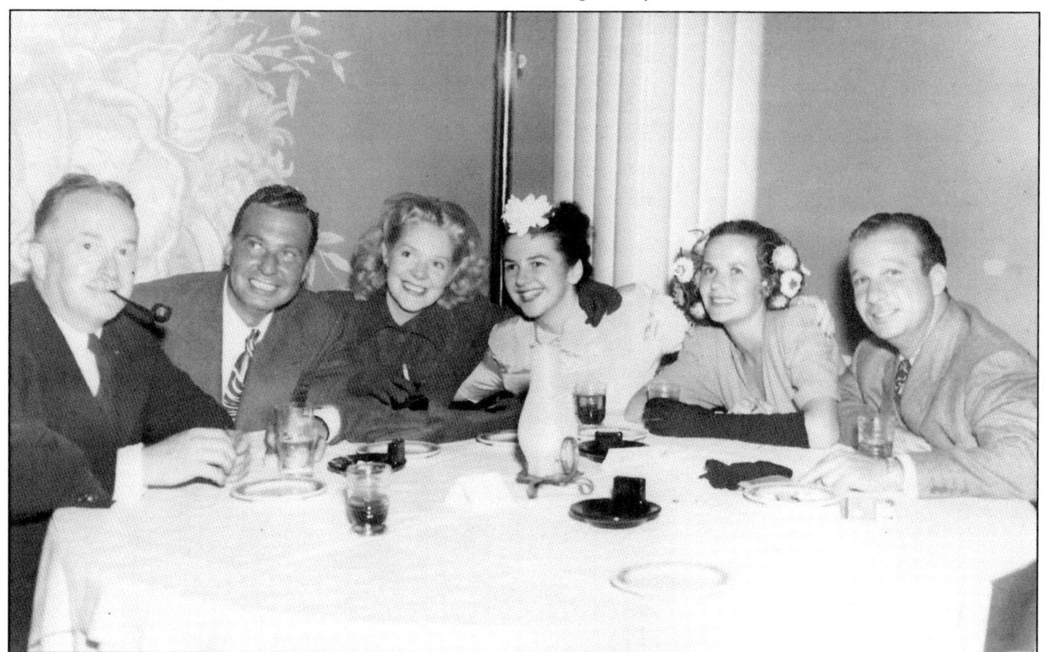

Phil Harris (second from left) was a singer, songwriter, musician, actor, and comedian. He is also known for his voice-over work as Baloo in Disney's *The Jungle Book* and as O'Malley in *The Aristocats*. Harris costarred, for eight years, in a series with actress, singer, and wife Alice Faye (third from left). Harris and Faye were married from 1941 until Harris's death in 1995.

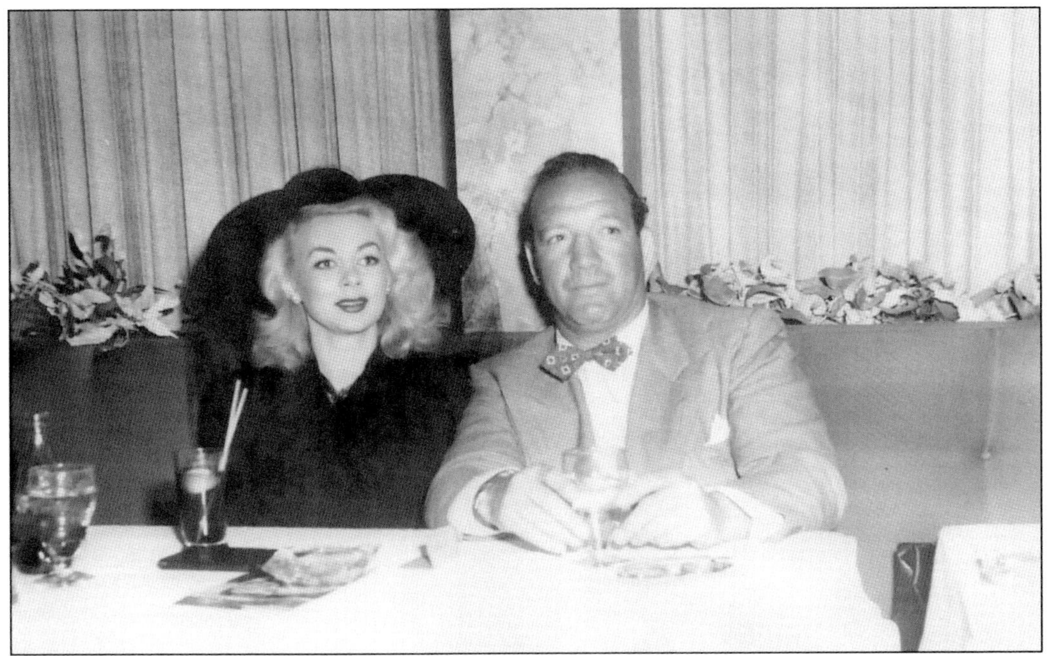

Maxie Rosenbloom, also known as "Slapsie Maxie," was a light heavyweight boxer who won 222 out of 298 fights. He became a character actor, usually cast as the big, clumsy but loveable personality in films, television, and radio. In the 1940s, he ran his namesake nightclub Slapsy Maxie's. Veda Ann Borg, originally a model, was a talented actress in over 100 films.

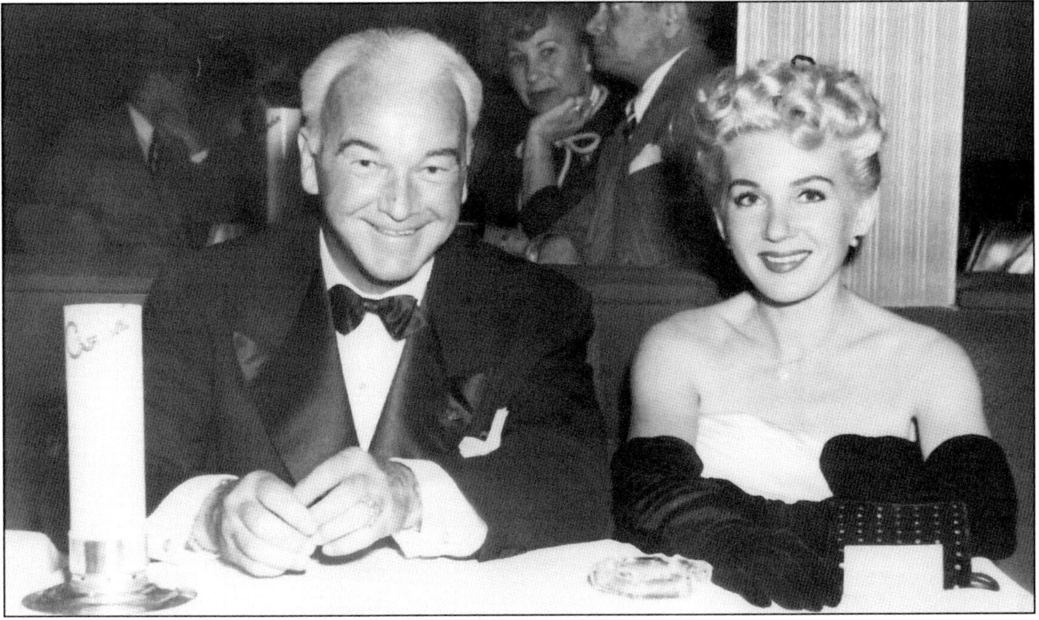

William Boyd is best known his lead role as the clean-cut Western hero in the *Hopalong Cassidy* films. He made 66 of these films, which he successfully lobbied to adapt for Saturday-morning television. Many "Hoppy" products were marketed, including lunch boxes, cowboy hats, and toy guns. Grace Bradley was an actress, singer, and dancer in the 1930s. She was married to Boyd from 1936 until his death in 1972. Bradley left acting to devote herself to Boyd's career.

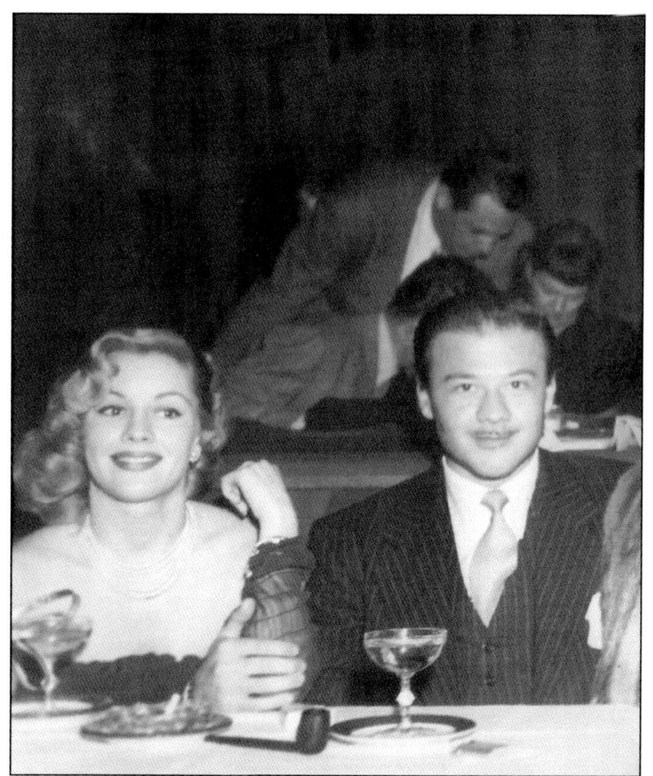

Austrian-born actor Turhan Bey was dubbed "The Turkish Delight" by his fans. He mainly appeared in films during the 1940s. He returned to film and did some television spots during the 1990s. Anita Ekberg was a Swedish actress, model, and sex symbol who may be best remembered for her role in Federico Fellini's *La Dolce Vita*.

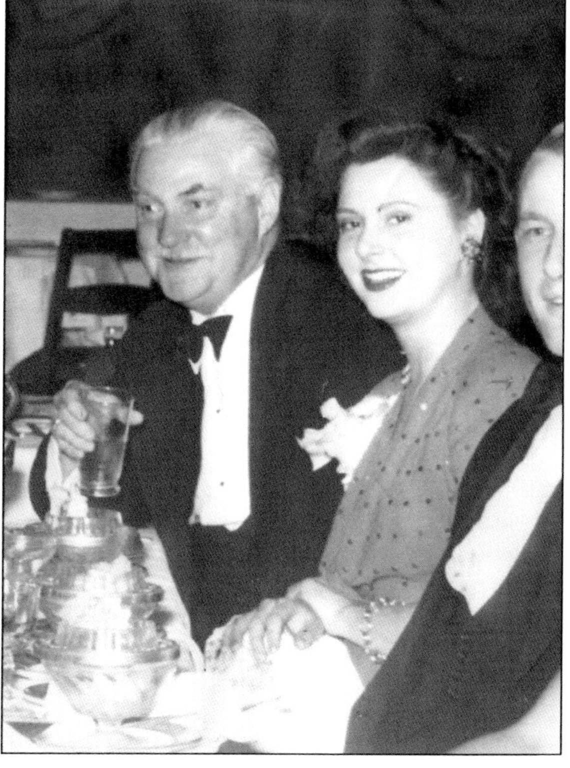

Actor of stage, film, and radio, Nigel Bruce was best known as Dr. Watson in *The New Adventures of Sherlock Holmes*, which aired on the radio from 1939 to 1947. He played Dr. Watson on film as well and appears in two Hitchcock films, *Rebecca* and *Suspicion*. Violet Campbell, his wife from 1921 until his death in 1953, was an actress with four movie credits.

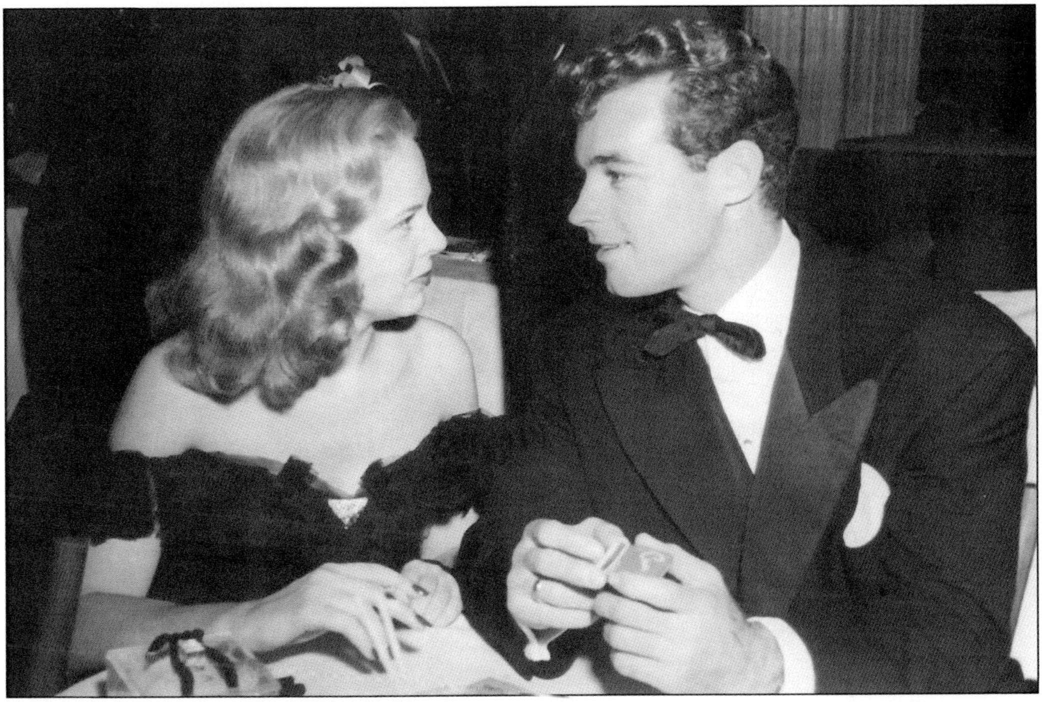

Guy Madison, with his strong, chiseled looks, landed lead roles in the 1940s and 1950s, in mostly Westerns. He was in 85 films, on television, and on radio. He starred as the lawman, Wild Bill Hickok, in television series *Adventures of Wild Bill Hickok* and received a special Golden Globe Award in 1954 for Best Western Star. Madison and wife, actress Sheila Connolly (below, left), were married from 1954 to 1963. Connolly may be remembered for her roles in various television series such as *Winner Takes All*, *The Star and the Story*, *Highway Patrol*, *The Millionaire*, or *The Lone Wolf*.

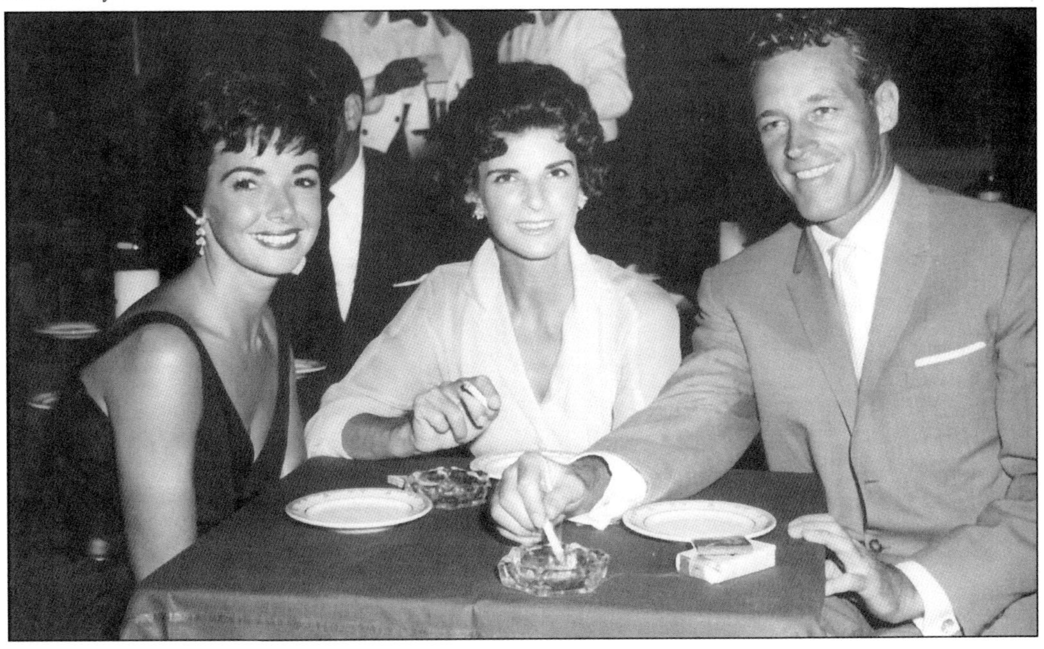

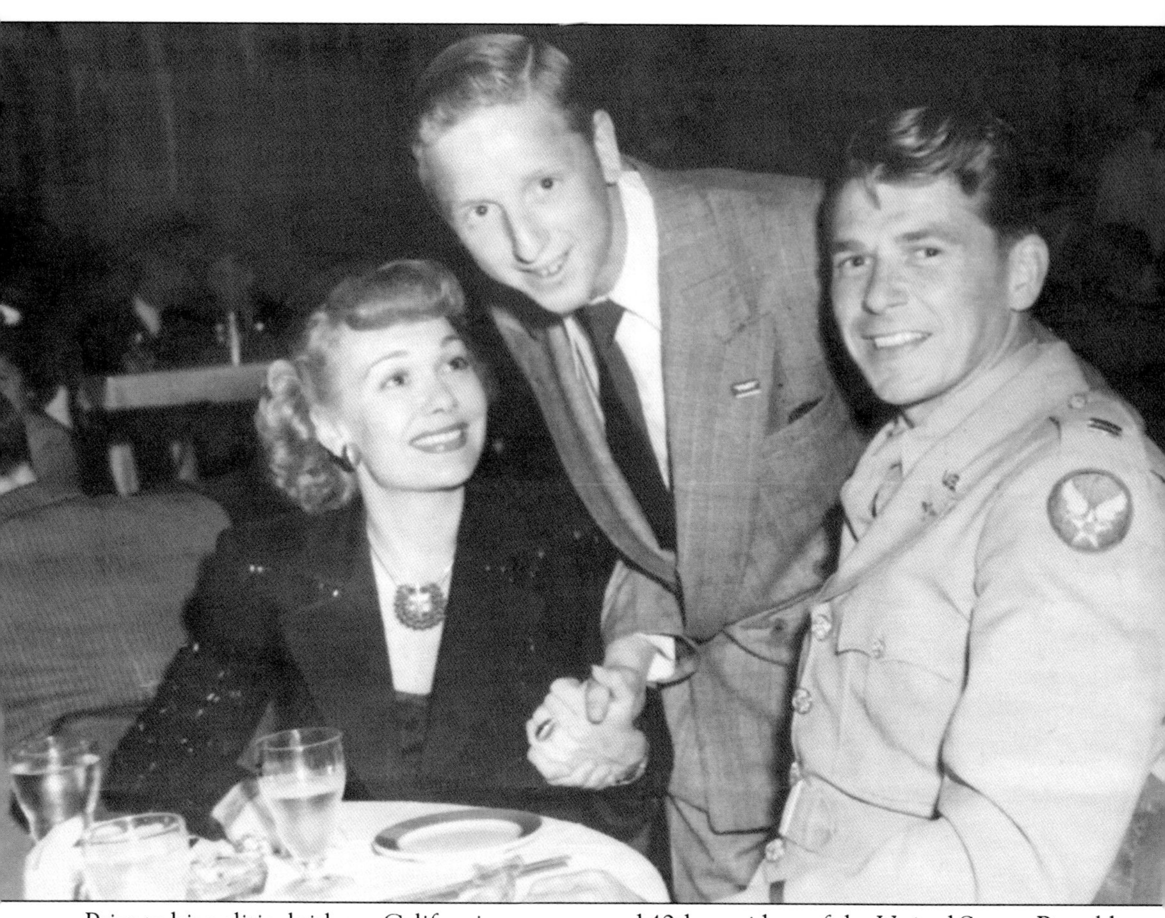

Prior to his political titles as California governor and 40th president of the United States, Ronald Reagan (right) was an actor. His first film credit was in 1937 for a starring role in *Love Is on the Air.* His lifelong nickname "The Gipper" derived from the movie *Knute Rockne, All American,* where he plays George Gipp. President Reagan regarded *Kings Row,* where he plays a double amputee, as his favorite acting role. His last film, *The Killers,* in 1964, is the only film where he plays a villain. In total, President Reagan had about 70 movie credits. Reagan's first wife, from 1940 to 1948, was actress Jane Wyman (left). Wyman received an Academy Award in 1948 for her role in *Johnny Belinda.* Dave Wolper (center) was a film and television producer of such hits as *Roots, The Thorn Birds,* and *Willie Wonka & the Chocolate Factory.*

Two

LEADING LADIES AND FAMOUS ACTRESSES

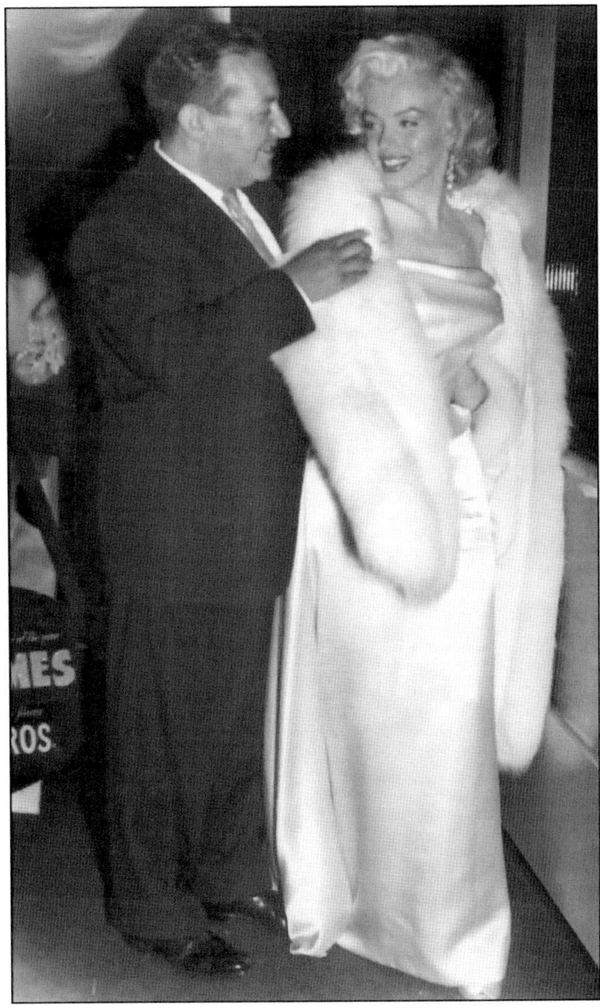

Iconic actress and sex symbol Marilyn Monroe frequented Ciro's nightclub in the 1940s and 1950s. She is seen here in Ciro's lobby with nightclub owner Herman Hover at a celebrity-filled birthday bash for gossip columnist Walter Winchell on May 13, 1953. Monroe began her career modeling for Blue Book Modeling Agency in the mid-1940s. She acted in various movies in the 1940s, but superstardom did not come until the early 1950s. She was typecast as the seductive, "dumb blonde," a role she tried to alter by taking acting lessons to add to her repertoire. Some noteworthy movies include *The Seven Year Itch* and *Some Like It Hot* (for which she received a Golden Globe). Although Monroe's rise to fame came gradually, her life ended abruptly when she died tragically of a barbiturate overdose in 1962 at age 36. Even after death, her popularity has not waned. Her life continues to be both a cautionary tale and a fantasy for many wide-eyed starlet hopefuls who seek fame and fortune. The last film she completed was *The Misfits* in 1961.

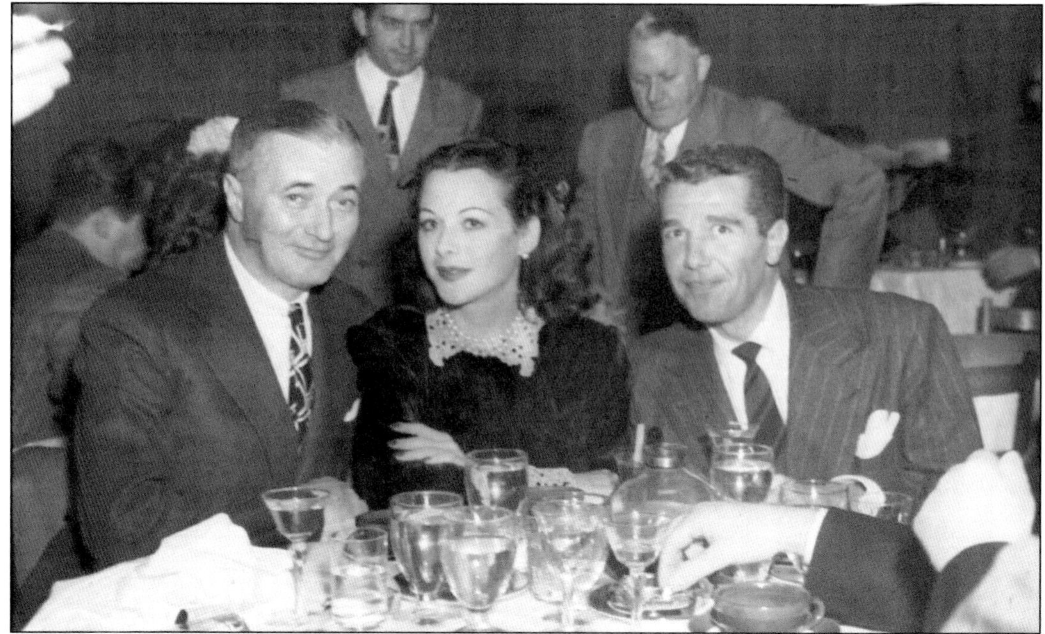

Hedy Lamarr was a popular and beautiful actress cast alongside leading men such as Spencer Tracy, Clark Gable, Victor Mature, and Robert Young, to name a few. Possibly, her best-known performance is in the Cecil B. DeMille 1949 film *Samson and Delilah*. She was the coinventor, along with composer George Antheil, of frequency hopping communication and spread spectrum technology. Her invention was useful for the US military during World War II and continues to be used in modern communication technology today. As a result of her contribution to technology, Lamarr was inducted into the National Inventors Hall of Fame in 2014.

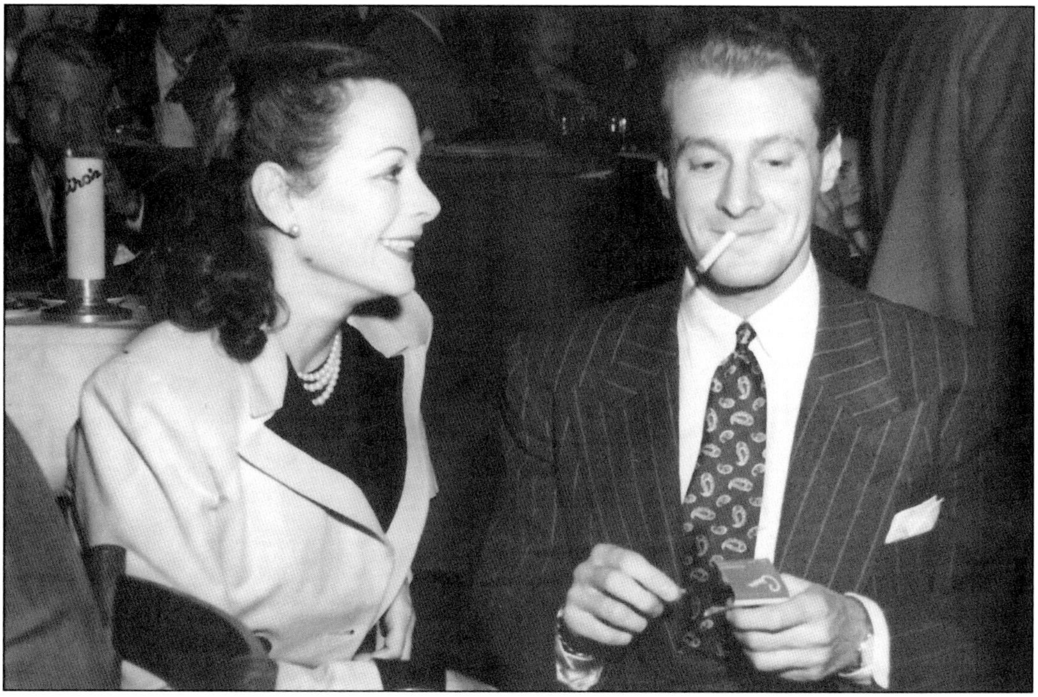

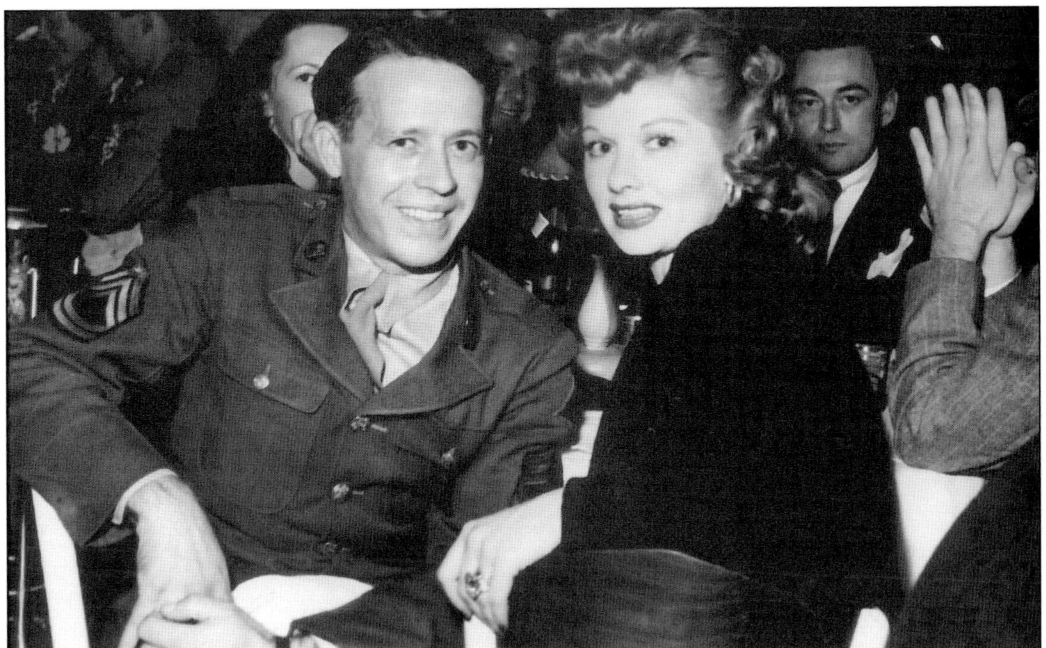

Lucille Ball was a beloved comedic television and film actress, model, and first woman to run a successful television studio. Ball was the star of wildly popular sitcom *I Love Lucy*, which aired from October 15, 1951 to March 6, 1957. In the list of *TV Guide*'s top 50 television shows of all time, *I Love Lucy* is second. The *I Love Lucy* show is still in syndication today.

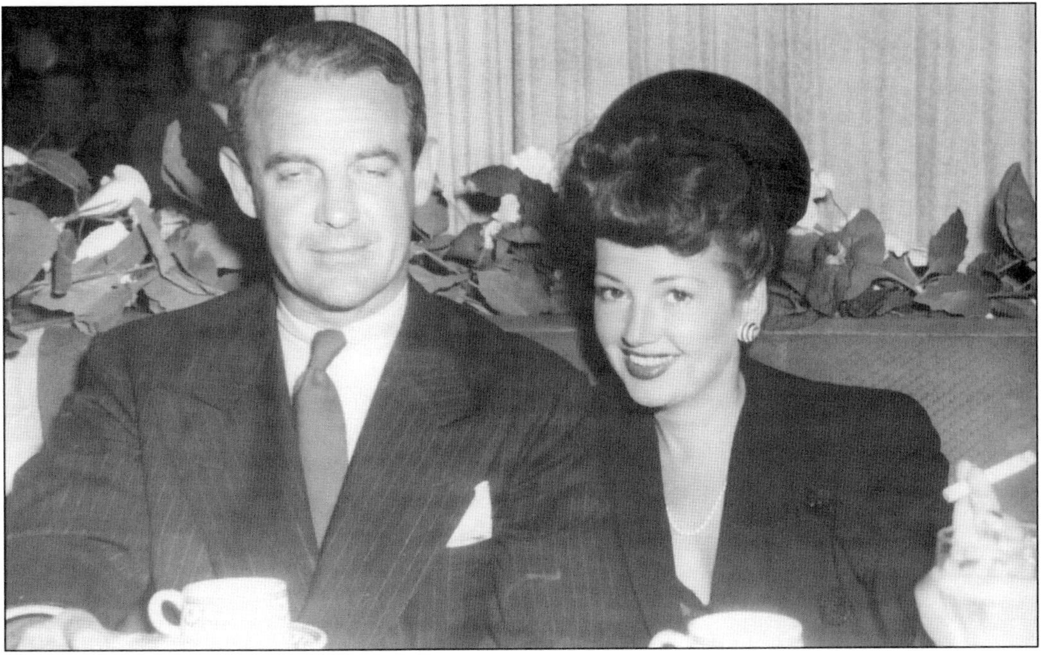

Arline Judge was an actress who appeared in mostly comedic, low-budget B movies during the 1930s and 1940s. She began as a dancer for Jimmy Durante's act. She gained much attention offscreen, via the tabloids, due to her numerous marriages; by some accounts, she was married seven times, while others report eight. She appeared in a few television programs through 1964.

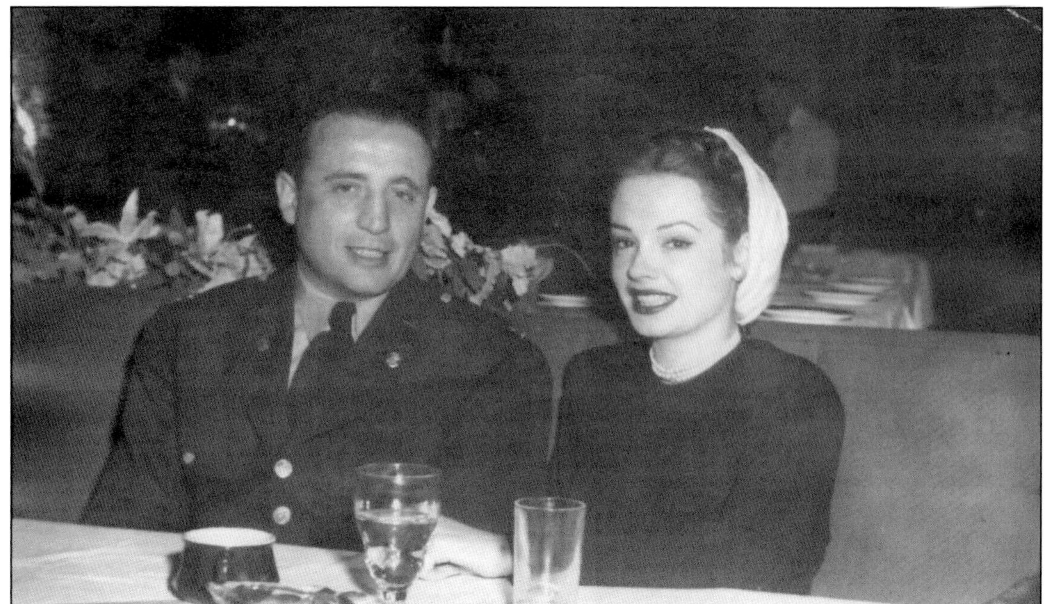

Jane Greer was a film and television actress who was discovered by Howard Hughes. Greer was known for her keen ability to demonstrate an array of facial expressions to convey emotions, a skill she attributed to facial exercises practiced after a partial facial paralysis at age 15. Greer may be best remembered for her femme fatale role in *Out of the Past*. Although Greer was a Democrat, she campaigned for Ronald Reagan in 1980 and 1984.

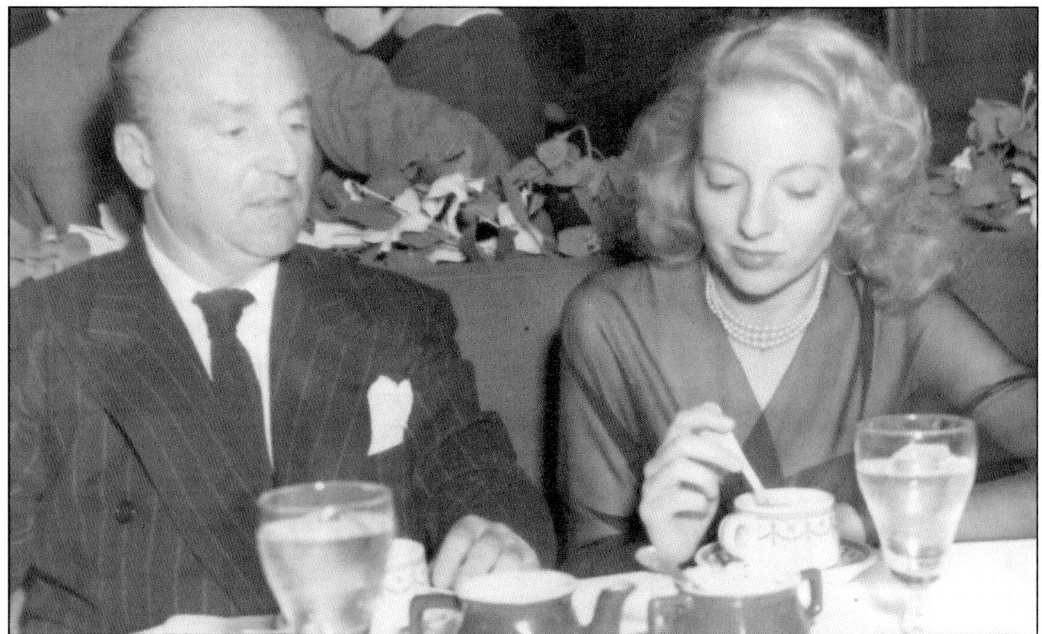

Arthur Hornblow Jr. was a film producer, and film actress Evelyn Keyes is best known as Scarlett O'Hara's younger sister, Suellen O'Hara, in the movie classic *Gone with the Wind*. She may also be remembered for her acting contributions in *The Seven Year Itch*, *Here Comes Mr. Jordan*, and *The Jolson Story*. In more recent years, Keyes had a recurring role on the television hit *Murder, She Wrote* from 1985 to 1993.

Janis Paige was an actress who was active in television, film, and musical theater for nearly 60 years. Paige received fame with her hit performance as Babe in the Broadway musical *The Pajama Game* in 1954. In the 1980s and 1990s, she appeared on several soap operas such as *General Hospital* and *Santa Barbara*.

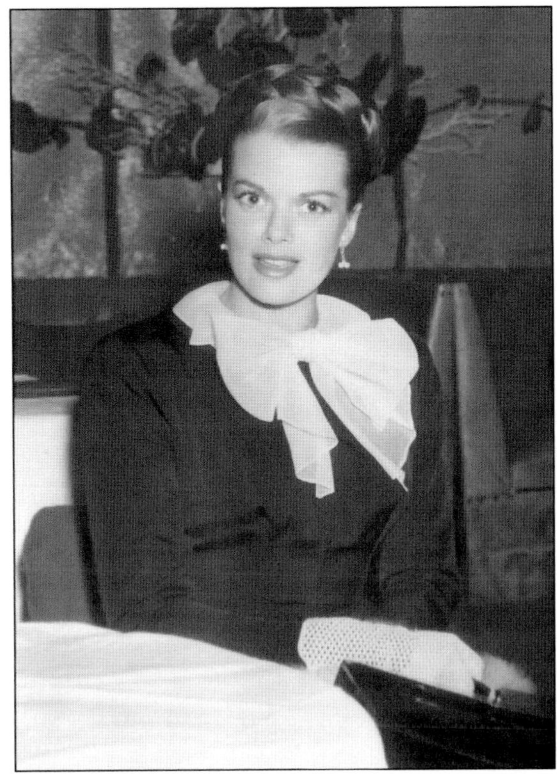

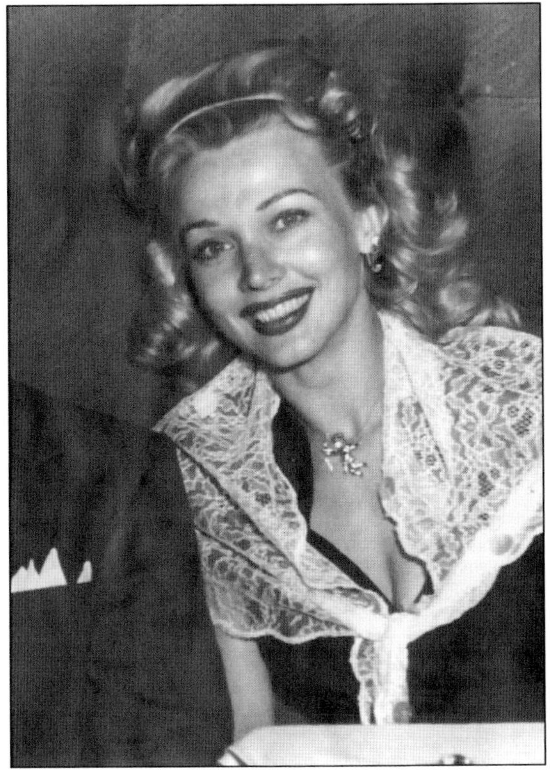

Carole Landis was a film actress contracted with 20th Century Fox and a stage actress. Her breakout role was as a cave girl in the 1940 film *One Million B.C.* During World War II, Landis was a popular pinup girl; she did USO tours with Jack Benny and Martha Raye and logged more than 100,000 miles visiting servicemen. In 1949, at age 29, Landis committed suicide by a drug overdose.

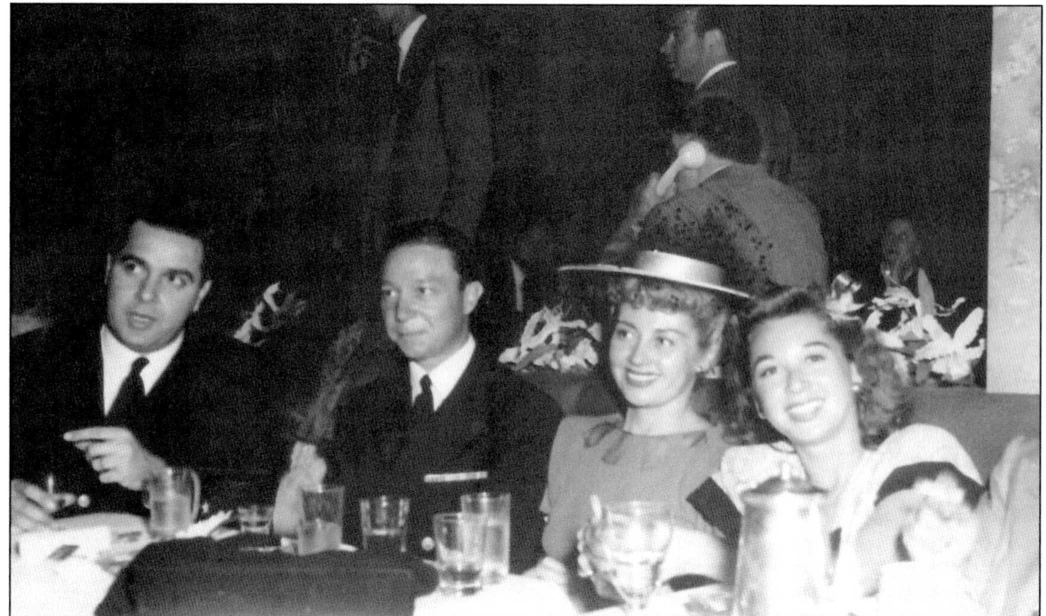

Actress Joan Blondell (second from right), the wisecracking sidekick, starred in over 100 films and television shows. She appeared in six films with James Cagney. For her work in the 1951 movie *The Blue Veil*, Blondell was nominated for an Academy Award for Best Supporting Actress. Blondell is also in the 1978 hit movie *Grease*. Her younger sister, Gloria Blondell (far right), was an actress and also the voice of Disney's Daisy Duck.

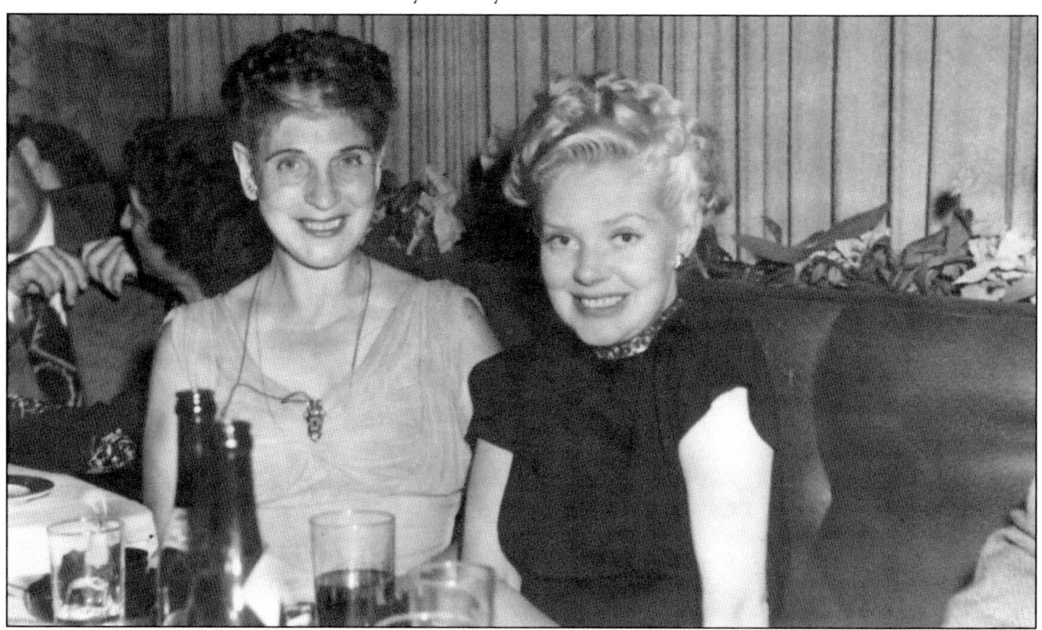

Alice Faye (right) was a popular actress, singer, and radio personality who virtually left acting after her second child was born in order to spend more time with her family. The *New York Times* called Faye "one of the few movie stars to walk away from stardom at the peak of her career." Faye introduced 23 songs to the hit parade and was considered, by many, the female version of Bing Crosby.

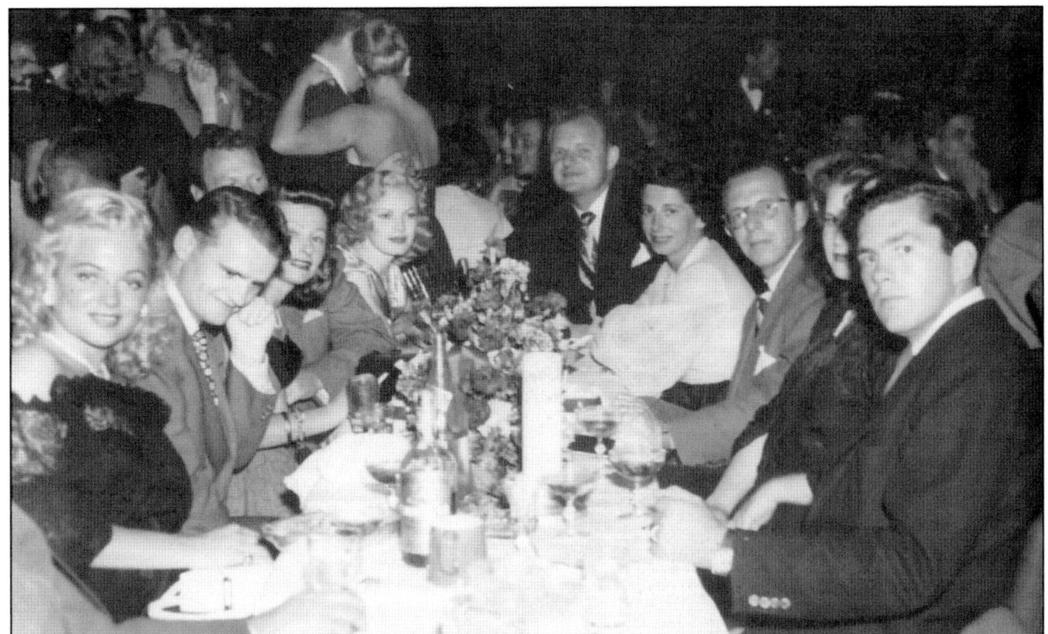

Actress June Haver (above, fifth from left; below, third from right) appears in many 1940s musicals. She was contracted with 20th Century Fox specifically to play the stand-in or alternate to Alice Faye and Betty Grable. Haver was often compared to Grable and was originally groomed by 20th Century Fox to hopefully achieve Grable's level of stardom. In 1945, Haver filmed *Where Do We Go From Here?* with her future husband, Fred MacMurray. After her last film, 1953's *The Girl Next Door*, Haver vowed to become a nun, which she did for a few months. She left the convent for health reasons and later wed MacMurray. They were married from 1954 to 1991.

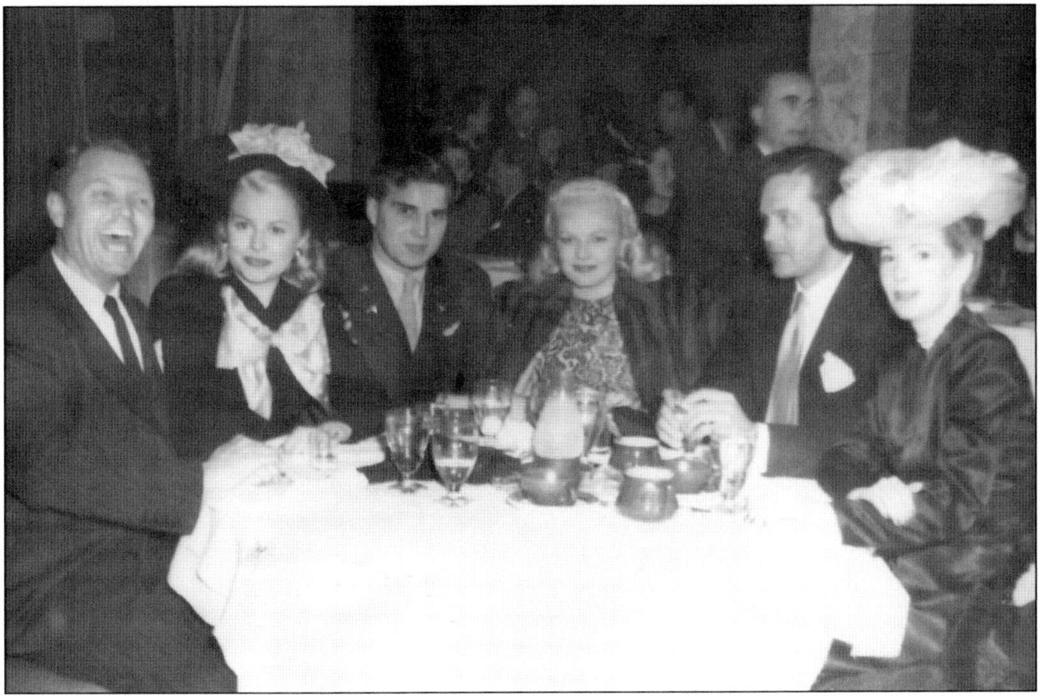

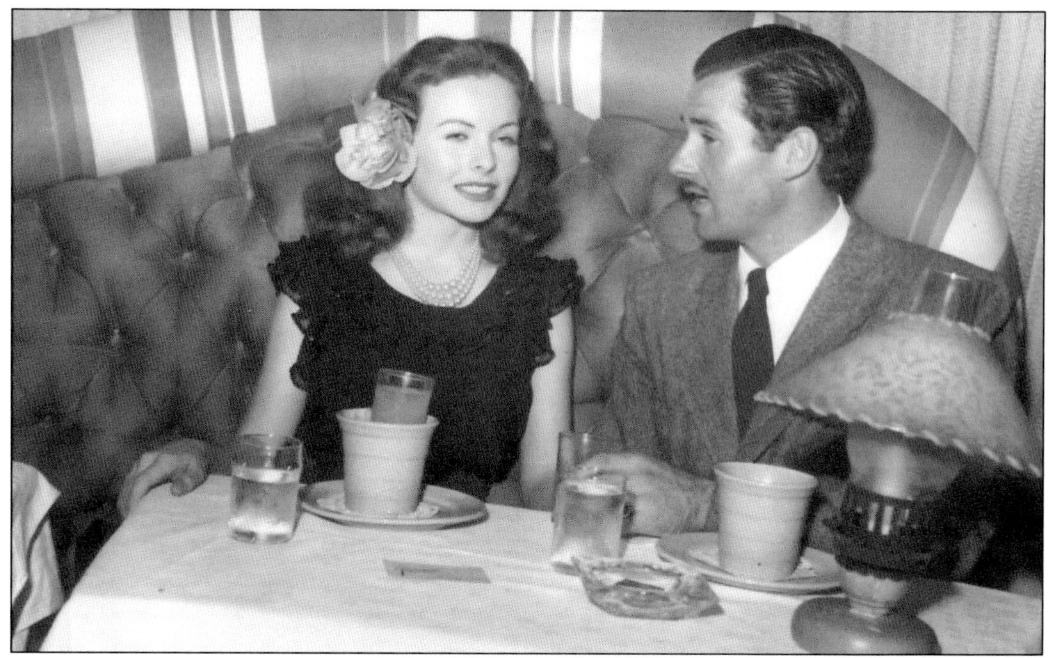

Jeanne Crain was a film and television actress who appeared in comedies and romances; her career spanned from 1943 to 1975. Crain received a Best Actress nomination for her lead role in the controversial movie *Pinky*, where she portrays a light-skinned black woman in love with a white doctor. Crain was a devout Catholic, had seven children (two of whom predeceased her), and fought fervently for the Republican cause in 1960. Paul Brinkman (above), Crain's only husband, was a former contract player for Radio-Keith-Orpheum (RKO). Although their marriage was rocky during some parts, they remained married from 1947 until Brinkman's death in 2003. The man in the image below is unidentified.

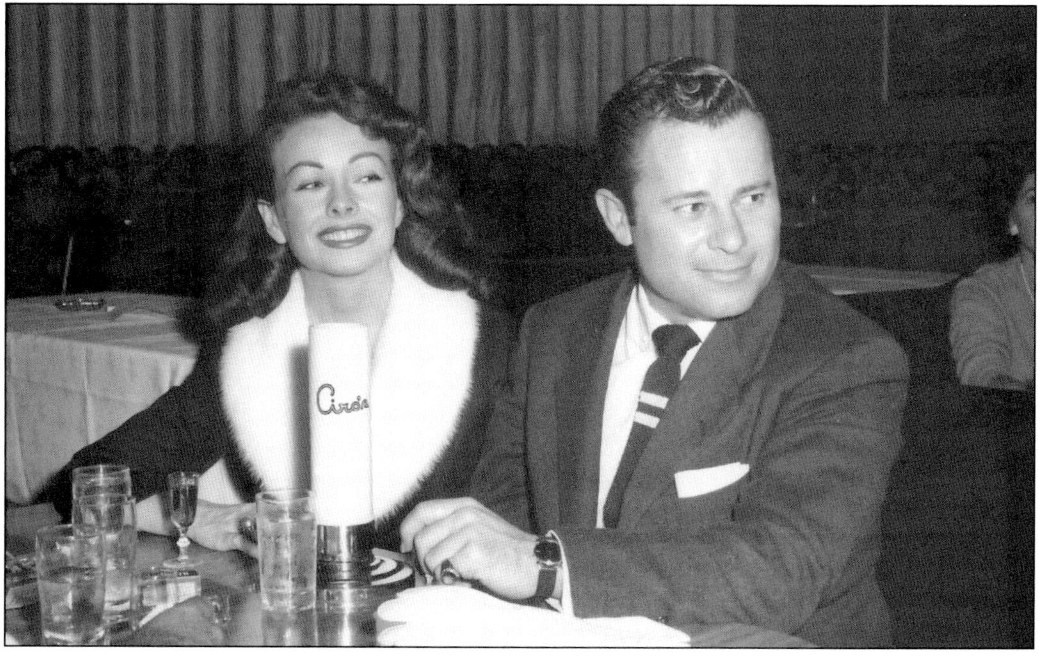

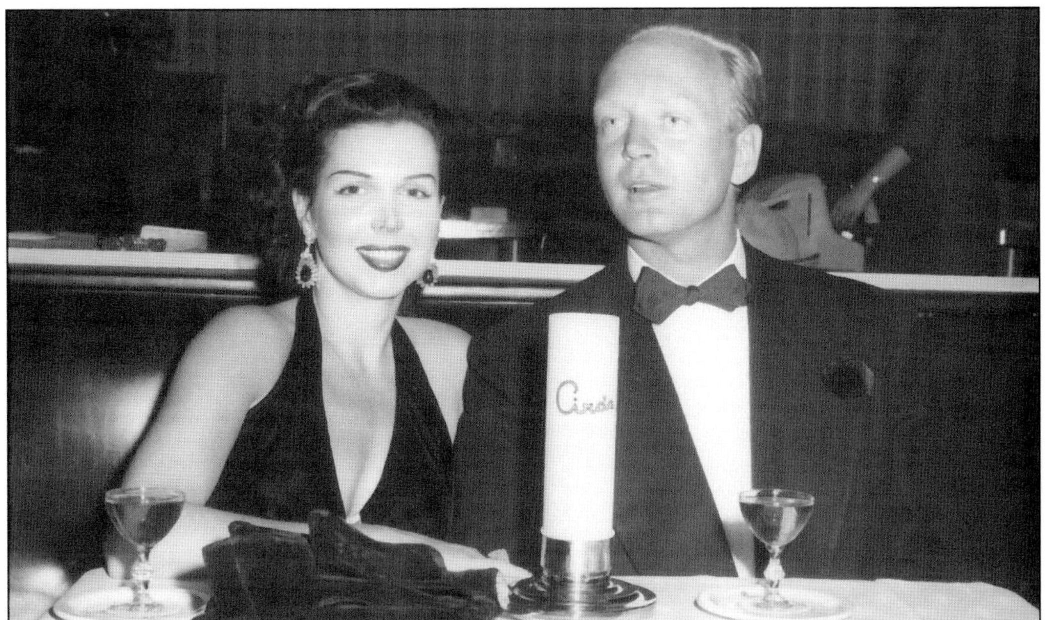

Actress, singer, and superb tap dancer Ann Miller was best known for her musical films during the 1940s and 1950s. Miller, who appeared older than she was as a teenager, began working as a dancer in nightclubs at age 13. She did so in order to help support her mother. Miller's acting career began with RKO at the same age; she lied and told them she was 18. A few of her best-known films with MGM include *Easter Parade*, *On the Town*, and *Kiss Me Kate*.

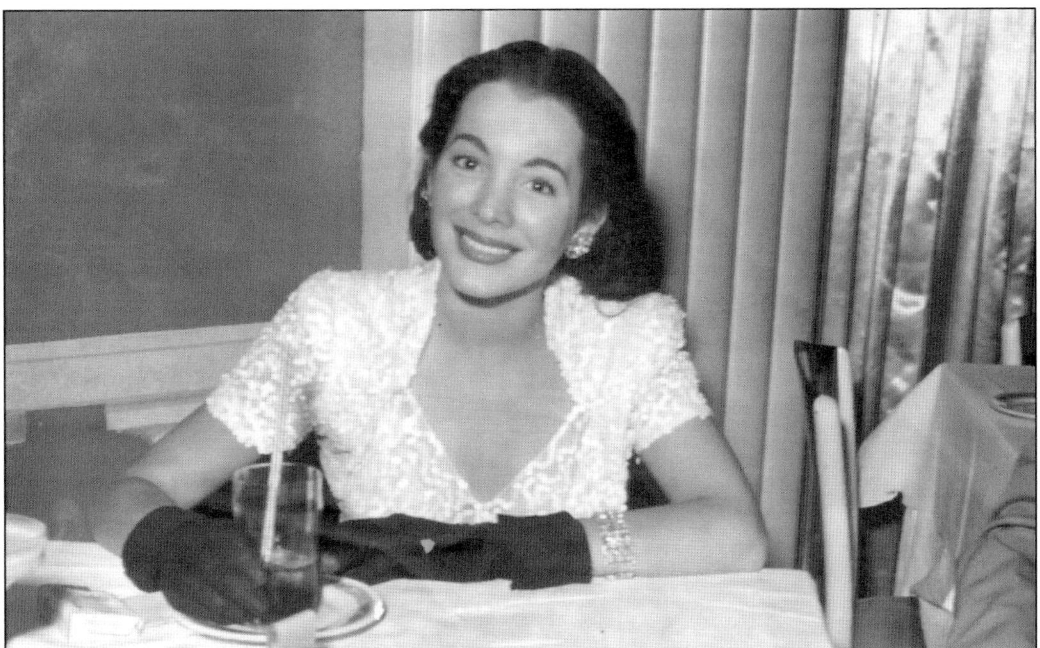

Actress Lita Baron, born in Spain, was best known for her work in *Champagne for Two*, *Jungle Jim*, and *Samba-Mania*. She performed as a singer and in dance numbers at Ciro's and other nightclubs with Xavier Cugat's band and singer Billy Daniels. She was married to actor Rory Calhoun from 1948 to 1970. Baron filed for divorce, citing Calhoun's numerous affairs.

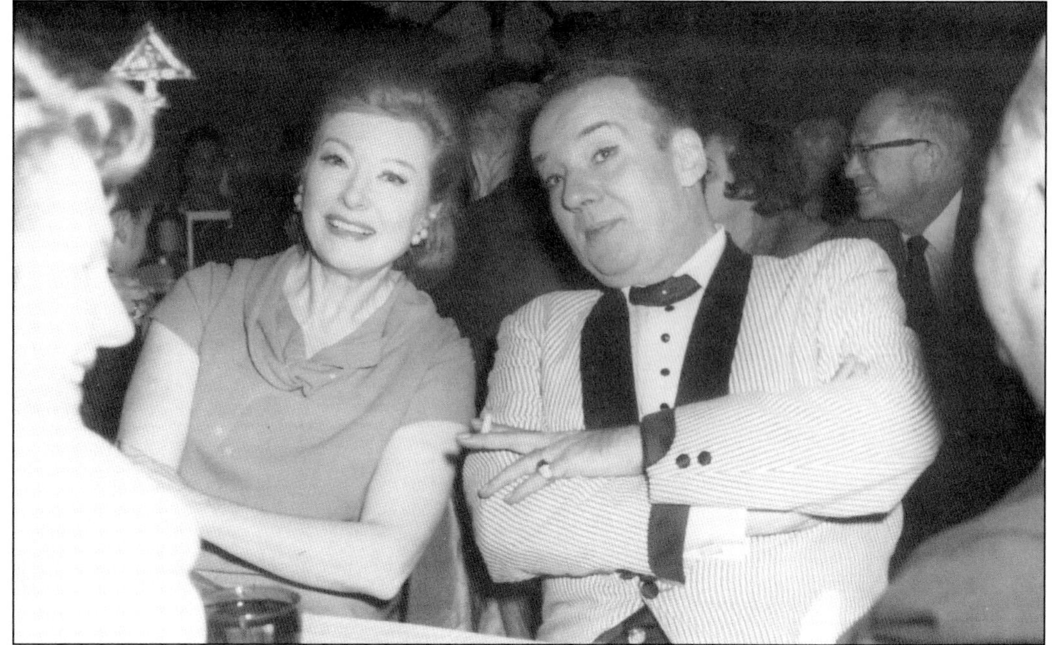

Greer Garson was a major MGM star of the 1940s. She was nominated for seven Academy Awards and won Best Actress in 1942 for the war drama *Mrs. Miniver.* She was married to actor Richard Ney from 1943 to 1947. Arthur Blake was a headlining nightclub comedian known for his impersonations, including female impersonations.

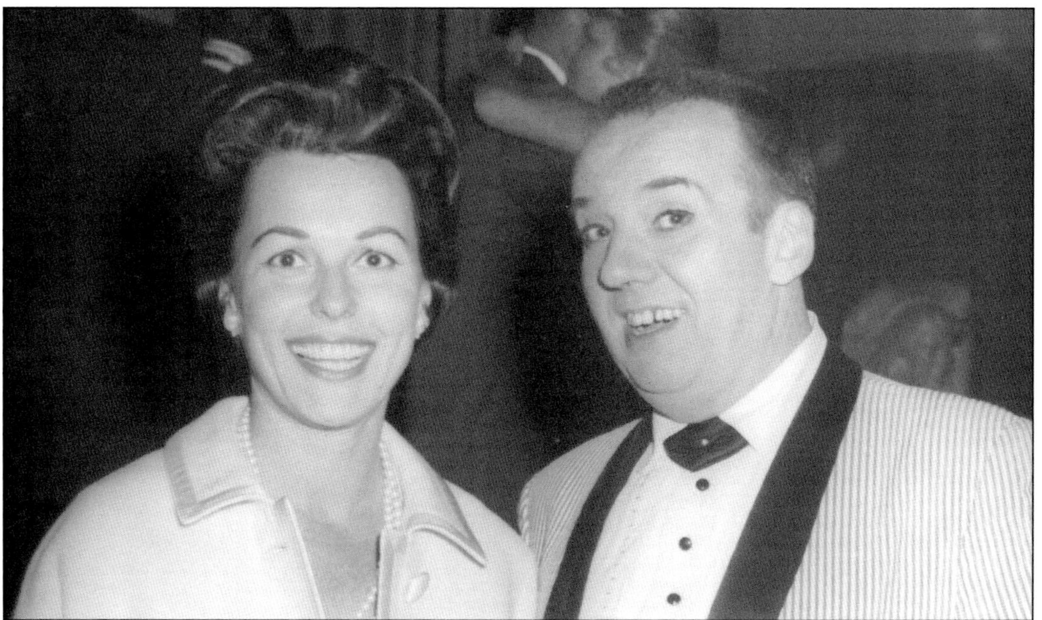

Bess Myerson was a model, actress, and the first Jewish American to be crowned Miss America, in 1945. She was on television in the 1950s and 1960s and had a political career that began in 1969 as a New York City commissioner. In the 1980s, her political career and aspirations ended as she was embroiled in conspiracy charges. Myerson is seen here posing with nightclub comedian Arthur Blake.

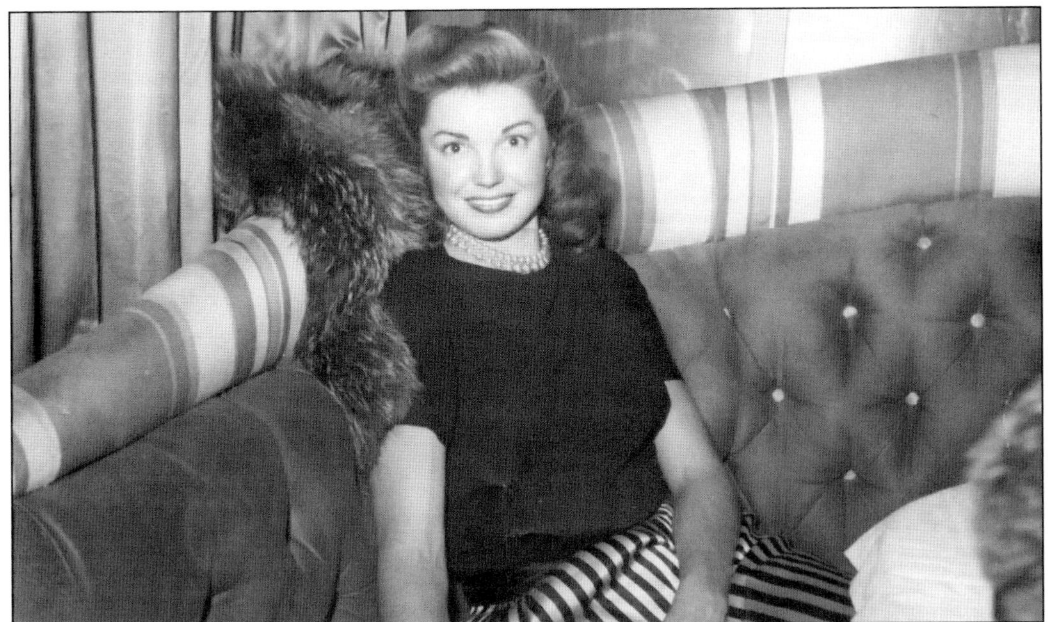

Esther Williams was a competitive swimmer and MGM film actress. Williams was known for her performances in major motion pictures in the 1940s and 1950s, with beautifully choreographed and perfectly synchronized swim sequences. A few of her best-known films are *Million Dollar Mermaid*, *Ziegfeld Follies*, and *Callaway Went Thataway*.

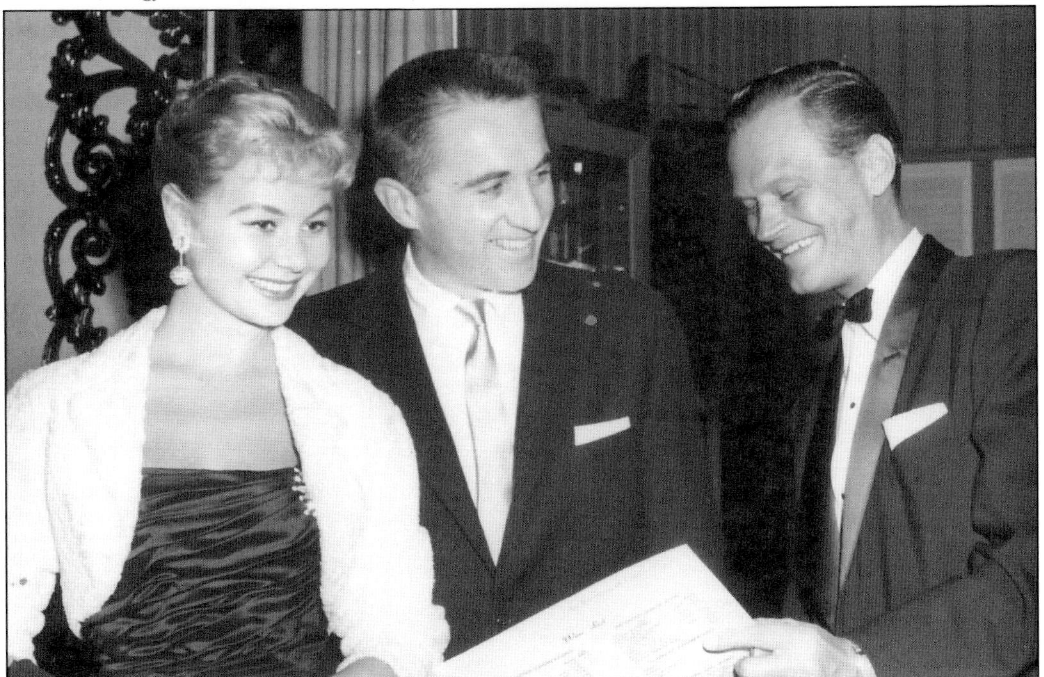

Mitzi Gaynor was a singer, actress, and dancer in numerous musical films. A few of her best know musicals include *There's No Business Like Show Business*, *For Love or Money*, and *South Pacific*. Jack Bean, Gaynor's husband, was her manager; he produced Gaynor's successful annual television musical specials in the 1960s and 1970s.

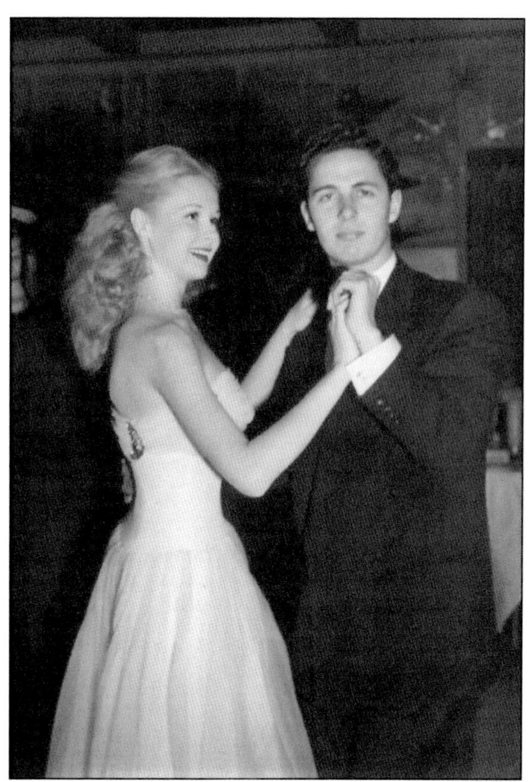

Joi Lansing was a successful model and actress. Her first acting roles, in 1948, were in the movies *The Counterfeiters*, *Easter Parade*, and *Julia Misbehaves*. She appears, uncredited, in one of the most popular movies of all time, *Singin' in the Rain*. She also plays the wife of Lester Flatt in the hit television comedy series *The Beverly Hillbillies*. Lansing was known for her pinup photographs and B movies. She died of breast cancer in 1972 at age 43.

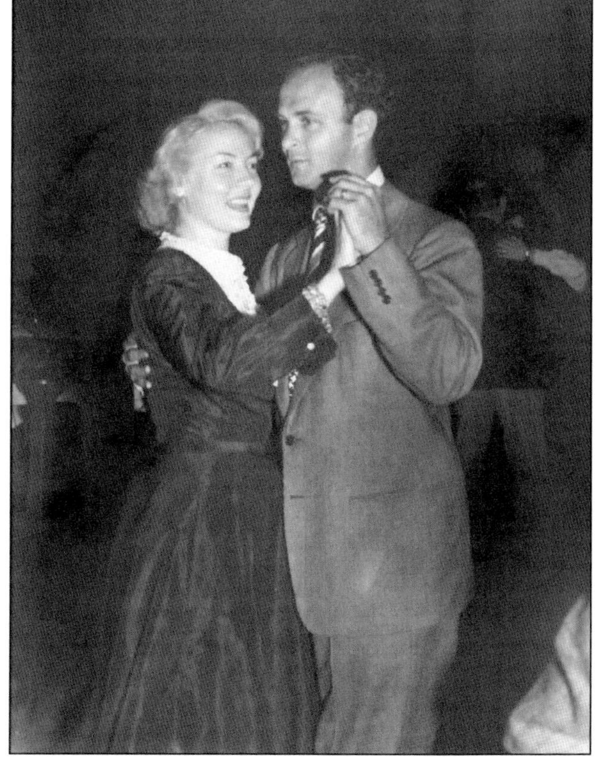

Audrey Totter began her career in the late 1930s on the radio. By the 1940s, she was a popular MGM movie star who appears in numerous film dramas as the female lead. In addition to MGM, Totter worked for 20th Century Fox and Columbia Pictures and was active from 1935 to 1987.

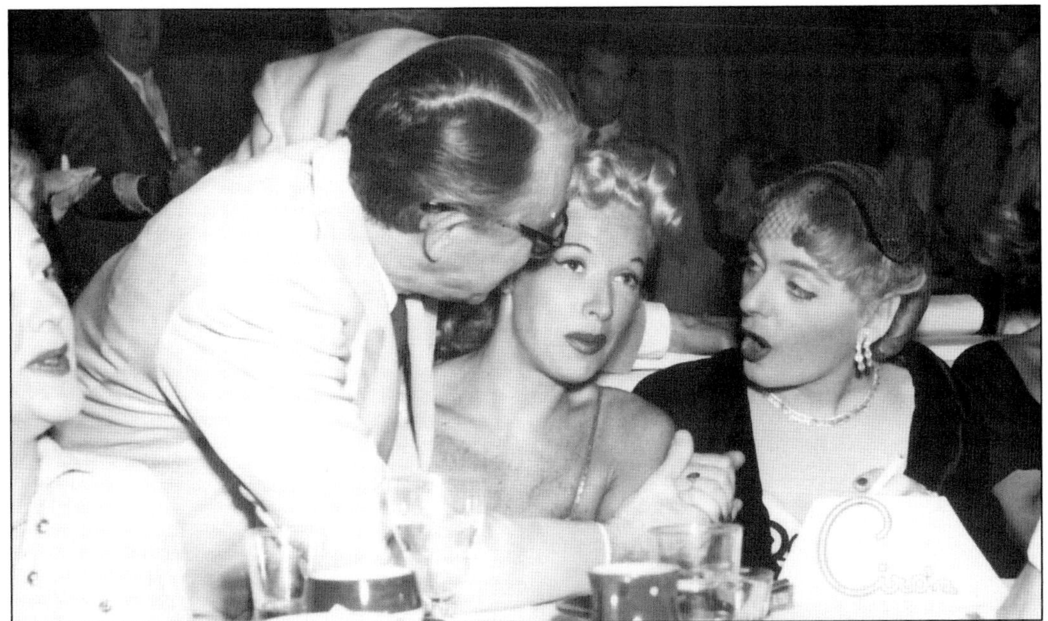

Christine Jorgensen (right) was an American nightclub entertainer, recorded singer, and actress who underwent hormone therapy and sex change operations in the early 1950s in Denmark. She became the face and witty spokesperson for the transgender community in the United States. She has been viewed as a pioneer who created questions in science, as well as in the minds of many Americans, regarding the definition of sexuality. Jorgensen was influential to many transsexual people during her day.

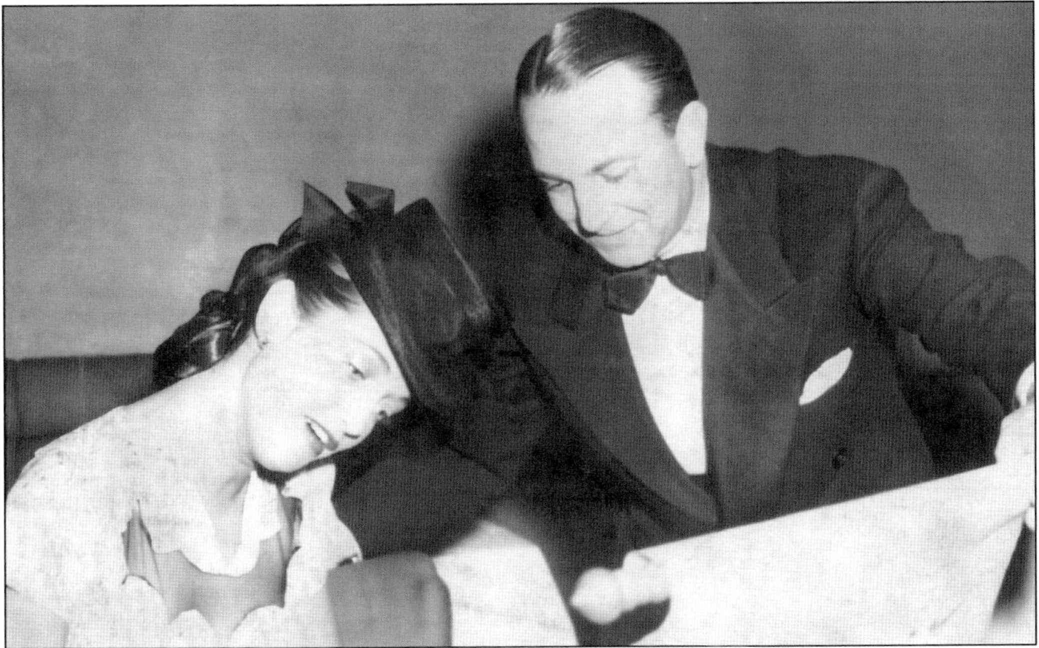

Dorothy Lamour began as a big band singer in the 1930s. In the 1940s, she was a popular actress who is best remembered in the series of comedy films with the beginning title *The Road to . . .* with Bob Hope and Bing Crosby. She appeared for the last time on-screen in 1987.

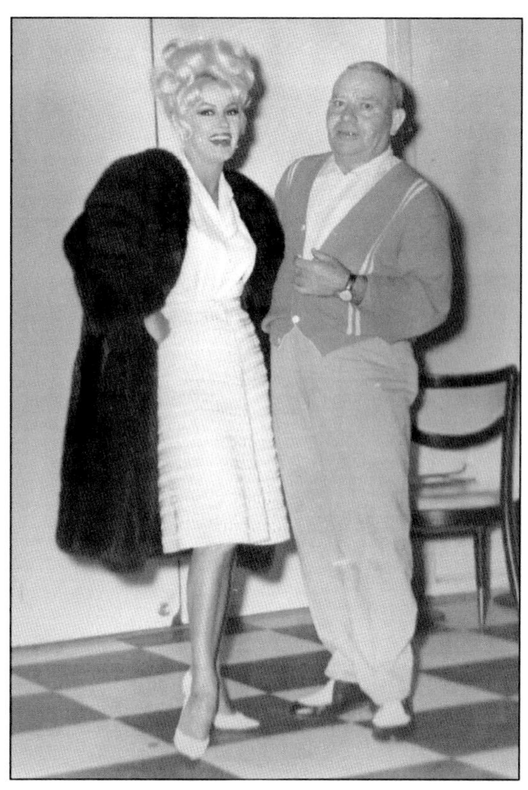

Mamie Van Doren was a voluptuous, platinum blonde actress, singer, nightclub performer, model, and sex symbol who was discovered by Howard Hughes. She appeared in movies mainly in the 1950s and 1960s. She also appeared in independent and foreign productions. In 1957, Van Doren was the lead in a B musical called *Untamed Youth*. This movie is noted as the first in American films where an actress sings rock-and-roll music in a musical.

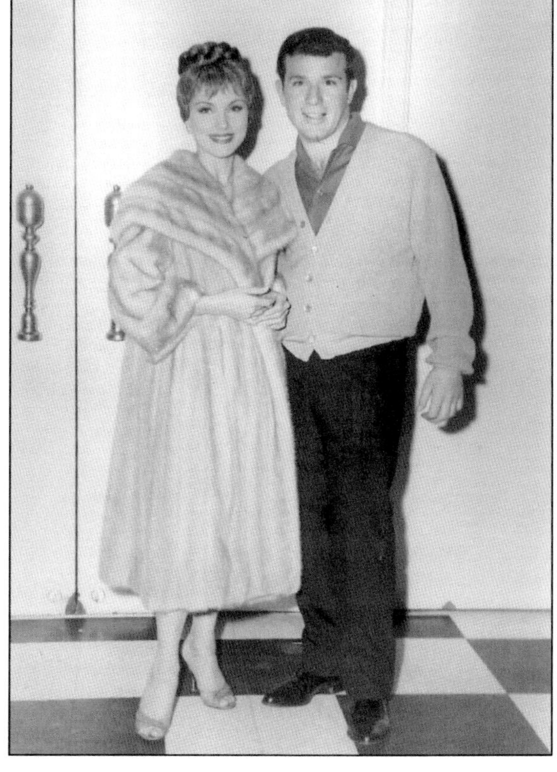

Actress Debra Paget's first movie was 1948's *Cry of the City*. She was cast as Lilia in the 1956 Cecil B. DeMille classic *The Ten Commandments* without having to audition. She also appears in Elvis Presley's debut film, *Love Me Tender*. In the mid-1960s, she retired from film after marrying a Chinese millionaire. She got divorced in 1980 and came out of retirement to host a Christian television program on the Trinity Broadcasting Network.

Actress Kim Novak was discovered while standing in line in Los Angeles, hoping to be an extra in a movie. She was signed to Columbia Pictures in 1954 and has been in such notable films as *Picnic*, *Pal Joey*, *Middle of the Night*, *Vertigo*, and *The Notorious Landlady*, to name a few. The last movie Novak made in the 1960s was *The Great Robbery*; then she retreated from the glare of a Hollywood life to Big Sur for four years. She returned to acting sporadically from 1970 to 1991. From 1986 to 1987, Novak appeared 19 times on the hit television show *Falcon Crest*. Novak left Hollywood in 1991 and has remained mostly out of the limelight. Her love of visual arts, nature, and animals has inspired her to paint, create poetry, and raise horses.

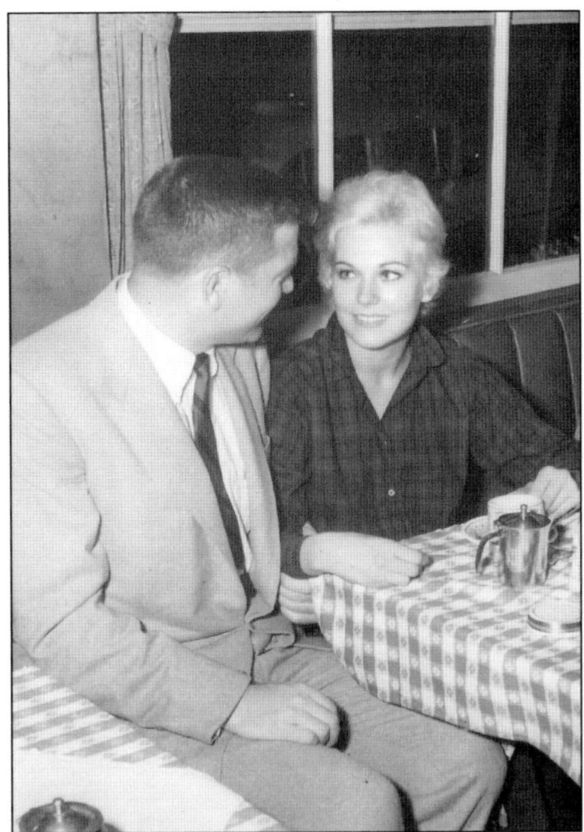

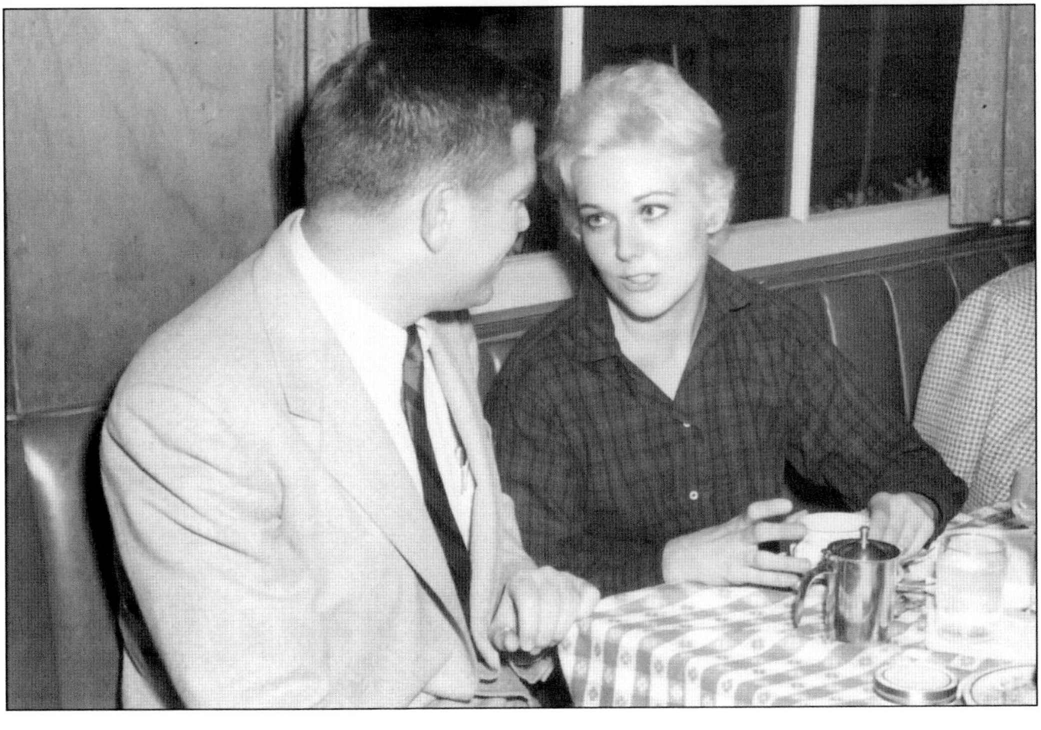

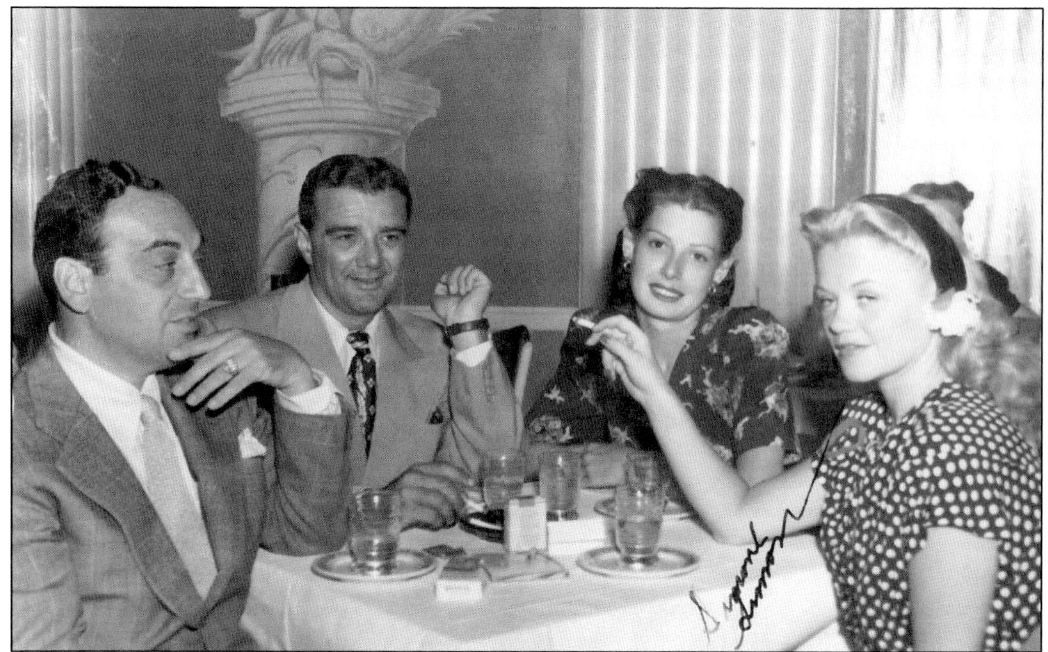

Simone Simon (right) was a French model and designer prior to becoming an actress. She appears in both French and American films from the 1930s to 1970s. Her work in the B horror film *Cat People* was memorable, but her acting career in America never completely took off. After World War II, she returned to Europe, where she continued to act in various French movies.

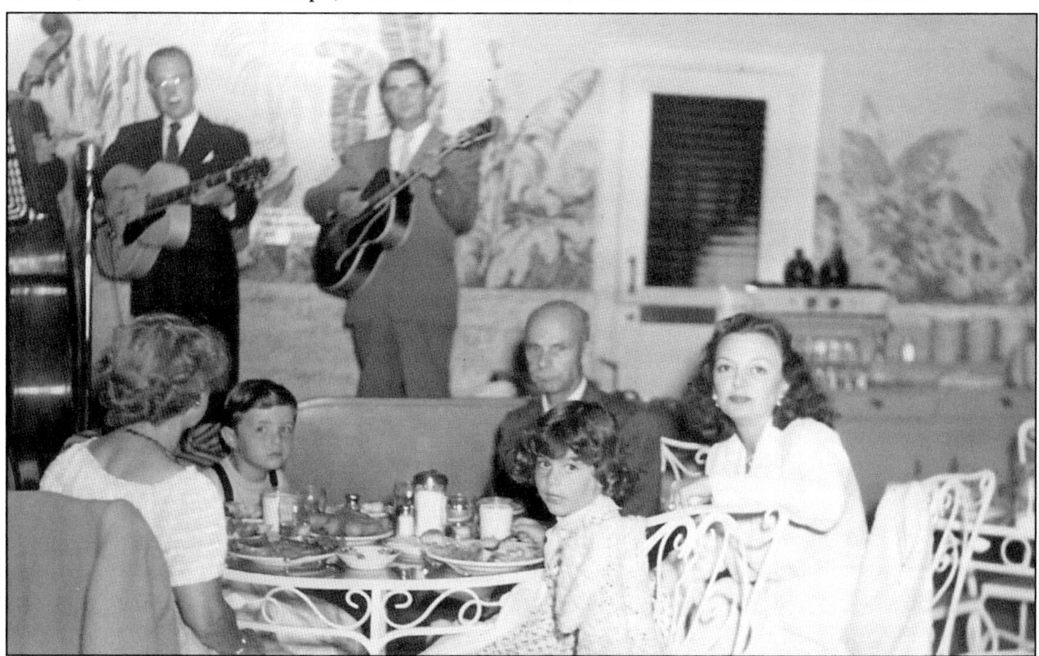

Tallulah Bankhead (right) was an outspoken, uninhibited radio show host and celebrated actress of stage, television, and film. She was in two British silent movies prior to coming to America, where she was a fixture on Broadway. In 1944, Bankhead filmed the memorable role of Constance "Connie" Porter in Hitchcock's movie *Lifeboat*.

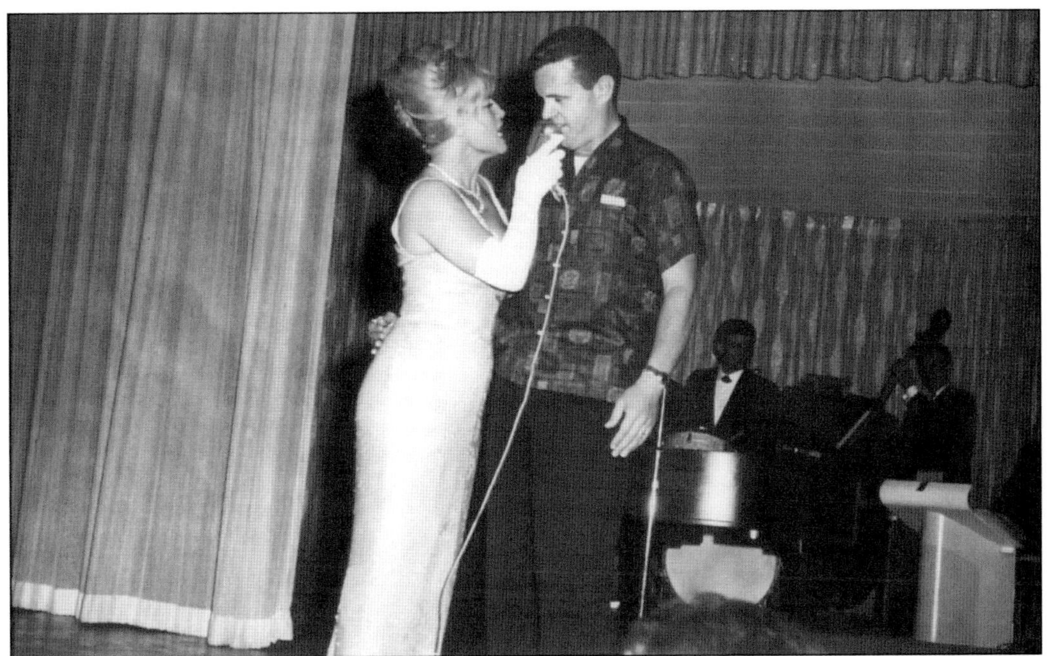

Denise Darcel was a French actress who played vampy roles in Hollywood films and on television after World War II. Her first movie role was in the 1948 *To the Victor.* In 1949, she was in *Battleground,* and in 1950, she played in *Tarzan and the Slave Girl.* In 1954, she had the lead role in *Vera Cruz* opposite Burt Lancaster and Gary Cooper. Her movie roles fizzled out in 1961.

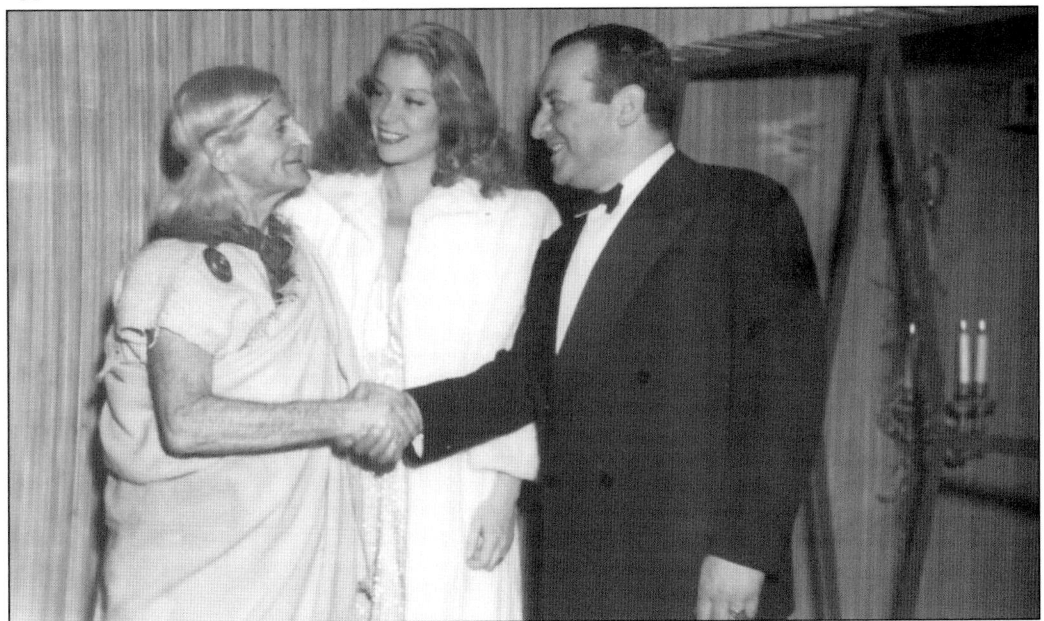

Mitzi Green began her career as a childhood actress for Paramount and RKO Pictures. She appears in *Tom Sawyer* and *Huckleberry Finn* in 1930 and 1931, respectively, and is the lead in *Little Orphan Annie*. Green performed in some movies as an adult but mostly turned her attention to performances onstage. She was the lead in *Babes in Arms* in 1937. "Brother" is pictured on the left and Ciro's owner, Herman Hover, is on the right.

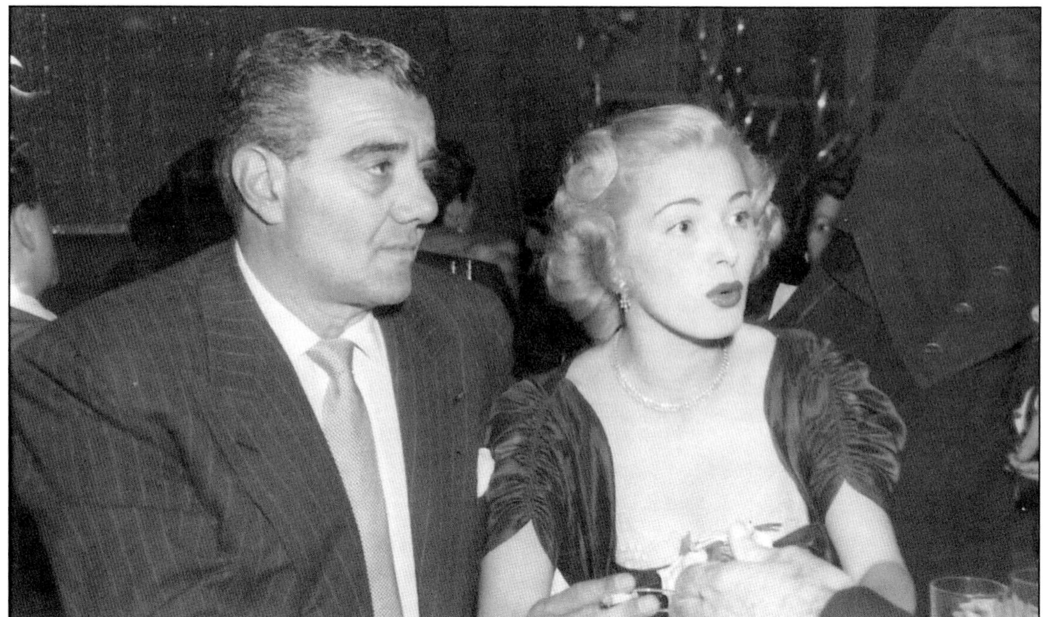

Versatile actress Eleanor Parker was known as the "Woman of a Thousand Faces." Parker was nominated for Best Actress three times, for her portrayal as a prisoner in *Caged*, in William Wyler's *Detective Story*, and for her performance in *Interrupted Melody*. She may be best remembered as the Baroness in the 1965 classic *The Sound of Music*. Parker has over 80 movie and television credits.

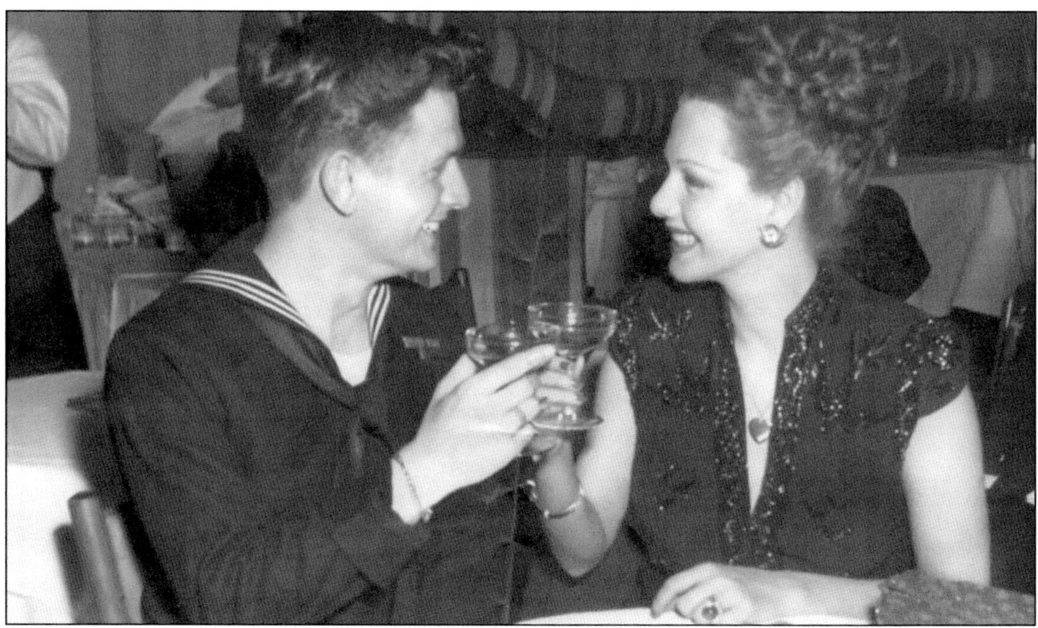

Maria Montez was a beautiful film actress from the 1940s who was born in the Dominican Republic and was of Spanish decent. Her popularity declined by the early 1950s, and she moved to France and appeared in films there. She may be remembered for her work in the films *Arabian Nights*, *Ali Baba and the Forty Thieves*, *Cobra Woman*, and *Portrait of an Assassin*. In 1951, Montez was found dead in her bathtub; she was 39.

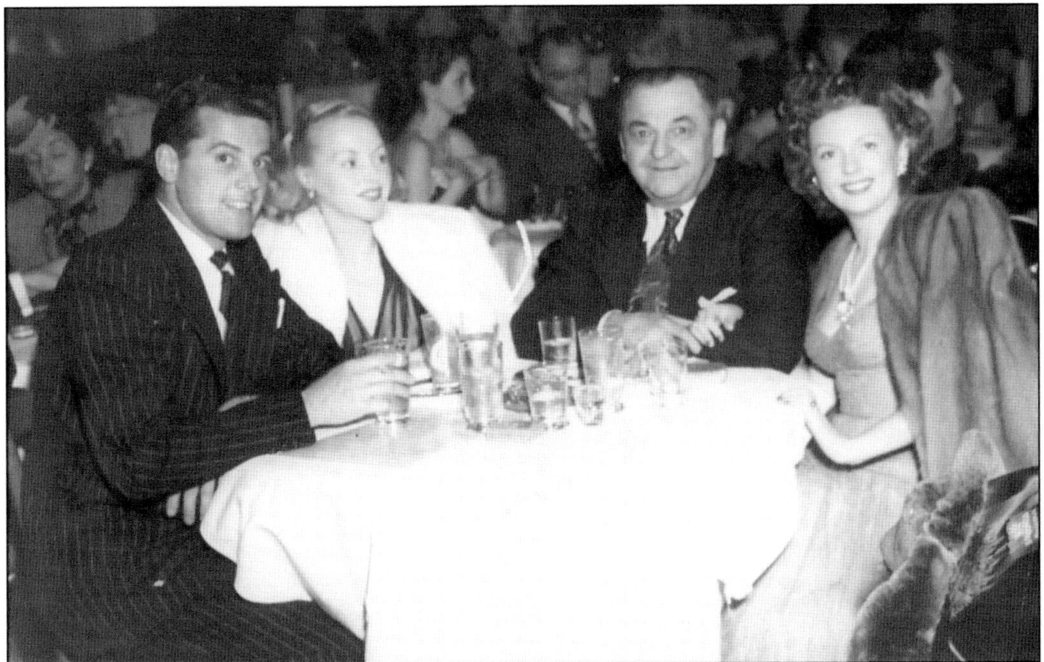

Martha Stewart (second from left) was an actress in film, television, and musical theater as well as a singer. Her film and television credits are limited, as she was only active from 1946 to 1964. She was married to comedian and singer Joe E. Lewis from 1946 to 1948. Stewart retired from acting in 1964.

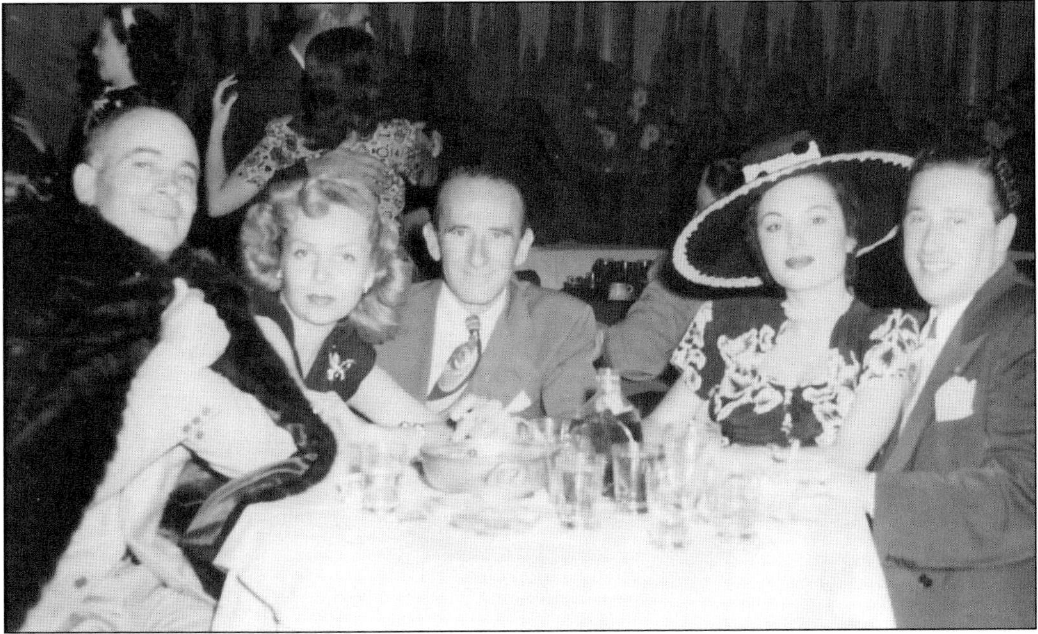

Margaret Sullavan (second from left) was an actress of film and stage. Sullavan preferred acting onstage to film. She made a total of 16 movies including *Three Comrades*, for which she received an Oscar nomination for her role as Pat Hollmann. She was active from 1929 until 1960. In 1960, at the age of 50, Sullavan died from an accidental barbiturate overdose.

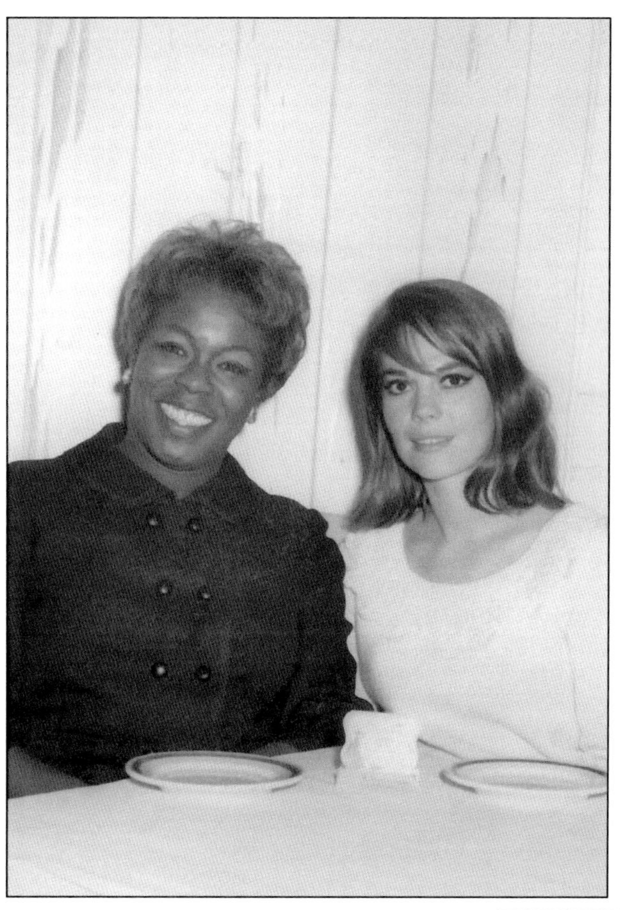

Grammy Award winner and Grammy Hall of Fame inductee Sarah Vaughan (left) was a jazz vocalist and pianist who sang with big bands prior to pursuing a solo career. Her long career spanned from 1942 to 1989. She recorded numerous songs; a few of her most well known titles include "Misty," "Summertime," "Whatever Lola Wants," and "The Banana Boat Song." Natalie Wood (right), daughter of Russian immigrants, was in 56 film and television movies over a short life span. She began her career as a child actress in 1943 at four years old. She appears in the Christmas classic *Miracle on 34th Street*. Wood stars in many classic films such as *Rebel Without a Cause*, *Splendor in the Grass*, *West Side Story*, *Gypsy*, and *Love with the Proper Stranger*. She received three Oscar nominations for her work. Wood died at age 43 in what was originally deemed a drowning accident. However, in 2013, after reopening of the case, the cause of death was classified as "drowning and other undetermined factors."

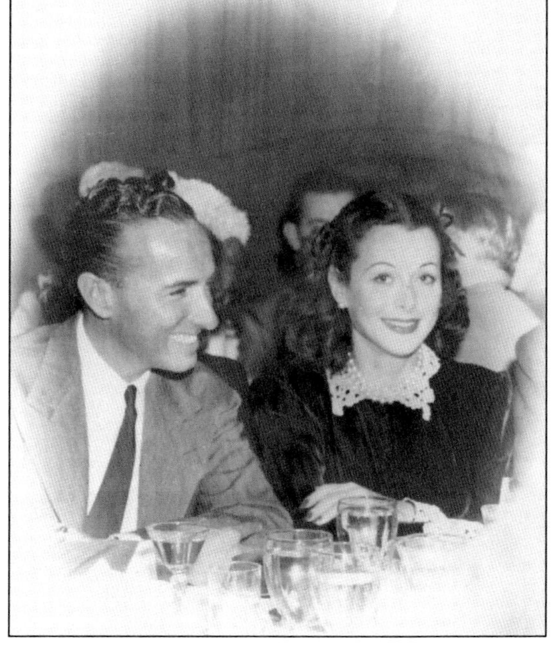

Actor and socialite Lloyd Pantages is pictured with beautiful MGM-contracted actress and inventor Hedy Lamarr. Pantages had one uncredited role in 1935 film *Dante's Inferno*. Lamarr was in about 35 films and appeared on various television series, game shows, and talk shows. For the war effort, Lamarr and composer George Antheil developed a frequency hopping system to improve radio-controlled torpedoes, preventing America's enemies from jamming radio frequencies. Prepunched paper rolls would unpredictably change the radio frequency, making radio jamming impossibly difficult. This complicated technology was later used in Bluetooth and Wi-Fi technology.

Three

Leading Men and Famous Actors

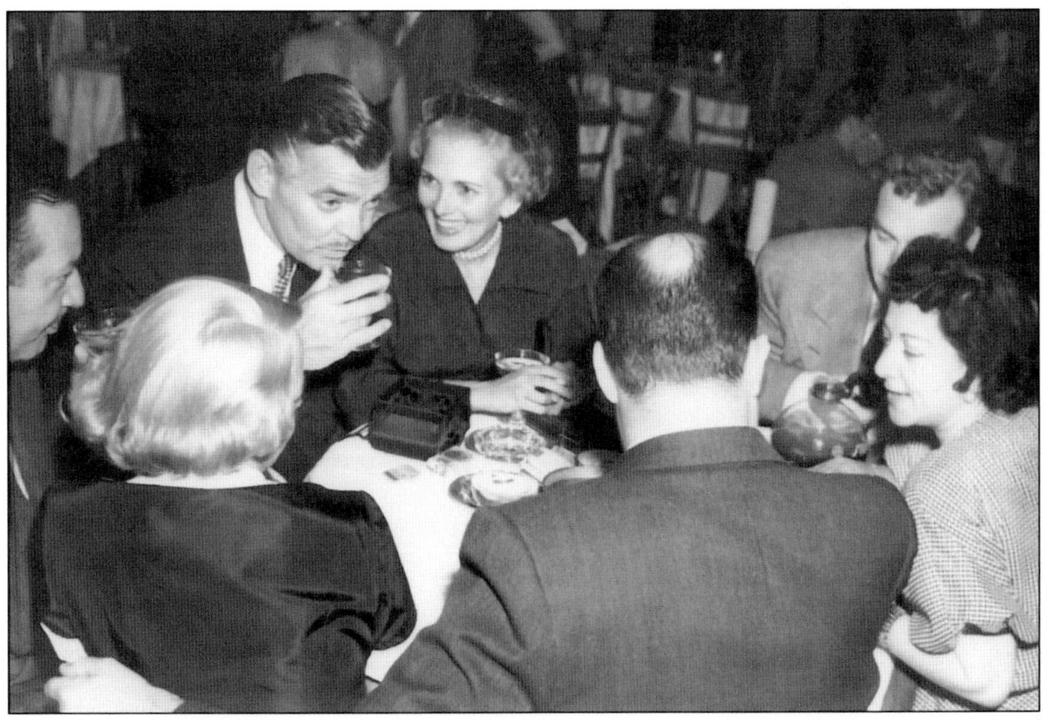

Screen legend Clark Gable, referred to as "The King of Hollywood" had a unique charisma and masculinity that translated into consistent box office success throughout his career. He is the male lead in more than 60 films but is undeniably best remembered as Rhett Butler in the epic *Gone with the Wind.* Some of his other critically acclaimed films include *It Happened One Night*, *Mutiny on the Bounty*, and his last film, *The Misfits.* Anita Colby (right of Gable) was a model and actress.

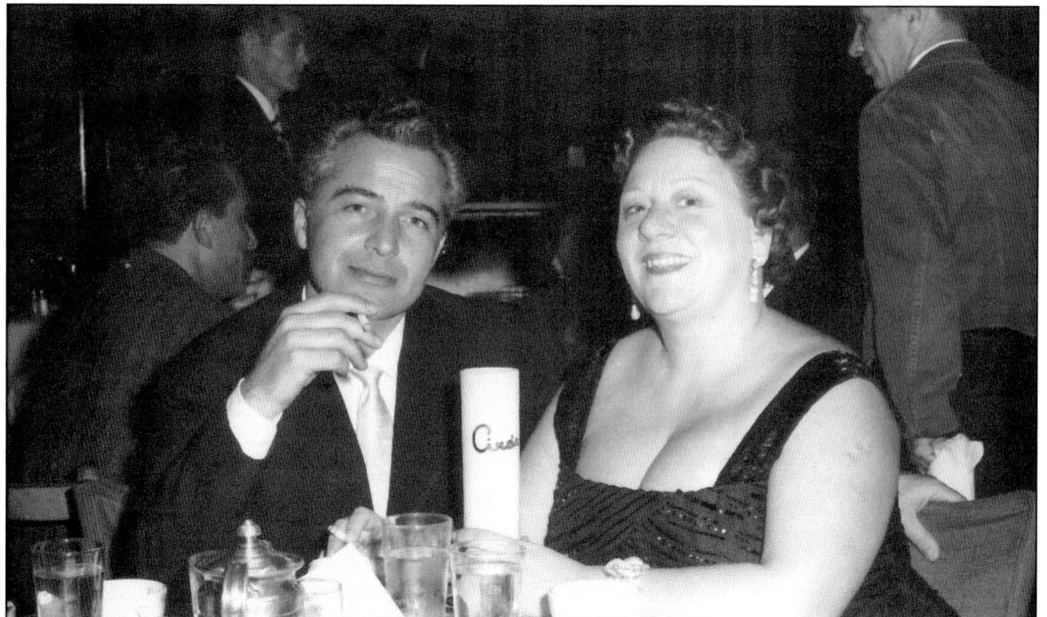

Rossano Brazzi, seen here with his wife, Baroness Lidia Bertolini, was an Italian actor. Prior to acting, Brazzi was a lawyer in Italy who became a respected stage director. He became an international star with his roles in *Three Coins in the Fountain* and *Summertime*, with Katharine Hepburn. He made films and television appearances mostly in Europe. Brazzi and Bertolini were married from 1940 until Bertolini's death in 1981.

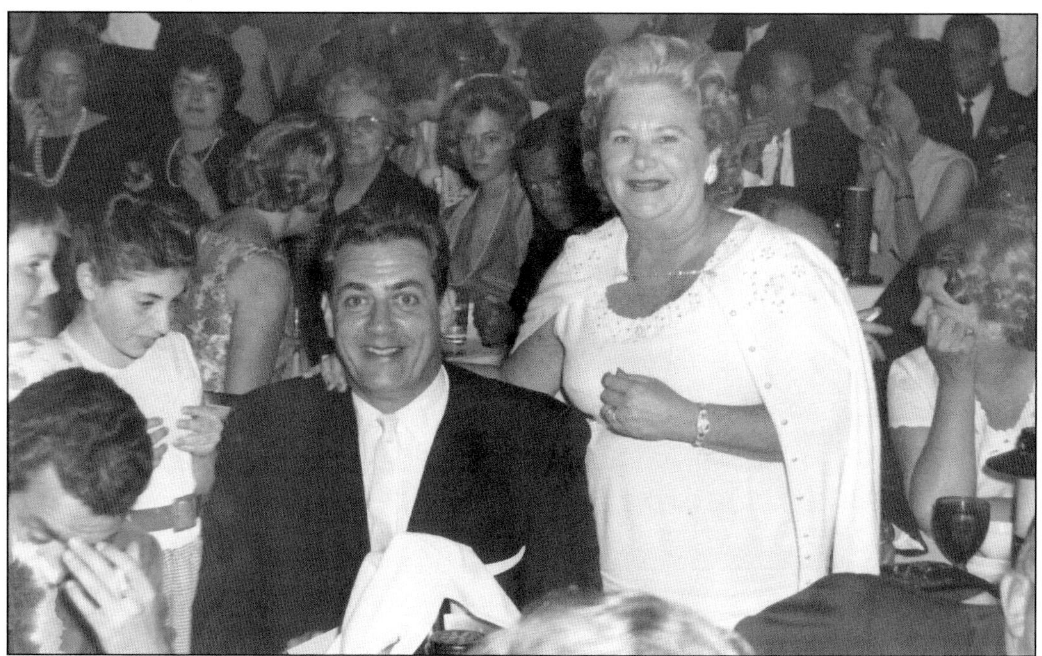

Raymond Burr was a television, radio, stage, and film actor who is best remembered for his television drama roles on *Perry Mason* and *Ironside*. He received two Emmys for his work on *Perry Mason* and six Emmy nominations for his work on *Ironside*. He is in Hitchcock's thriller *Rear Window*, playing the suspected murderer. Burr was involved in numerous charitable endeavors.

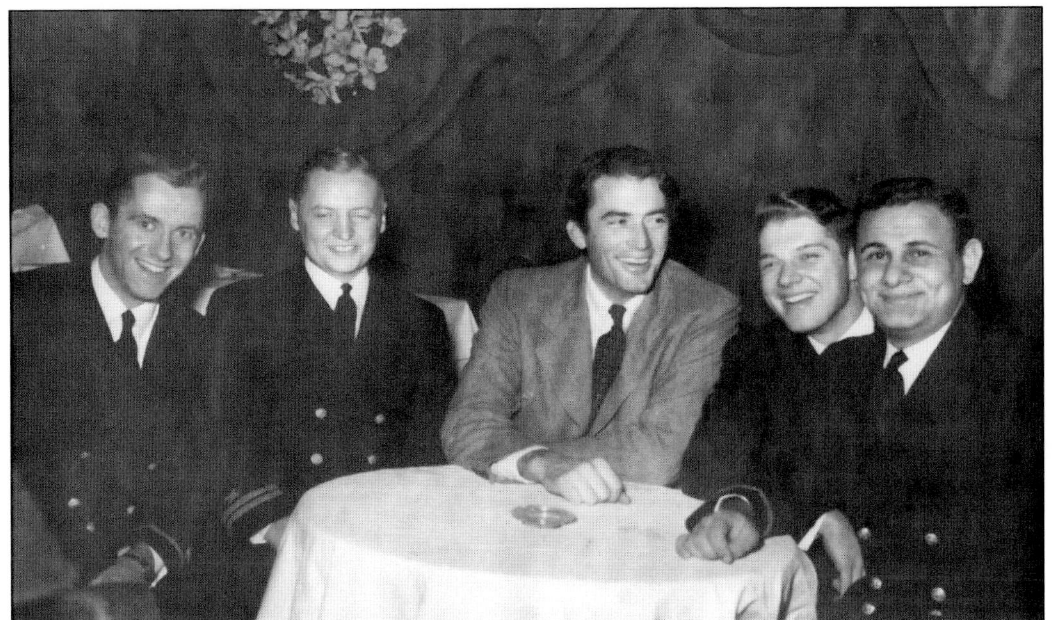

The American Film Institute ranked Gregory Peck (center) as one of the best male actors of all time. He appears in Westerns, thrillers, melodramas, war movies, and comedies. He was nominated five times for Best Actor and received an Academy Award in his most notable performance as Atticus Finch in *To Kill a Mockingbird*. Several other memorable performances include his work in *Spellbound*, *The Yearling*, *Gentleman's Agreement*, and *Roman Holiday*.

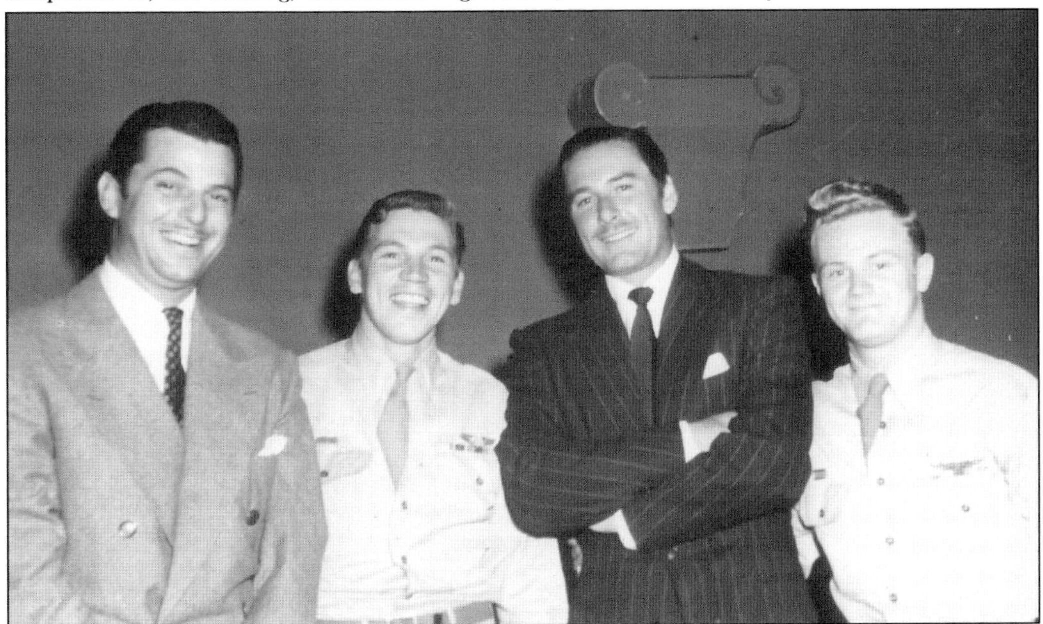

John Carroll (far left) was an actor in various Western, action, drama, and comedy productions. A few of his best known movies include *Zorro Rides Again*, *Only Angels Have Wings*, *Go West*, and *Flying Tigers*. Errol Flynn (second from right) was an Australian American actor known for his swashbuckler movies. He stars in nine movies with Olivia de Havilland, including *The Adventures of Robin Hood*. He died at age 50 of a heart attack.

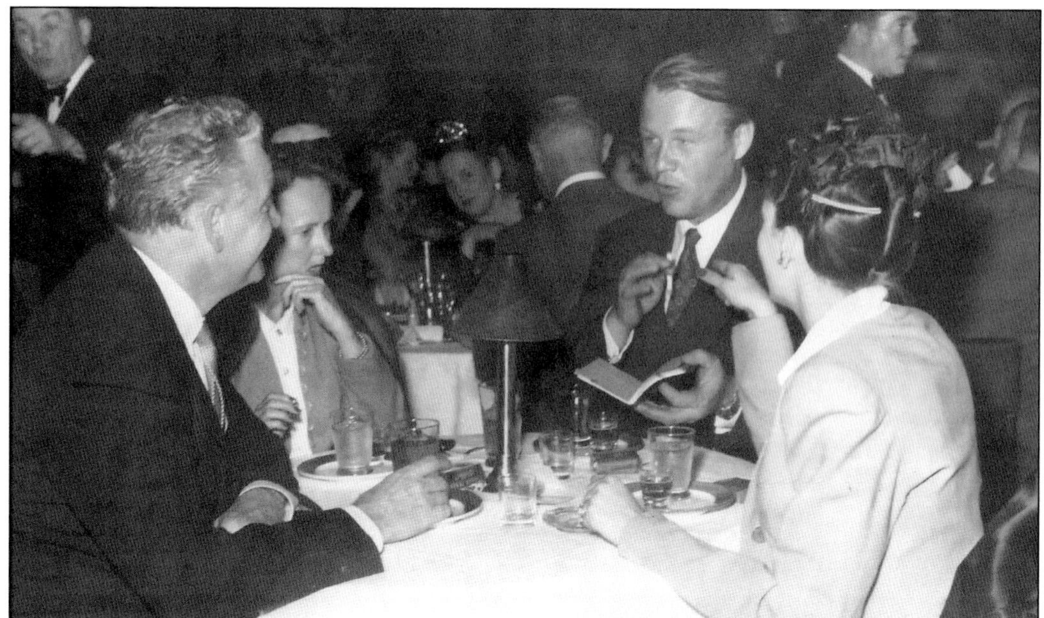

Wayne Morris (middle right) was an actor and World War II ace fighter pilot. Morris's few notable film credits include *Kid Galahad*, *Paths of Glory*, and *The Bushwhackers*. While filming a 1940s movie about flying, *Flight Angels*, he became interested in aviation and consequently became a pilot. During World War II, he was a Navy flier and awarded Air Medals and Distinguished Flying Crosses for his contribution to the war effort. Morris died of heart failure at age 45.

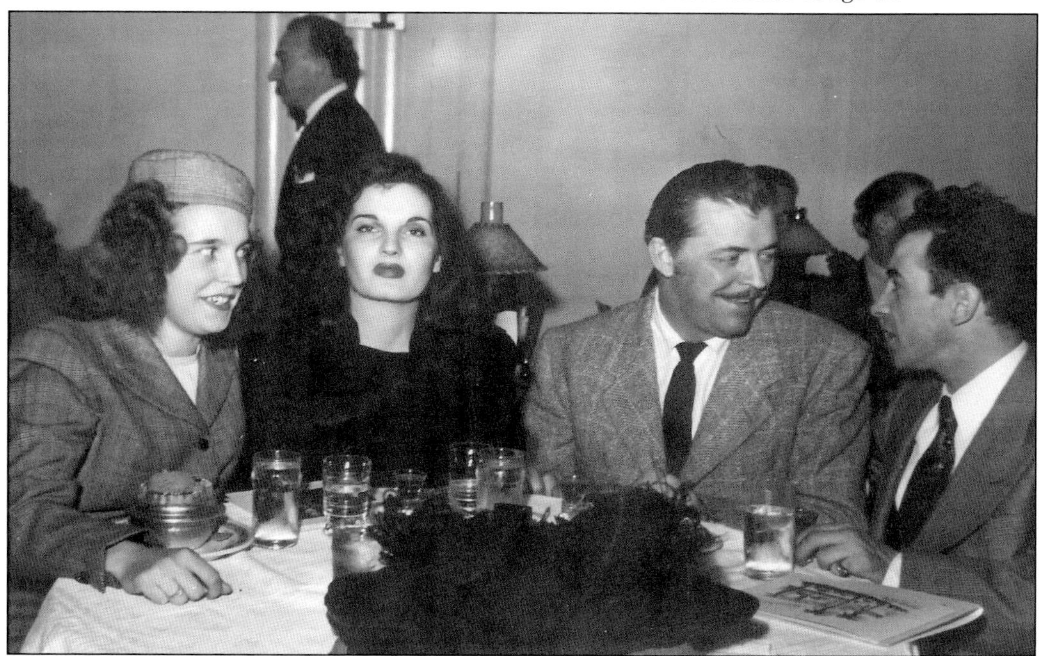

Lyle Talbot (second from right) was a television, film, and stage actor who is best known for his character Joe Randolph in television comedy *The Adventures of Ozzie and Harriet*. His career spanned over 50 years, and he appears in more than 150 films, in both supporting and lead roles in B movies. Talbot was a founding member of the Screen Actors Guild (SAG).

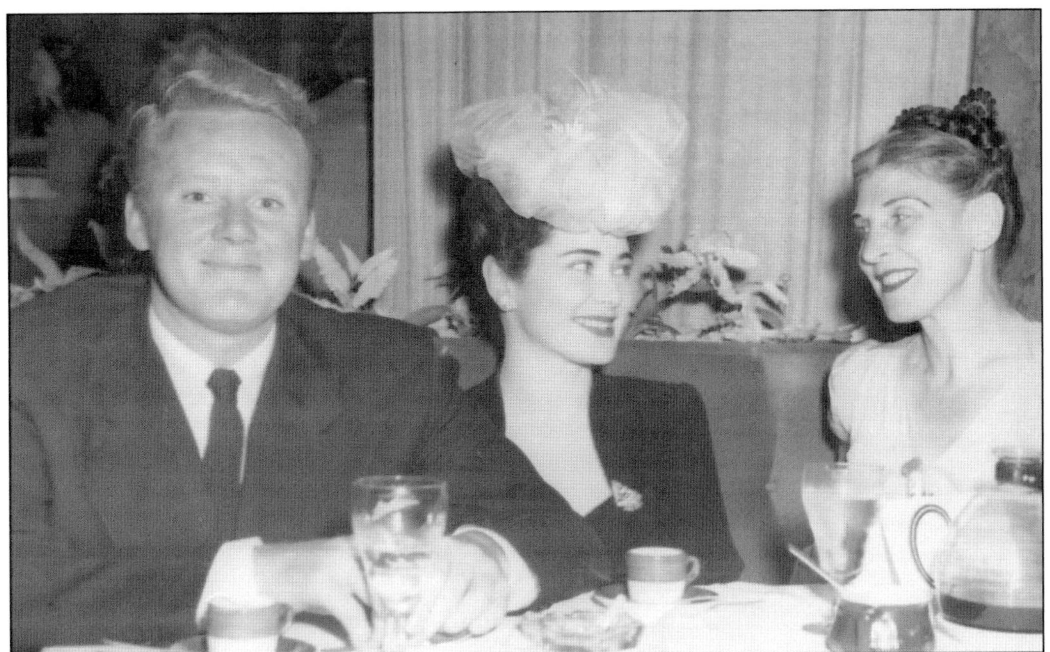

Van Johnson was a dancer, singer, and actor onstage and in film and television. He had a wholesome and amiable boy-next-door look about him and was often cast into roles highlighting and capitalizing on his looks. He was a major star for MGM in the 1940s and 1950s. A few of Johnson's most popular movies include *The Caine Mutiny*, *Battleground*, and *Brigadoon*.

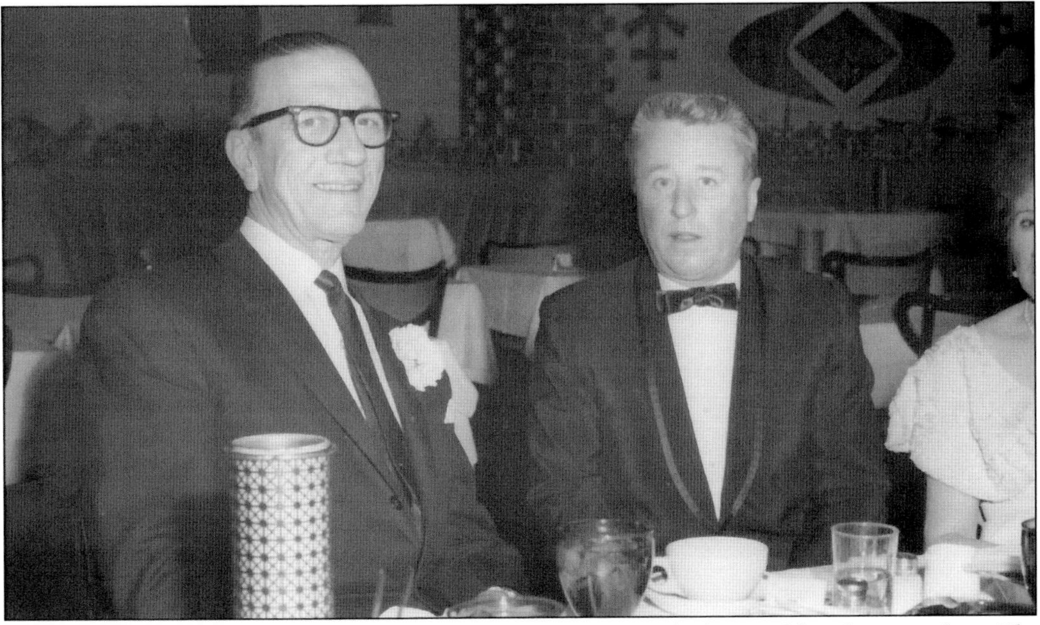

George Gobel (right) was a comedian and actor best known for his weekly television show *The George Gobel Show*, which aired from 1954 to 1960. Gobel and his business manager, David O'Malley, produced the *Leave It to Beaver* television program from 1957 to 1961. Gobel performed on Broadway, in Las Vegas, in film, on game shows, and made numerous guest appearances on talk shows. He was active from 1953 until 1988.

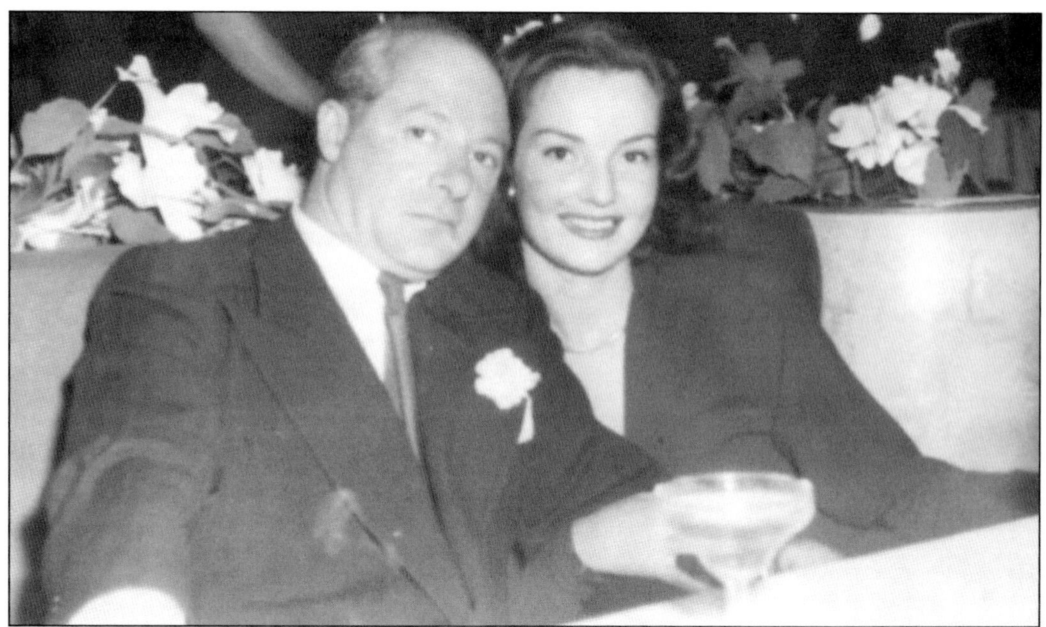

George Jessel was a multitalented comedic entertainer who was active from 1919 to 1978. Jessel began entertaining in vaudeville at age 10 to help support his family after his father had passed away. By age 11, he was Eddie Cantor's partner in a vaudeville act. Jessel was an actor, singer, songwriter, and Academy Award–winning producer. In total, he produced 24 films. He was toastmaster at many political events and gatherings. In the early 1950s, he had a radio show called *The George Jessel Show*, and from 1953 to 1954, the show became a televised series. From 1954 to 1956, he guest starred on *The Jimmy Durante Show*, which aired on NBC.

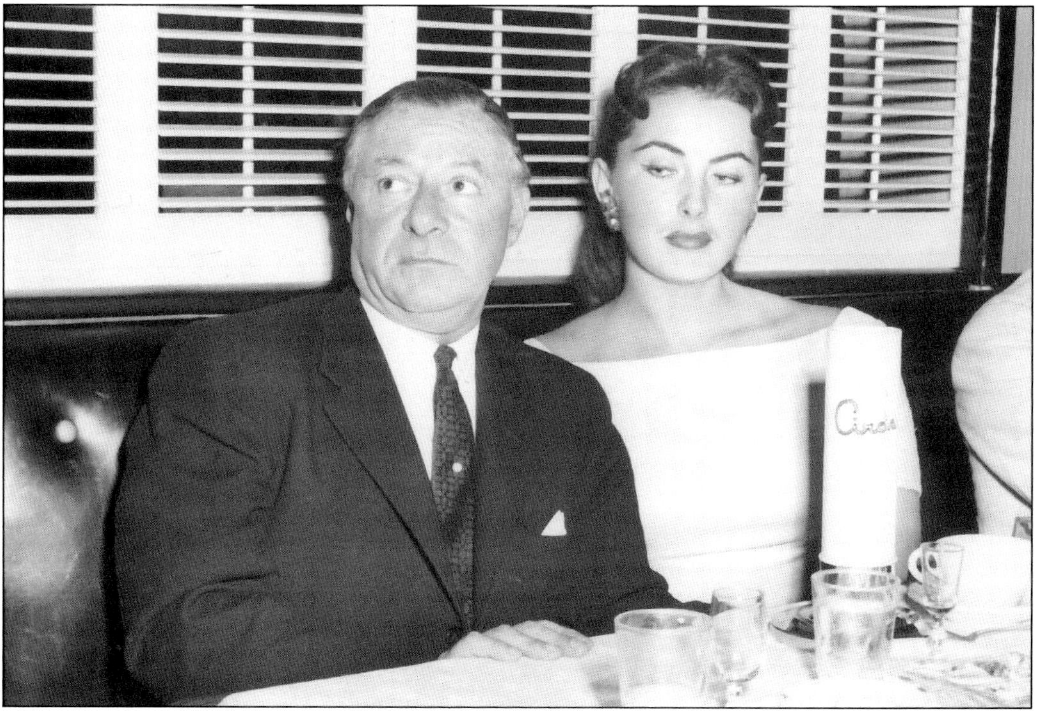

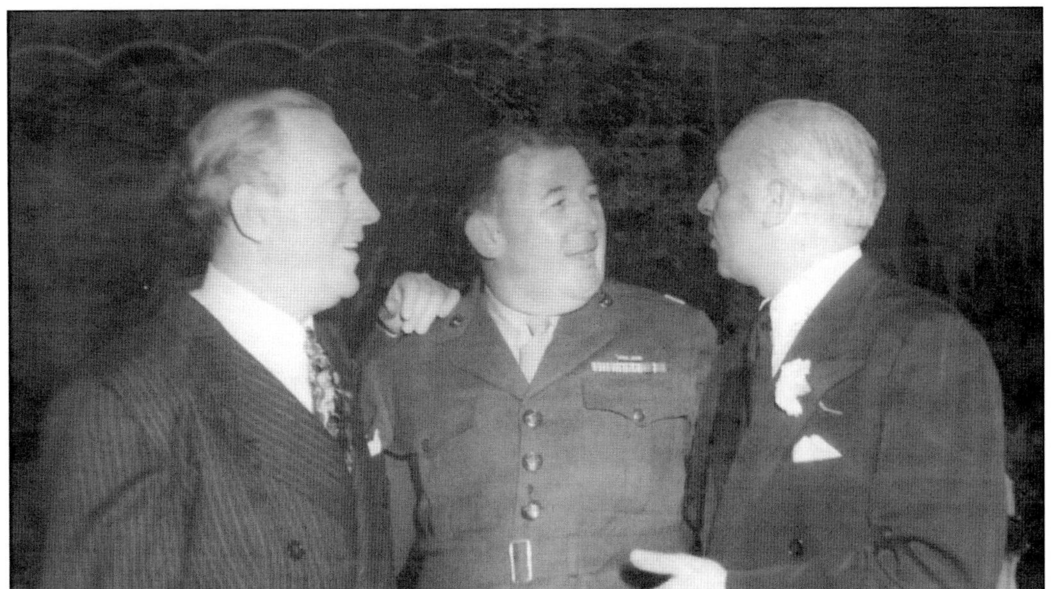

Pat O'Brien (far left) was a television, film, and radio actor with over 100 screen credits. He is best remembered for his role as a football coach in the movie *Knute Rockne, All American*, where, in his climatic speech, he encourages his team to "win one for the Gipper." Ronald Reagan plays the part of George Gipp, a football player who dies during the film. Walter Winchell (far right) was an influential radio and television personality but mostly known for his gossip column from the 1920s to the 1960s.

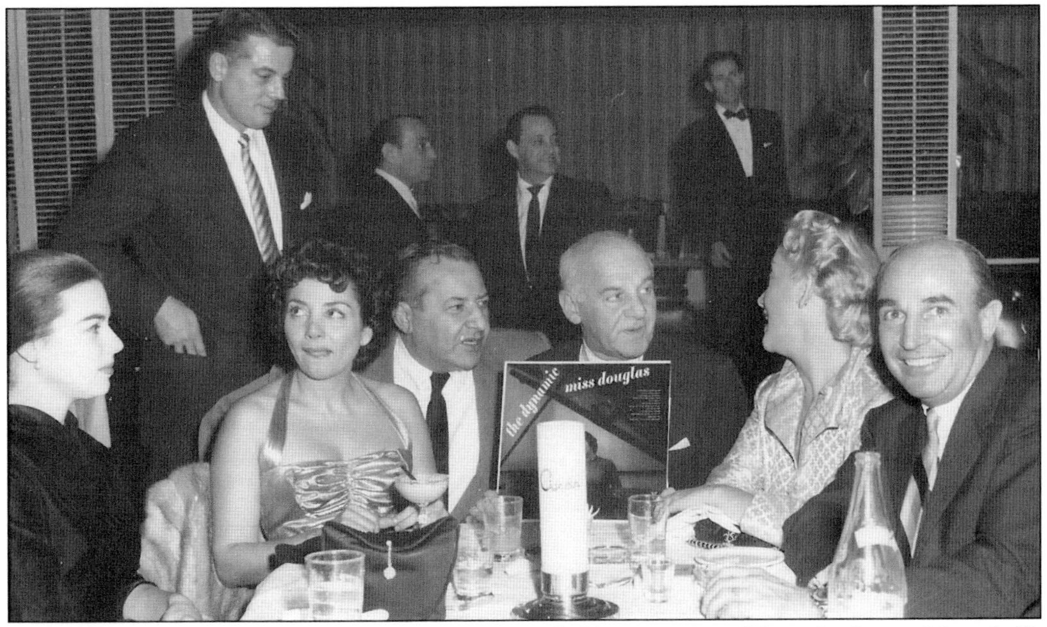

In this photograph are Hover's wife Yvonne Hover (left), singer "Miss" Douglas (second from left), Ciro's owner Herman Hover (third from left), and Walter Winchell (third from right). Winchell was the first to have a syndicated gossip column, in 2,000 papers from the 1920s to 1960s and with 50 million readers. He was known for exposing tantalizing information about powerful people in the industry and popular celebrities.

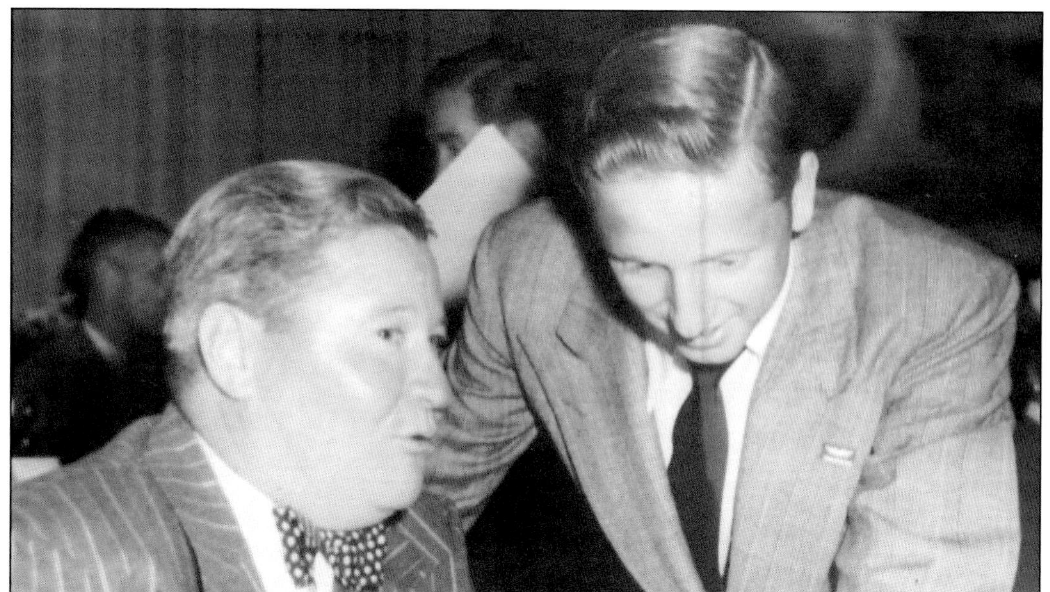

Comedic actor Jack Oakie (left) appears in 87 films, mostly from the 1930s and 1940s. He received a Best Supporting Actor nomination for his role as Benzino Napaloni in Charlie Chaplin's *The Great Dictator.* Television and film producer Dave Wolper (right) produced highly popular shows and films such as *Roots, The Thorn Birds, L.A. Confidential,* and *Willy Wonka & the Chocolate Factory.* Wolper produced numerous documentaries, and in 1971 received an Academy Award for *The Hellstrom Chronicle*, a film about insects.

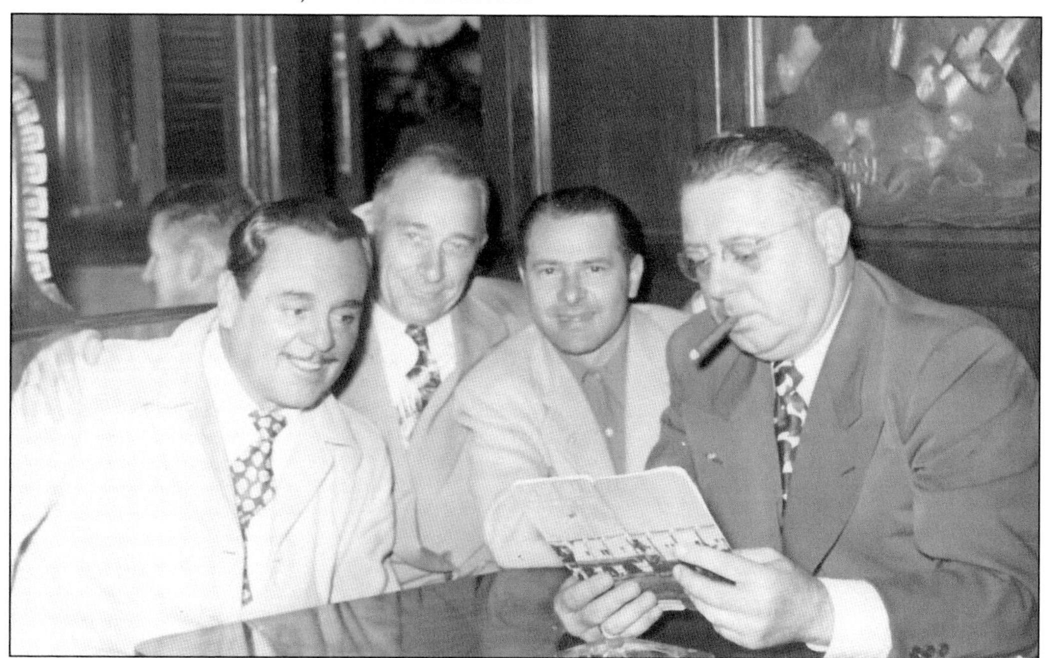

Leo Carrillo (far left) was an actor, political cartoonist, and conservationist. He appeared on Broadway and in more than 90 films. He is possibly best remembered for his role as Pancho in the television series *The Cisco Kid.* Due to his 18-year dedication and service to the commission of California beaches and parks, a state beach located west of Malibu was named in his honor.

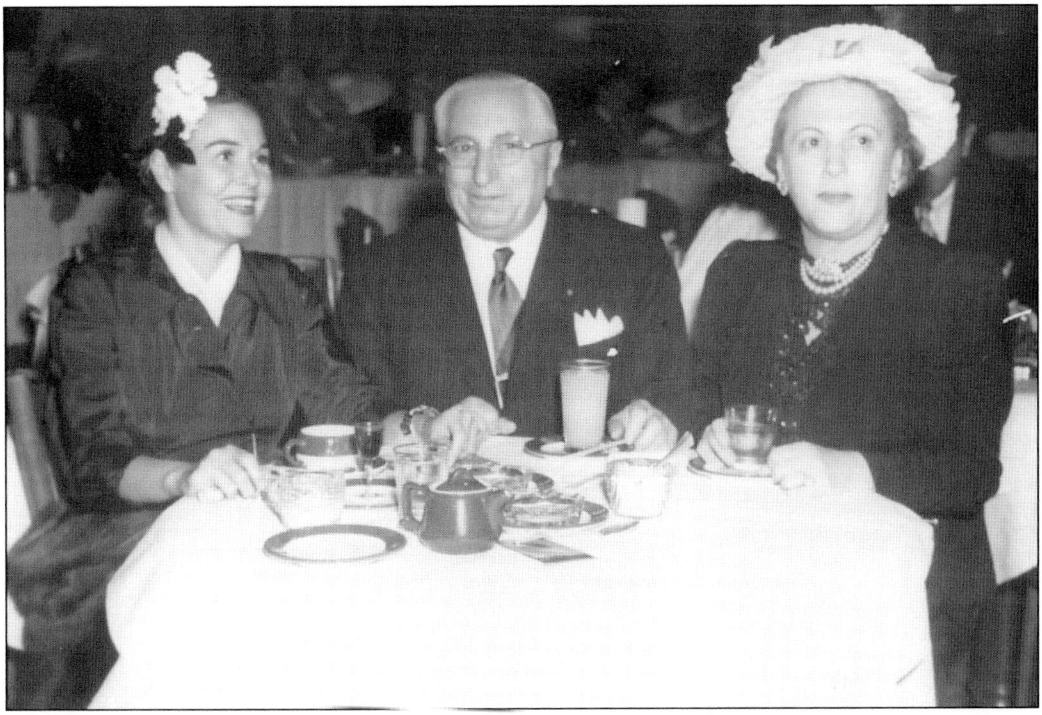

Louis B. Mayer, with his wife, Lorena (left), was a film producer and cofounder of Metro-Goldwyn-Mayer (MGM). Mayer made MGM into a thriving studio and was considered the most influential person in Hollywood from the 1920s to the late 1940s. He was gifted at developing stars and creating wholesome entertainment.

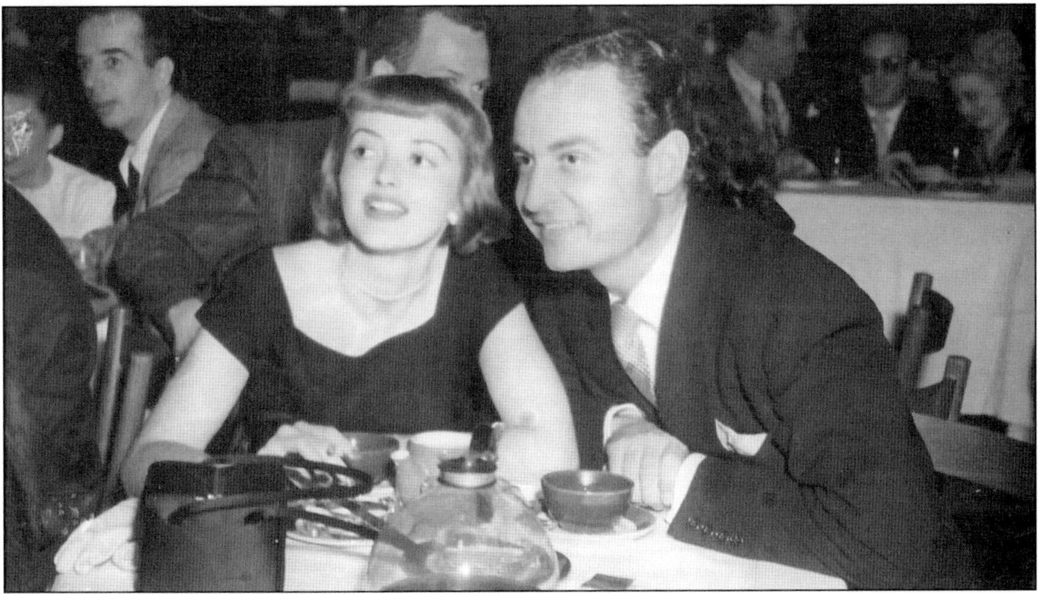

The well-liked and well-known A.C. Lyles worked his way up from an office boy at Paramount Pictures to film producer. He is best known for producing various low-budget, profitable Westerns during the 1950s and 1960s. He produced nine episodes of *Rawhide* and, in recent years, was a consulting producer on HBO's award-winning *Deadwood* from 2005–2006.

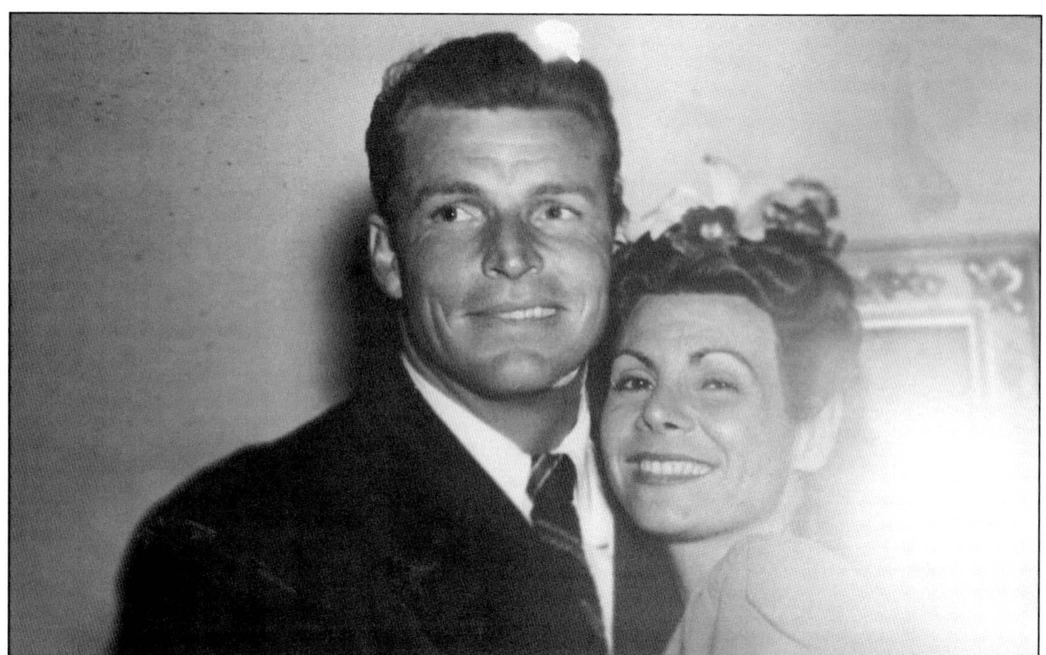

Buster Crabbe was a freestyle swimmer gold medalist in the 1932 Olympics. Crabbe was also an actor in sci-fi serials and low-budget Western films in the 1930s and 1940s. In the 1950s, he was in serial pirate movies and active on television, playing lead roles in anthologies such as *Million Dollar Rookie* and *Cowboy for Chris*.

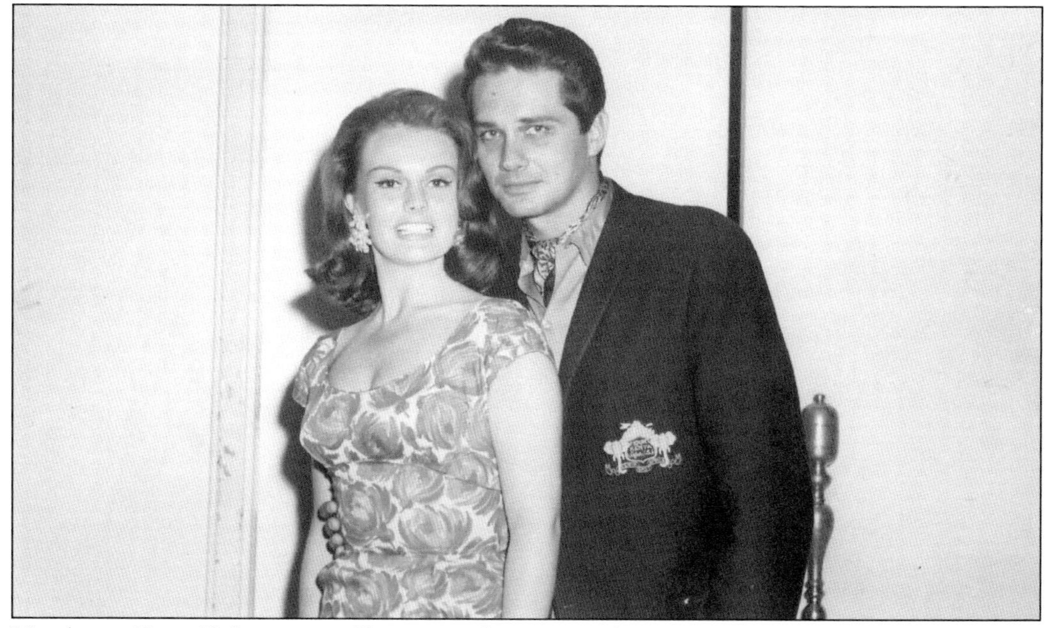

Handsome Brett Halsey was a film actor who appeared in numerous European and B movies in the 1950s and 1960s. In the 1970s and 1980s, he was seen on daytime soap operas and in a handful of films here and there. He was married to second wife, Luciana Paluzzi, from 1960 to 1962. Paluzzi was an actress in movies such as *The Green Slime* and *Muscle Beach Party* and a Bond girl in *Thunderball*.

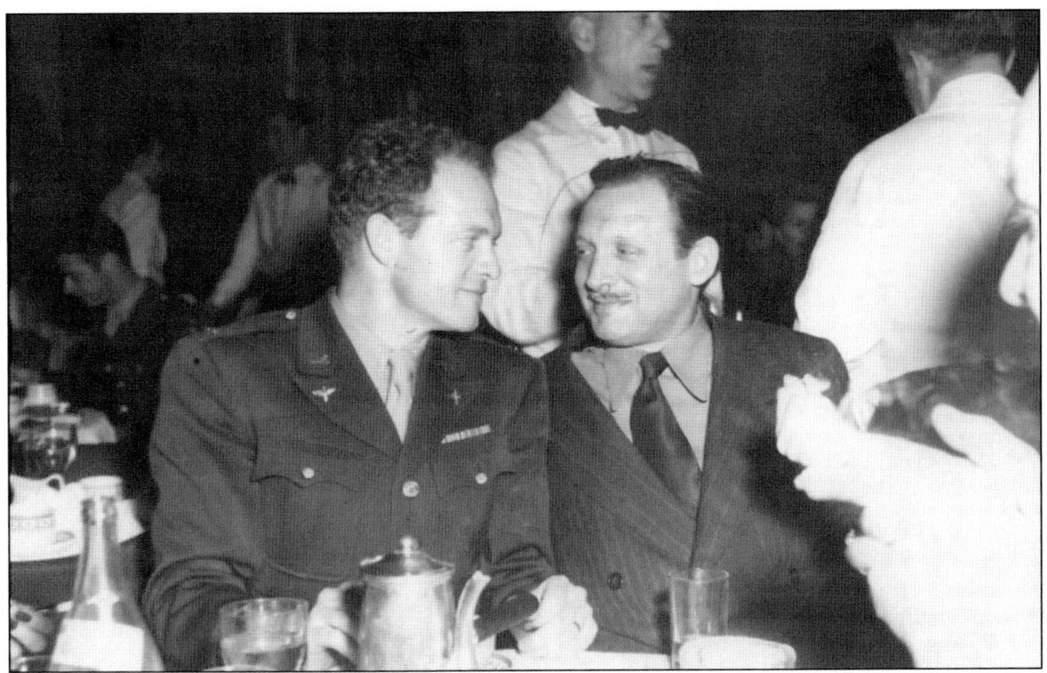

Van Heflin (above, left; below, second from left) was a film, radio, and stage actor. He mainly appeared in supporting roles but, in the 1940s, played the lead role in numerous films. Katharine Hepburn saw Heflin in a play and helped him secure a role opposite her in the 1936 film *A Woman Rebels*. Heflin was in the hit play *The Philadelphia Story*, which ran from 1939 to 1940 with 419 performances. A few of the well-known movies he stars in, made during the 1940s and 1950s, include *The Three Musketeers*, *Madame Bovary*, and *Shane*. He won a Best Supporting Actor Academy Award in 1942 for *Johnny Eager*. Heflin had a smattering of roles in the 1950s and 1960s. His last performance was in *A Case of Libel* on Broadway from 1963 to 1964. Heflin died of a heart attack at age 60 in 1971.

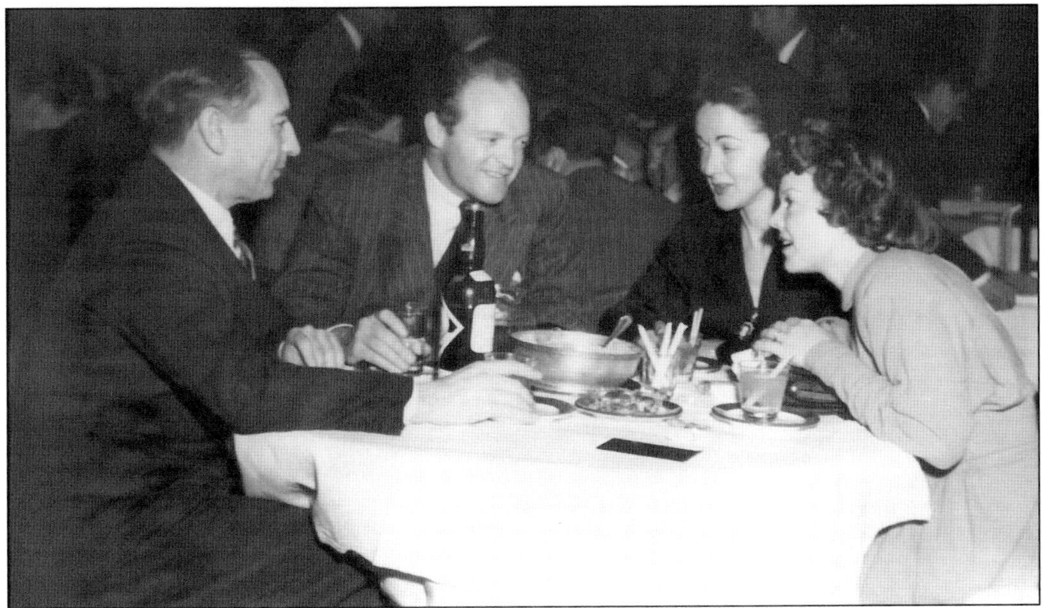

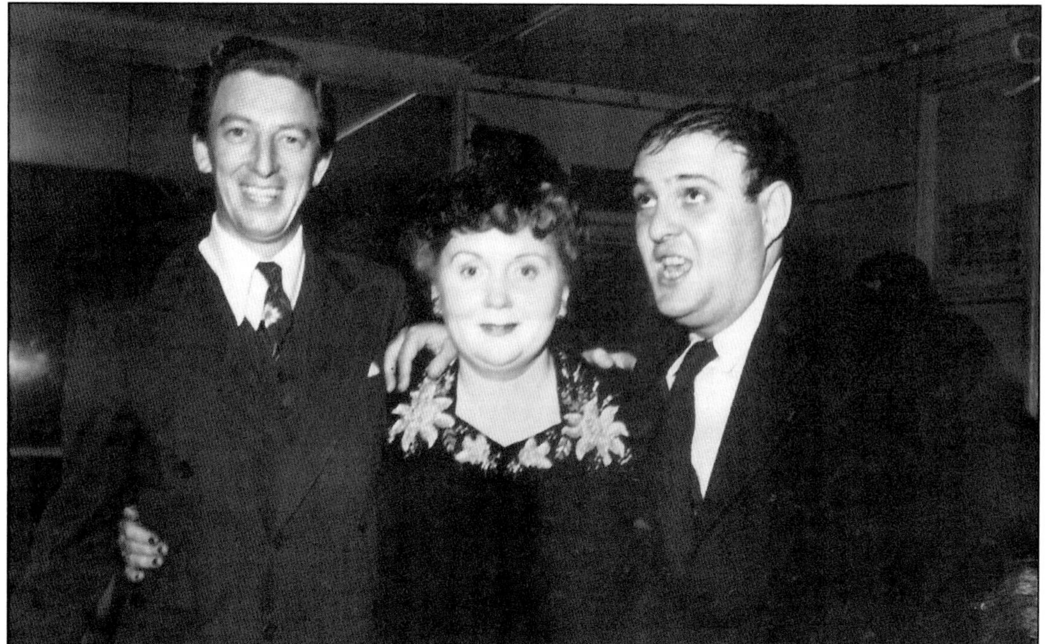

Film and stage actor Ray Bolger (left) is best remembered as the Scarecrow in the classic movie *The Wizard of Oz*. He had success in vaudeville, Broadway, and television as well. Comedian and actor of stage and screen Zero Mostel (right) is best known for his onstage portrayal of Tevye in *Fiddler on the Roof*. He won three Tony Awards during his career.

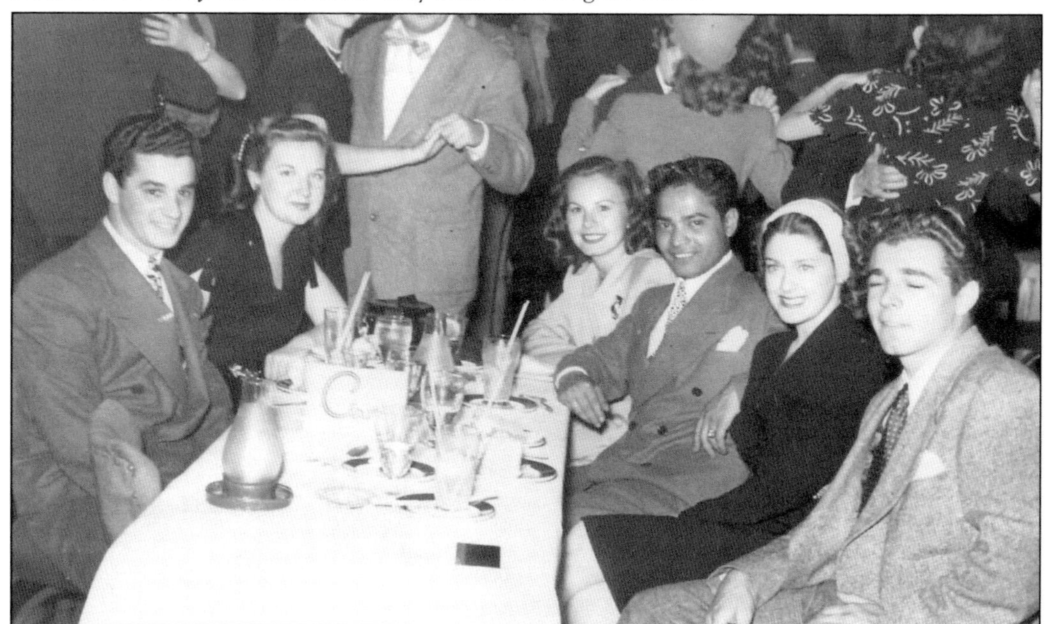

Born in India, Sabu Dastagir (third from right) was a film actor in America and Britain. At age 12, Dastagir, an impoverished orphan, met British location crew members who discovered him. He ended up playing a major role in *Elephant Boy* as a result. Dastagir was often typecast in various exotic-looking parts, such as Mowgli in the well-received 1942 movie *Jungle Book*. Dastagir died at age 39 of a heart attack.

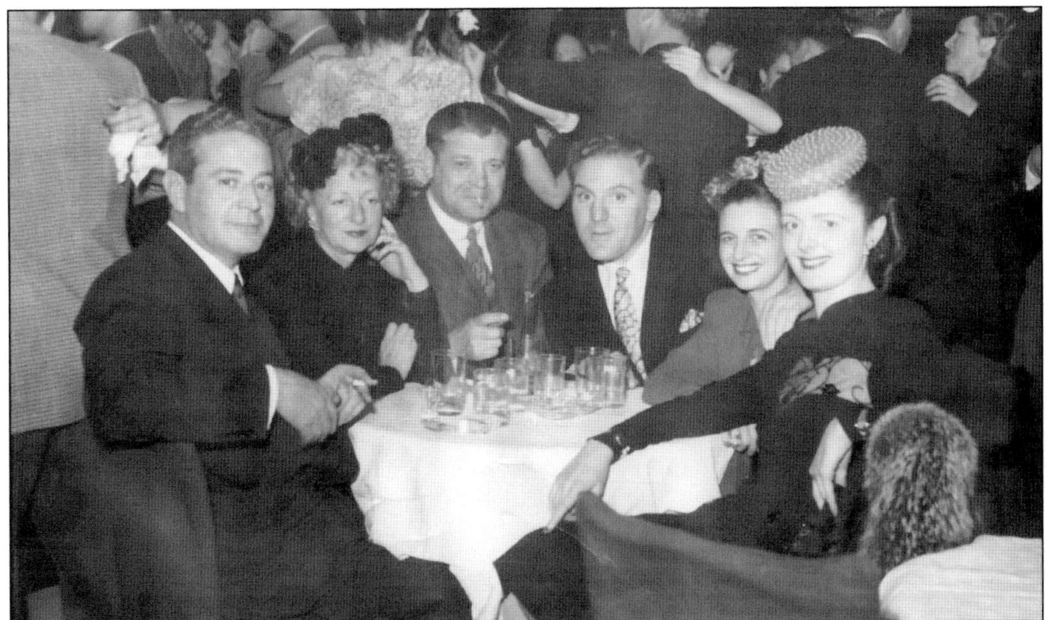

William Bendix (third from right) was a character actor known for his roles as a thug or likeable lug. He worked in film, television, onstage, and on radio. He received an Academy Award nomination in 1942 for his work in *Wake Island*. His popularity grew during his work on the radio show *The Life of Riley*, which ran for nine years, then became a movie, and later was a television show. He was also the lead as Babe Ruth in 1948 film *The Babe Ruth Story*.

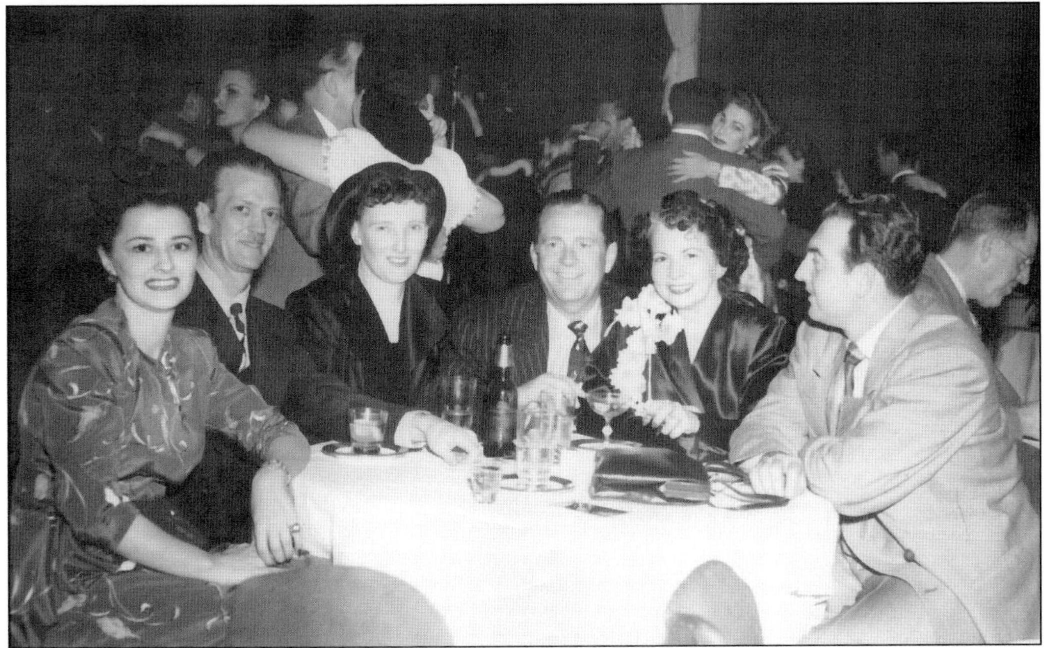

James Dunn (center) worked onstage, in vaudeville, in silent movies, in feature and B movies, and in television. He appears in Shirley Temple's first three feature movies in 1934: *Baby Take a Bow*, *Stand Up and Cheer*, and *Bright Eyes*. In 1945, he received an Oscar for Best Supporting Actor in *A Tree Grows in Brooklyn*.

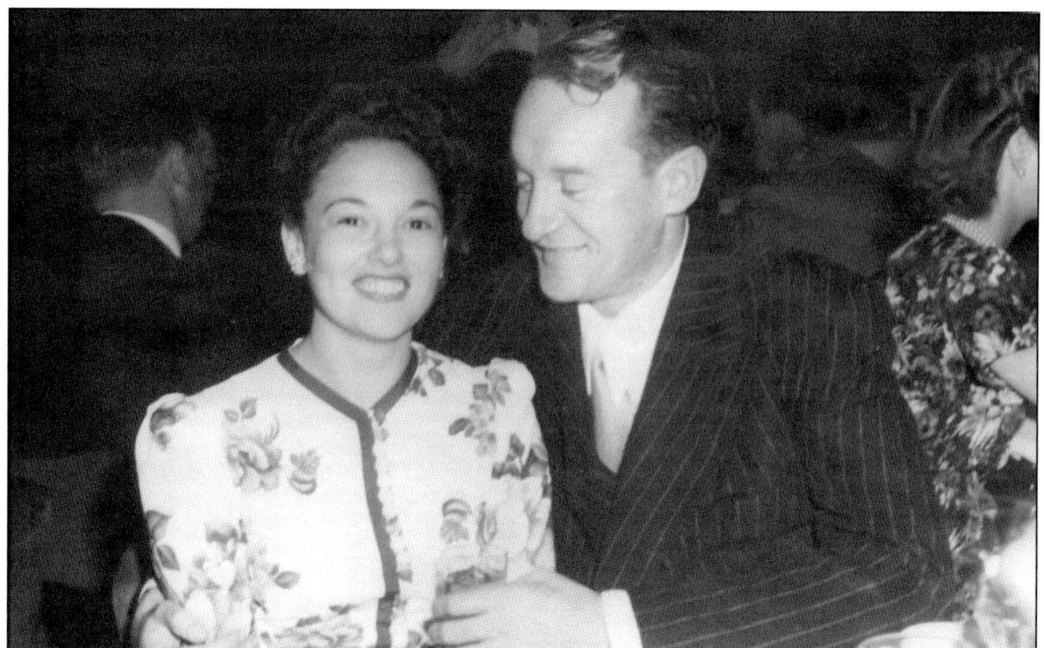

George Sanders was an English actor in film and on television, a music composer, singer-songwriter, and an author. His best-known work includes *Rebecca*, *Samson and Delilah*, *All About Eve* (for which he won Best Supporting Actor), *King Richard and the Crusaders*, and *Jungle Book* (in which he voices Shere Khan). Sanders died in 1972 of suicide.

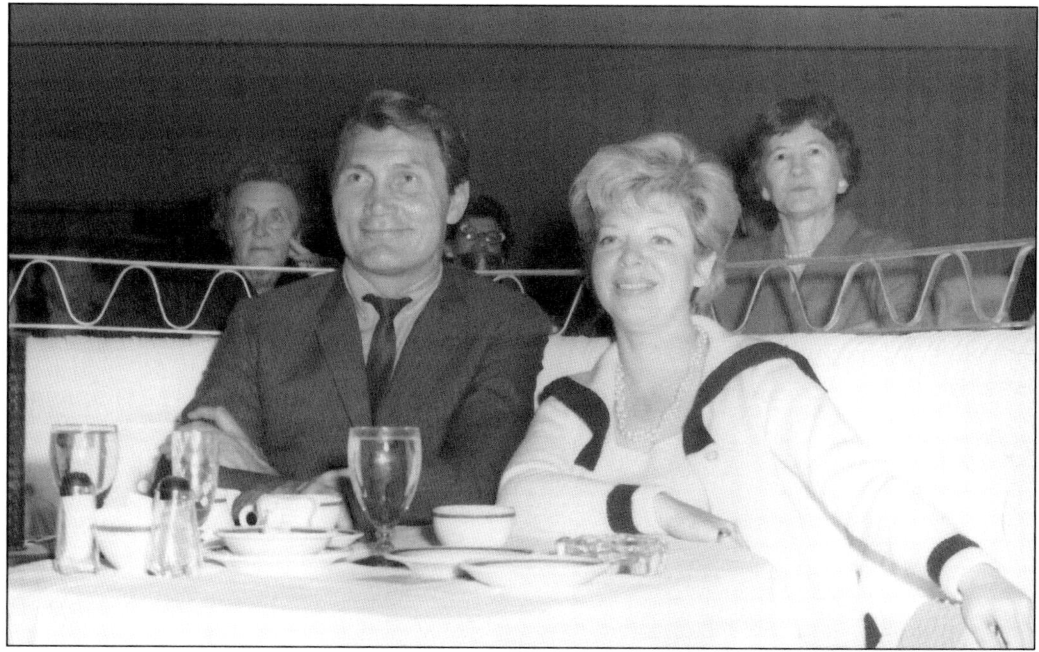

Jack Palance was an actor of film, stage, and television who appeared in many villainous roles in Westerns and melodramas in the 1950s. He was nominated for Best Supporting Actor three times, first in the film *Sudden Fear* in 1952 and next for the film *Shane* in 1953. He finally won the coveted Best Supporting Actor award in 1991 for *City Slickers*.

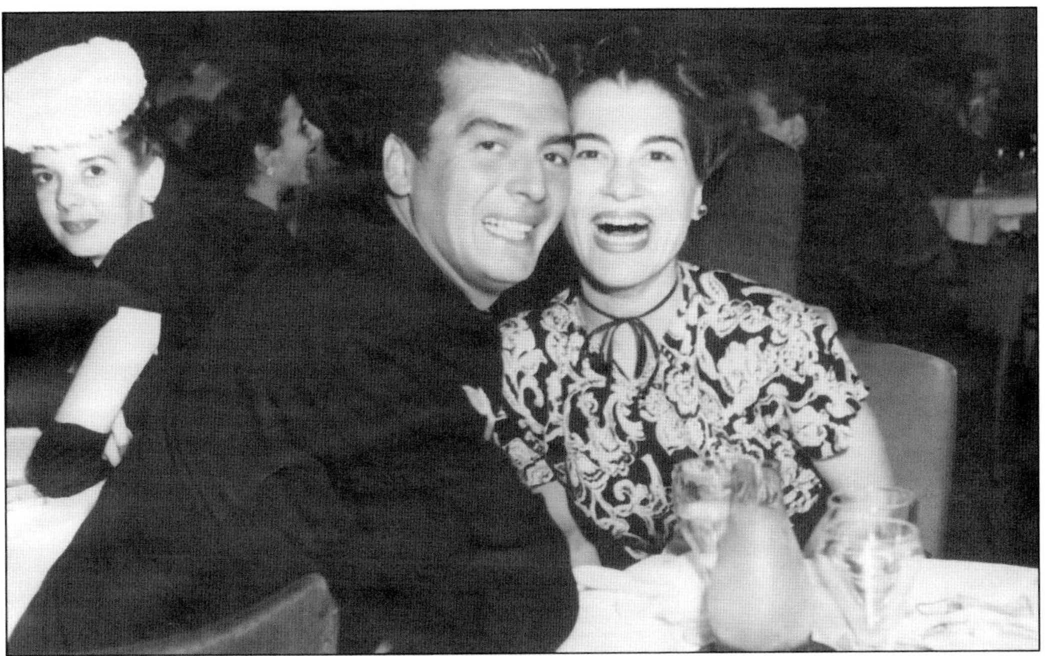

Television, film, and stage actor Victor Mature, with his strong physique, was cast in numerous Western and biblical films during his career. Some of his most notable films include *My Darling Clementine*, *Kiss of Death*, *Samson and Delilah*, and *The Egyptian*. In 1952, he was in *Million Dollar Mermaid*, costarring with Esther Williams.

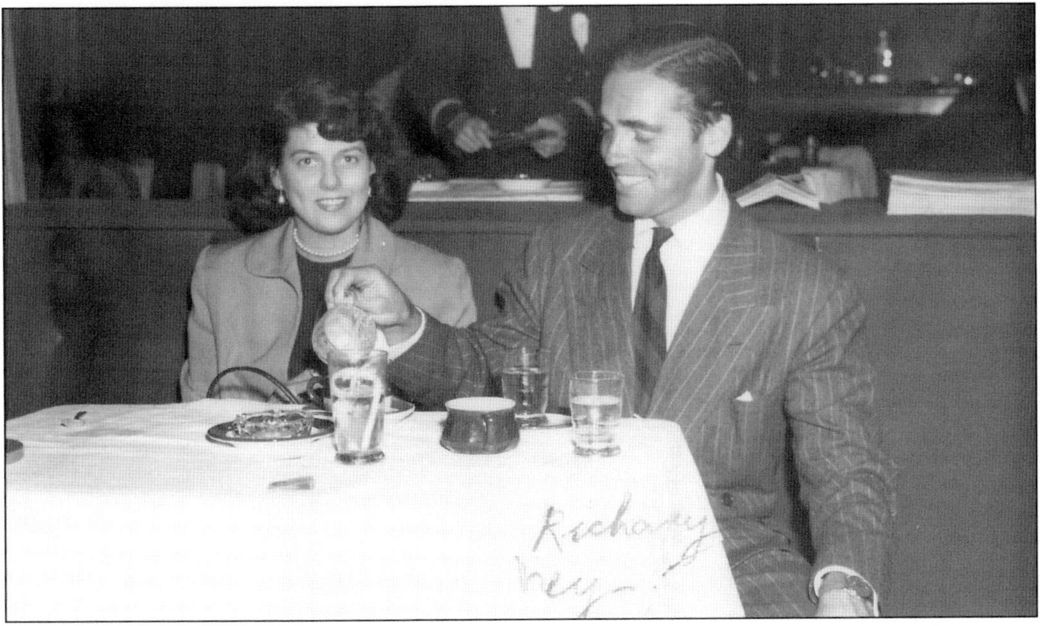

Richard Ney, an actor of stage and film, accrued 40 television and film credits during his acting career. He appears in the 1942 award-winning movie *Mrs. Miniver*. In 1943, he married the lead in *Mrs. Miniver*, Greer Garson, who was 10 years his senior. A few other movies he appears in are *The War Against Mrs. Hadley, Midnight Lace, and Premature Burial*. Ney left acting in the 1960s and became an investment counselor and author.

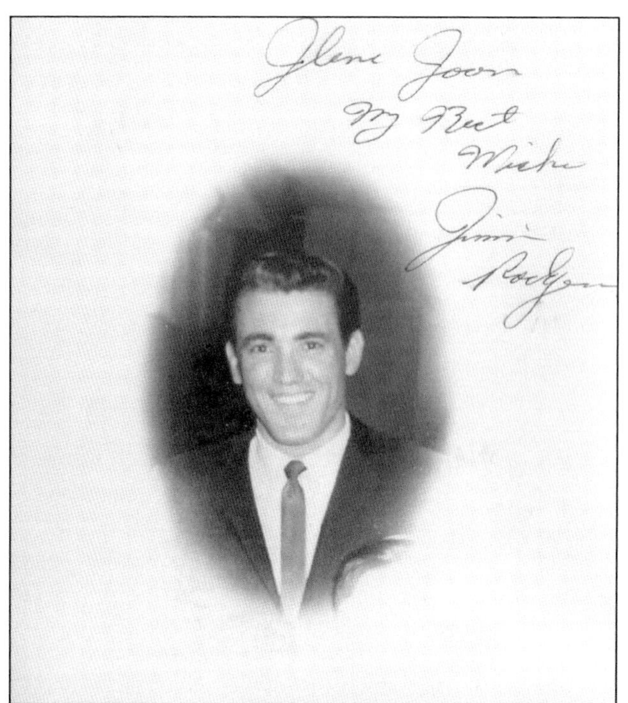

Jim Rogers is the son of famous 1920s and 1930s actor and humorist Will Rogers and brother of writer, actor, and political commentator Will Rogers Jr. Jim was best known for his work in the 1942 film *Dudes Are Pretty People* and 1943 films *Calaboose* and *Prairie Chickens*. He has 13 film credits.

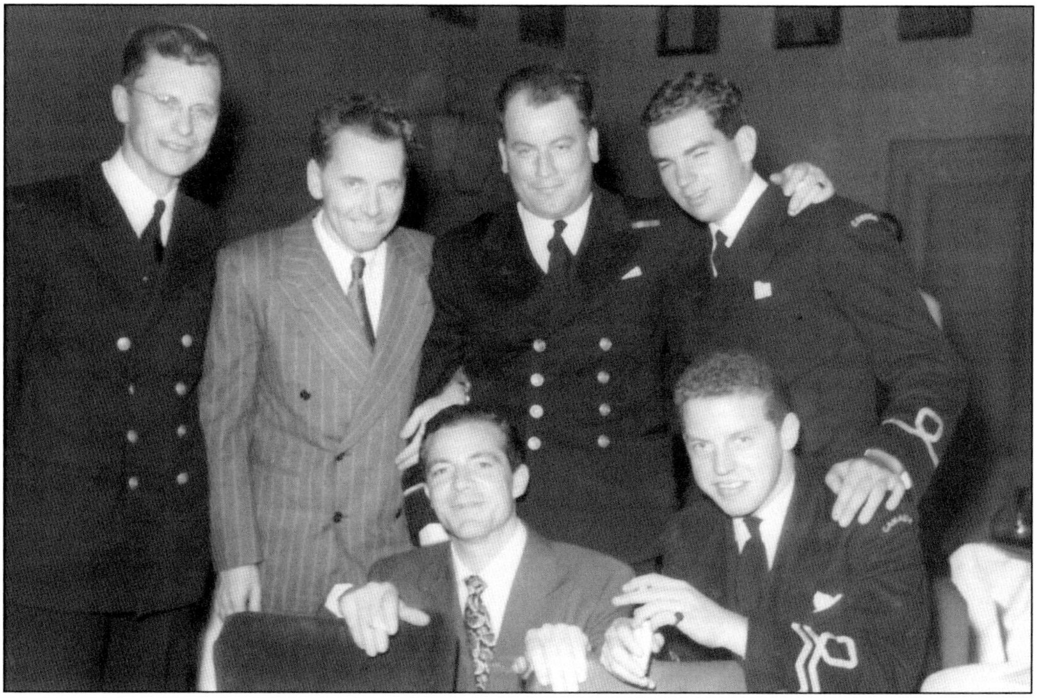

Dana Andrews (bottom left), was a stage actor and major film star in the 1940s. A few of the many noteworthy films he acts in are *Laura*, *The Best Years of Our Lives*, *In Harm's Way*, and *Where the Sidewalk Ends*. He retired from film acting in the 1960s, became the Screen Actors Guild (SAG) president in 1963, and appeared in public-service announcements on television about alcoholism in 1972. Later, his work entailed investing in real estate.

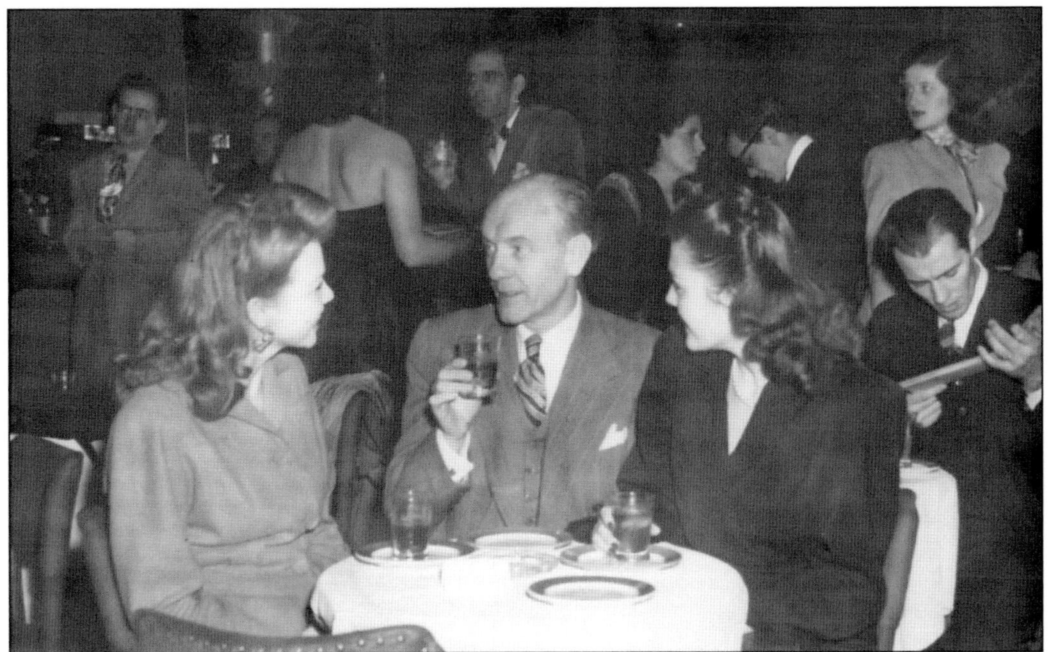

Earl Carroll was a theatrical producer, songwriter, composer, and director. Carroll owned two theaters, one in New York and one in Hollywood. His nightclub provided patrons with a meal and a theater production showcasing beautiful showgirls in elaborate costumes. Carroll's neon sign in front of his Hollywood theater (now located next to Universal Studios in Los Angeles, on City Walk), displayed "Thru These Portals Pass The Most Beautiful Girls In The World." His girlfriend, Beryl Wallace (both, right), was an actress, singer, dancer, and one of many women who performed in Carroll's productions. Carroll and Wallace died in a plane crash in 1948.

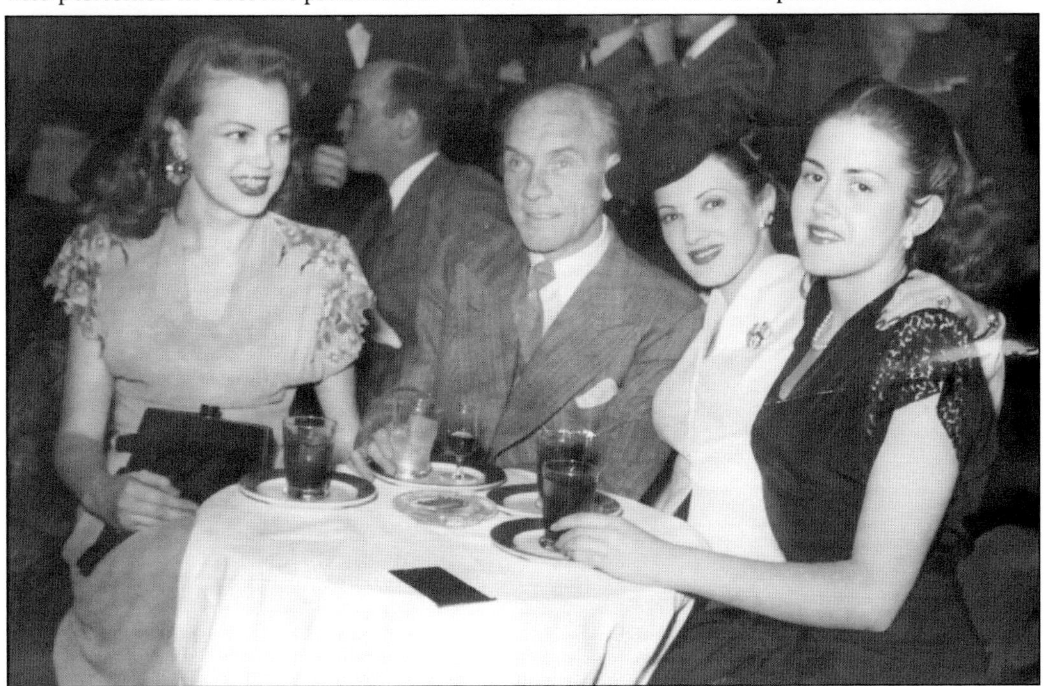

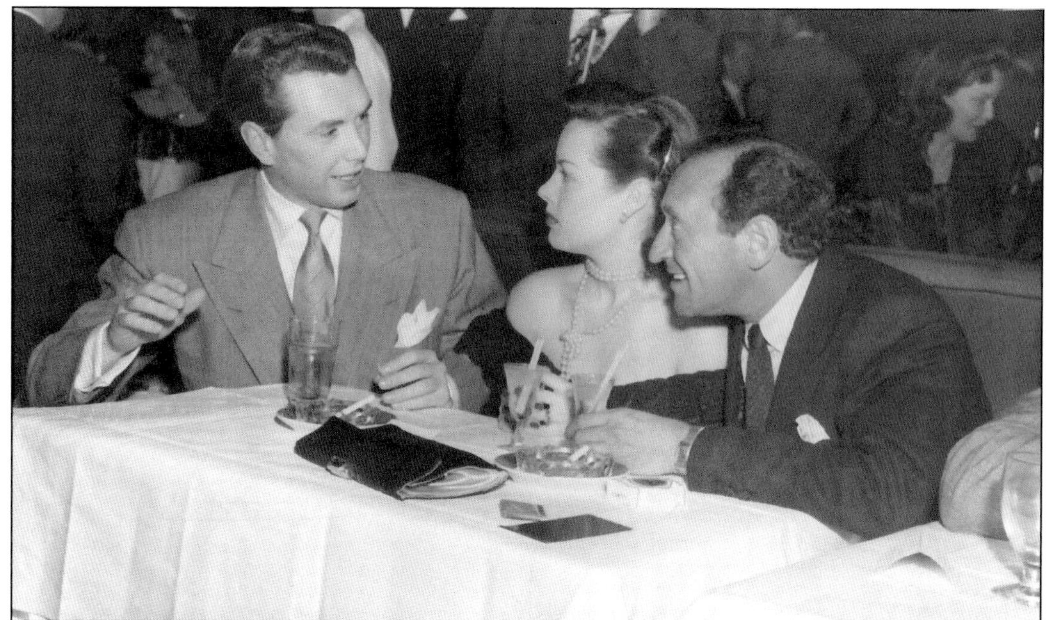

Robert Hutton (left) was a contracted actor with Warner Bros. studios, for several years, who resembled Jimmy Stewart. When Stewart enlisted in the Army for World War II, Hutton received some roles Stewart would have played. After Hutton's contract with Warner Bros. ended, he went to England where he acted in movies and television shows as well as wrote and directed for several years. Harry Ritz (right) was an actor who was part of a comedy team called the Ritz Brothers.

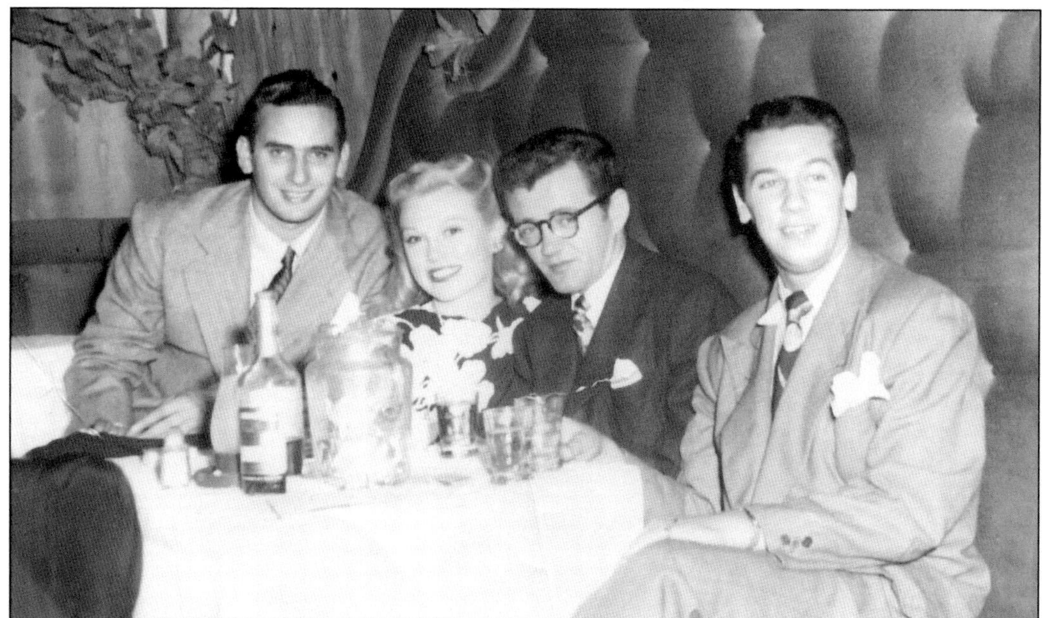

Actor Robert Walker (second from right) had a boy-next-door look that resonated with audiences. He appears in movies such as *The Vanishing Legion*, *Till the Clouds Roll By*, *Madame Curie*, and *Thirty Seconds Over Tokyo*. He was best known for his role in Alfred Hitchcock's 1951 film *Strangers on a Train*. Walker struggled with mental illness and alcoholism. He died at age 32 from an adverse reaction to alcohol and sedative medication prescribed by his psychiatrist.

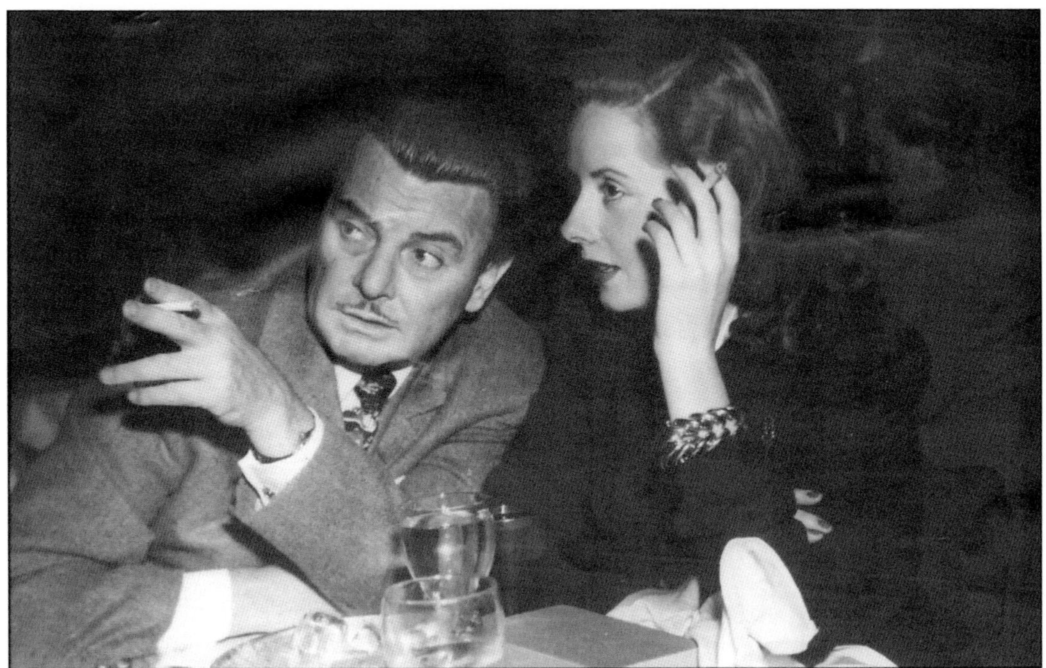

George Brent was an Irish actor who appeared in American film, television, and stage roles. He played lead roles during the 1930s and 1940s and costarred with Bette Davis in 13 films. *Dark Victory*, *The Spiral Staircase*, *Jezebel*, *Baby Face*, and *42nd Street* are some of the films considered to be Brent's finest work. In the late 1940s, Brent slid into B movie roles and through 1960 he could be seen on various television shows. Although Brent retired in 1953 from film, his true last film was a made-for-television production in 1978 titled *Born Again*.

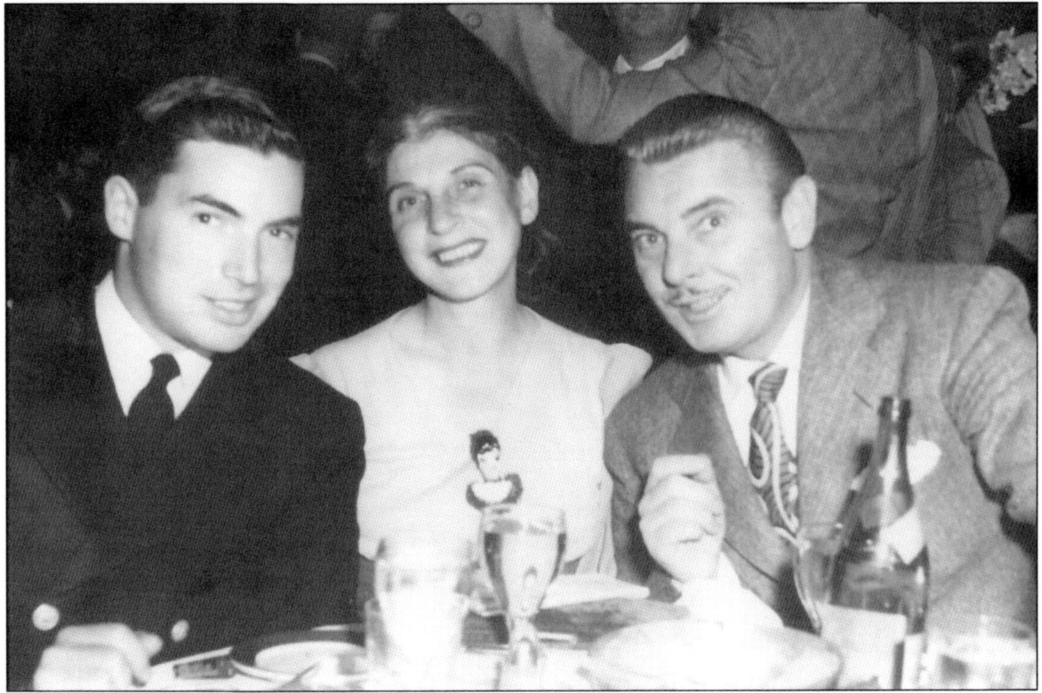

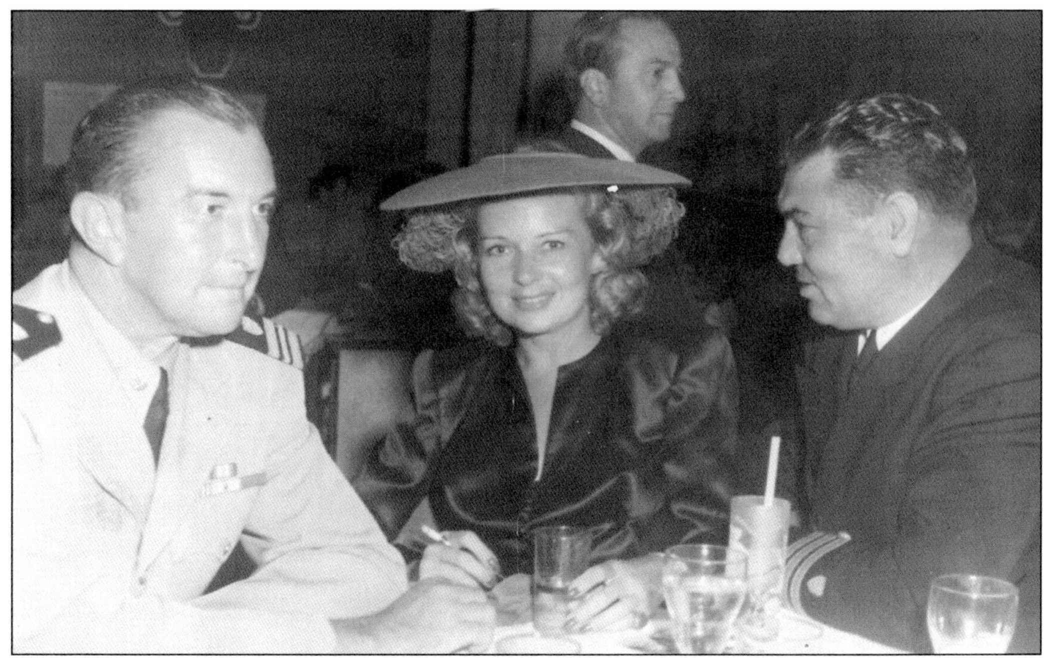

Jack Dempsey (right) was one of the most popular professional boxers in American history. He was the heavyweight champion from 1919 until 1926. Of his 85 recorded fights, Dempsey won 65, lost 6, had 11 draws, and had 1 no contest. After Dempsey retired from boxing (following his rematch with Tunney), he appeared in the 1933 film *The Prizefighter and the Lady*. In 1935, he opened a successful restaurant in New York City that remained open until 1974.

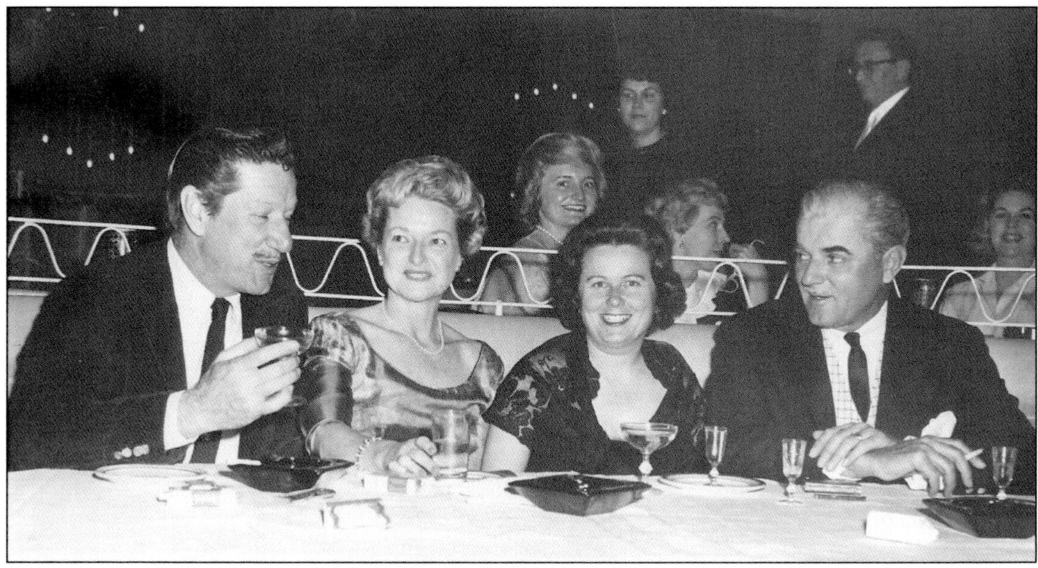

Richard Boone (left) was an actor of stage, film, and television who is best known for starring in Westerns. He was the lead on the hit television series *Have Gun – Will Travel*, which aired from 1957 to 1963. His acting career began when he debuted on Broadway at age 31. In 1964, he won a Golden Globe, Outstanding Television Drama Series, for his anthology *The Richard Boone Show*. Boone was in over 50 films. He is related to American pioneer Daniel Boone and singers Pat Boone and Debby Boone.

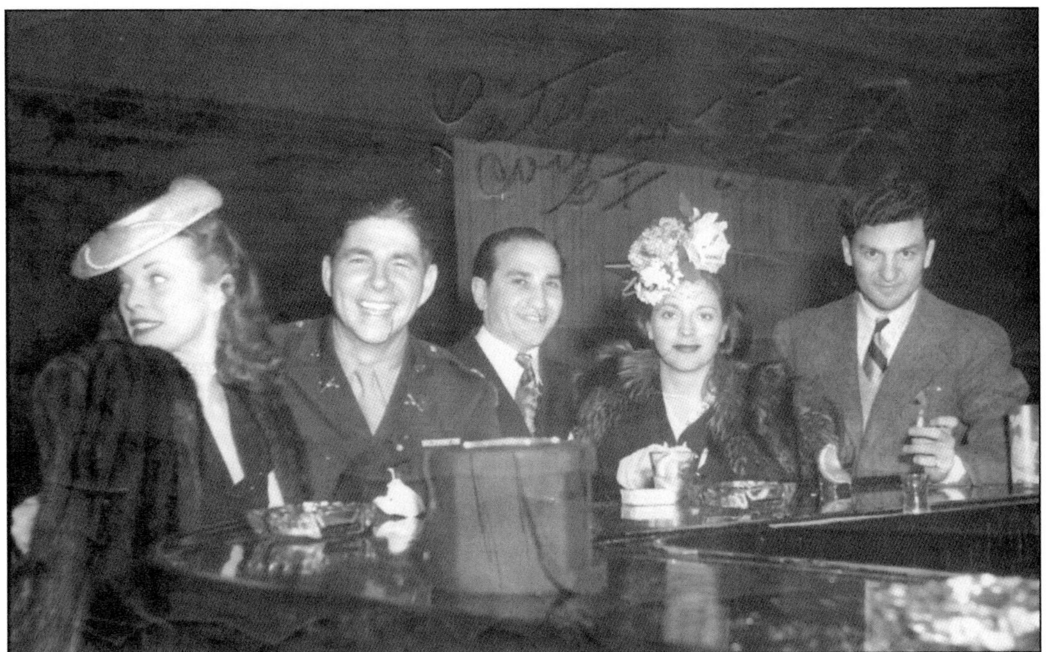

Lester Cowan (center) was a film producer of dramas, comedies, and gangster movies in the 1930s and 1940s. Some of his best-known productions include *The Story of G.I. Joe* with Robert Mitchum and two of W.C. Fields's most popular movies, *You Can't Cheat an Honest Man* and *My Little Chickadee*.

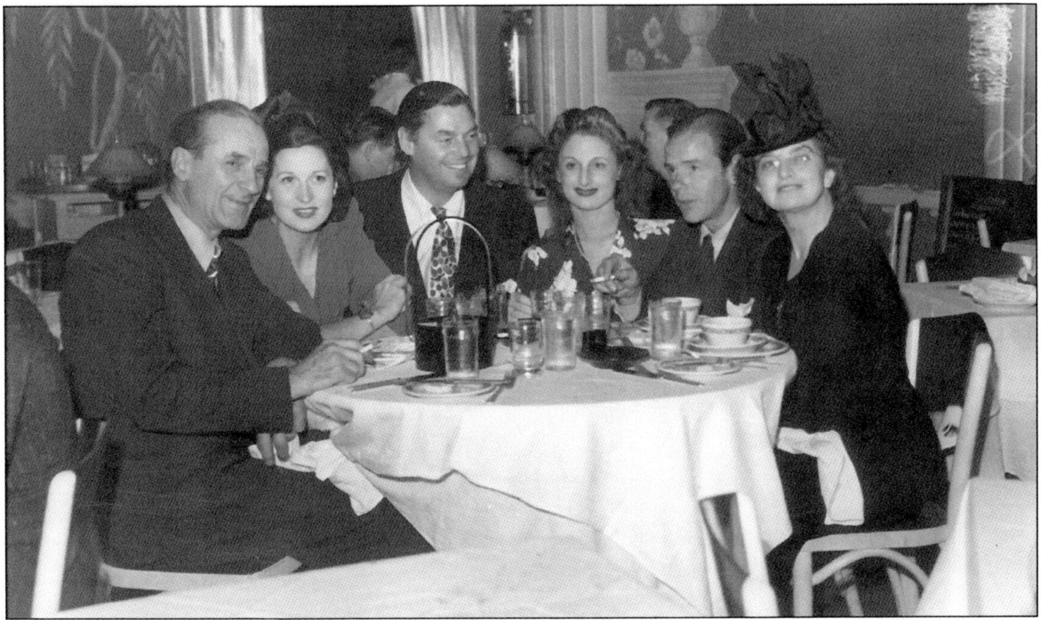

Competitive swimmer and actor Johnny Weissmuller (center) won five Olympic gold medals and one bronze during the 1920s—four during the Paris Olympics and two during the Amsterdam Olympics. As an actor, he was best known as the lead in the Tarzan films from the 1930s and 1940s. He had a seven-year contract with MGM and plays Tarzan in six movies. He subsequently signed with RKO and appears in an additional six Tarzan films.

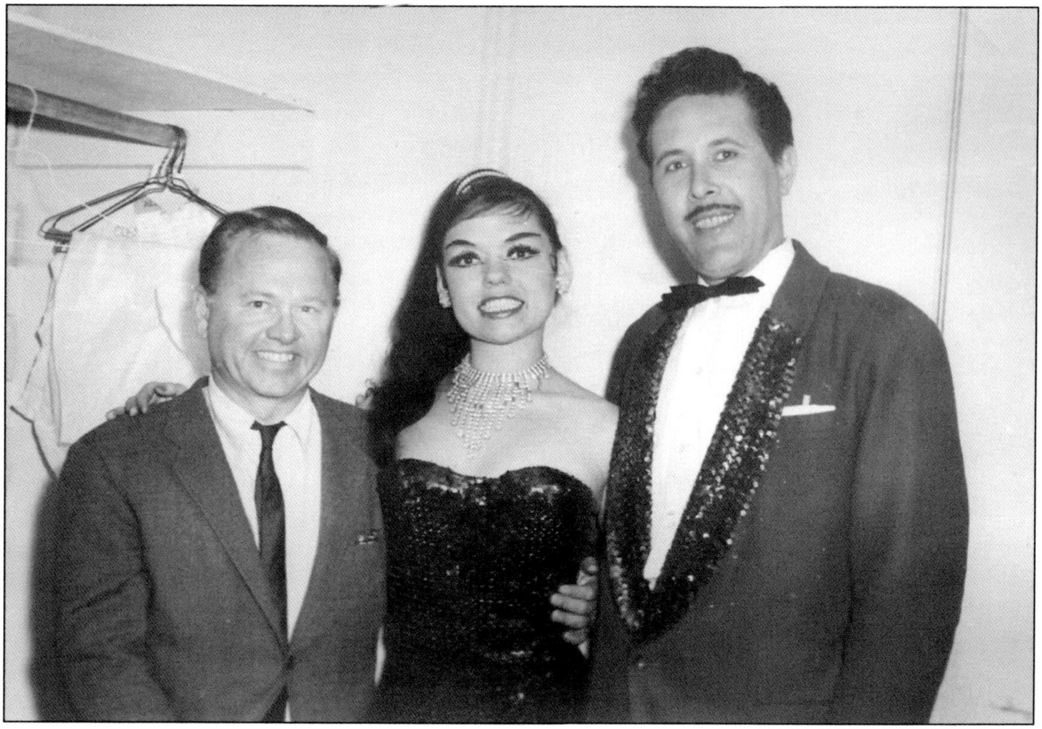

Above, Mickey Rooney (left) poses with two unidentified nightclub performers. Below, Rooney (left) is pictured with orchestra leader, bandleader, composer, and violinist Paul Whitman. Whitman was an exceptionally popular band director of numerous ensembles in the 1920s, reportedly earning over one million dollars a year during that time period.

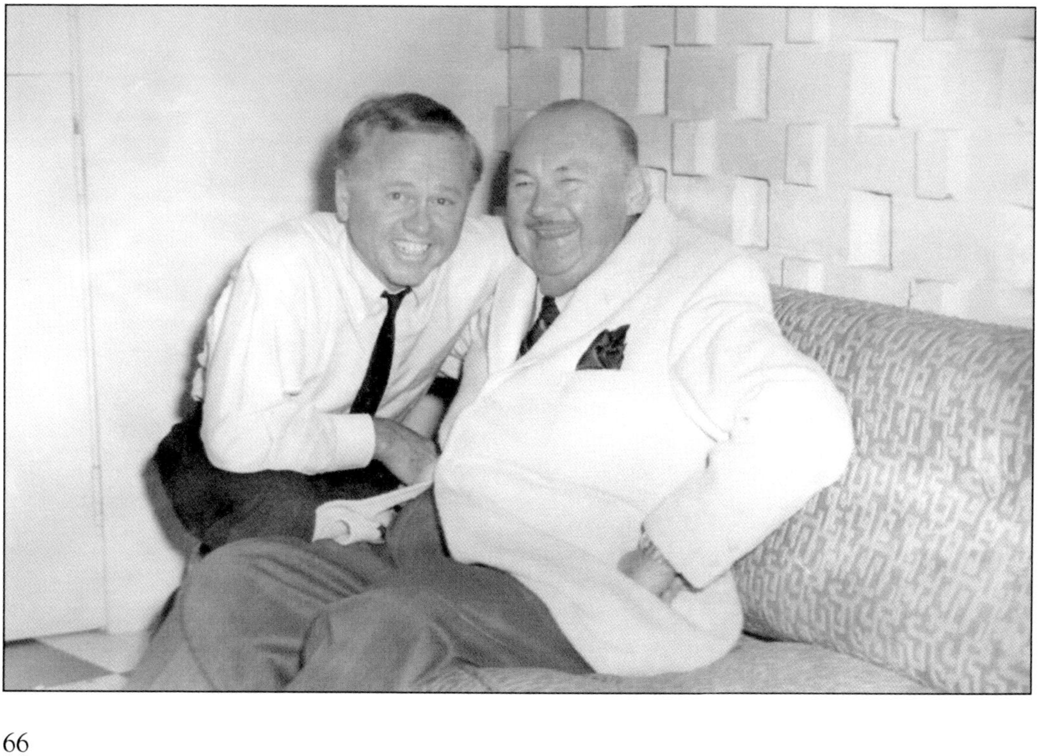

Mickey Rooney (both, left) was a versatile entertainer and actor of film, television, and stage. He had the longest acting career in American history, spanning over 90 years. Rooney began as a childhood actor in vaudeville and silent films. His talent was multifaceted, as he could sing, dance, play various instruments, and act in serious as well as humorous roles. Rooney appeared in over 300 films over his long career and received numerous accolades including two Academy Awards, two Golden Globes, and one Emmy Award. He appears in such American classic films as *National Velvet*, *The Human Comedy*, *A Midsummer Night's Dream*, and *Babes in Arms*. During World War II, Rooney entertained over two million troops on radio and stage. His numerous career successes did not always translate to his personal life. He was married eight times and struggled with alcohol and painkiller addiction. Regardless of his weaknesses, Rooney will be remembered as one of the greatest entertainers in American history.

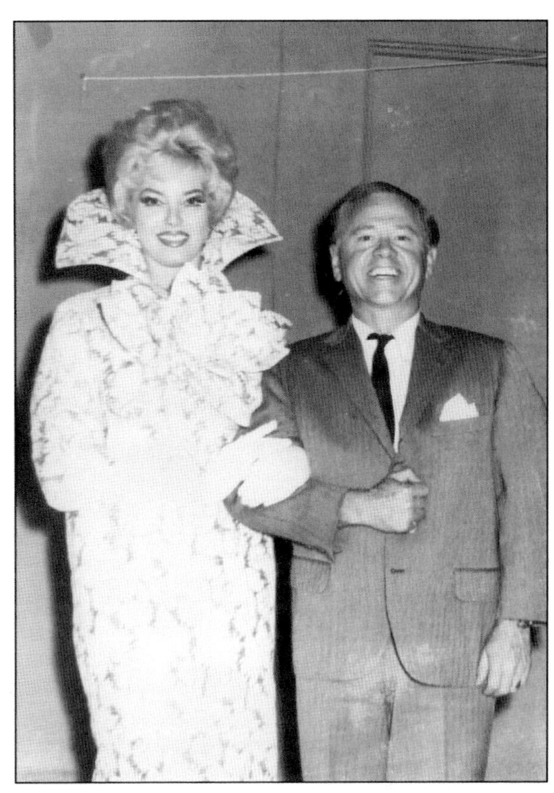

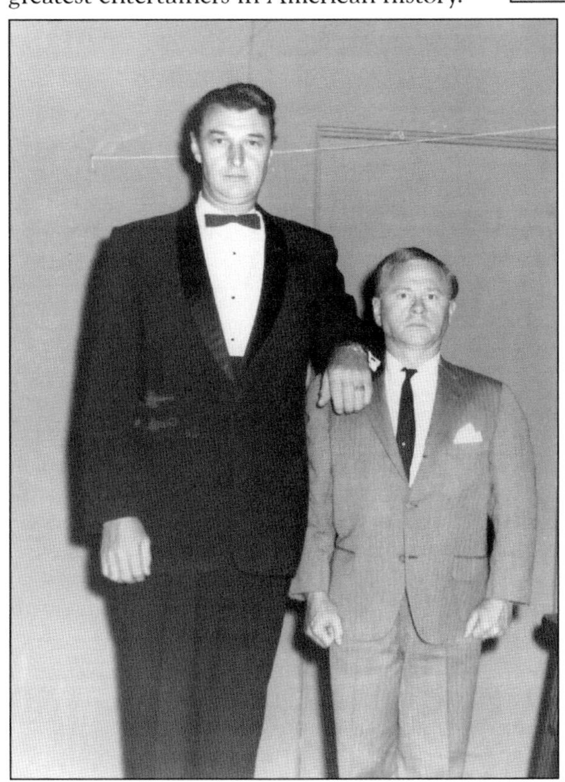

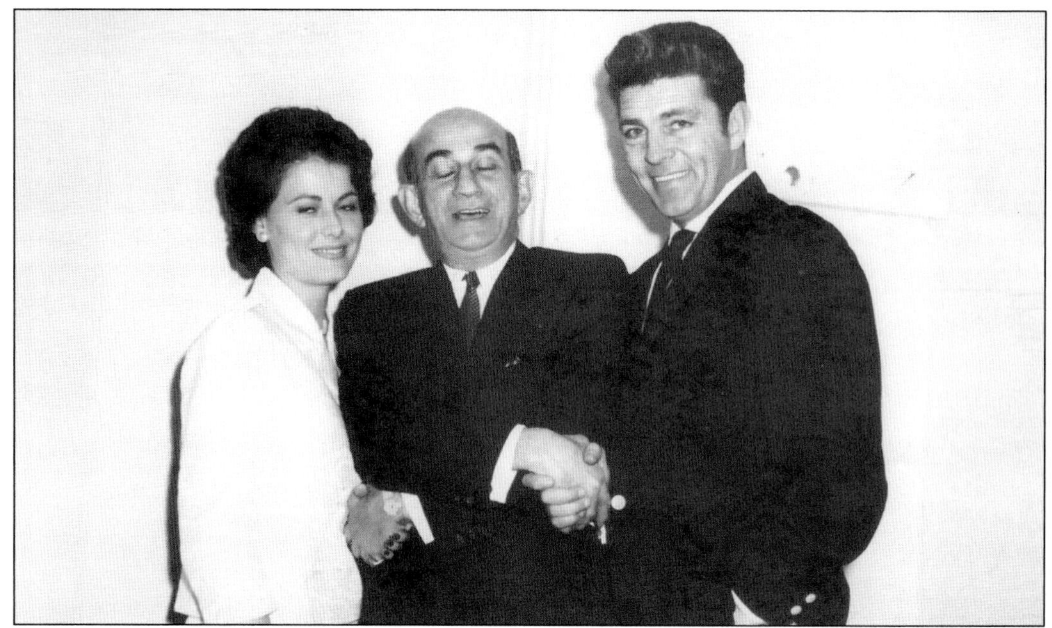

Horse-savvy Dale Robertson (right) was a television and film actor who appears in numerous Western movies and television shows. Robertson was in *Tales of Wells Fargo* from 1957 to 1962, *Iron Horse* from 1966 to 1968, and *Death Valley Days* from 1968 to 1972. In the 1980s, he was in several episodes of two hit nighttime soap operas *Dynasty* and *Dallas*. Myron Cohen (center) was one of the top headlining comedians in nightclubs during the 1950s and 1960s.

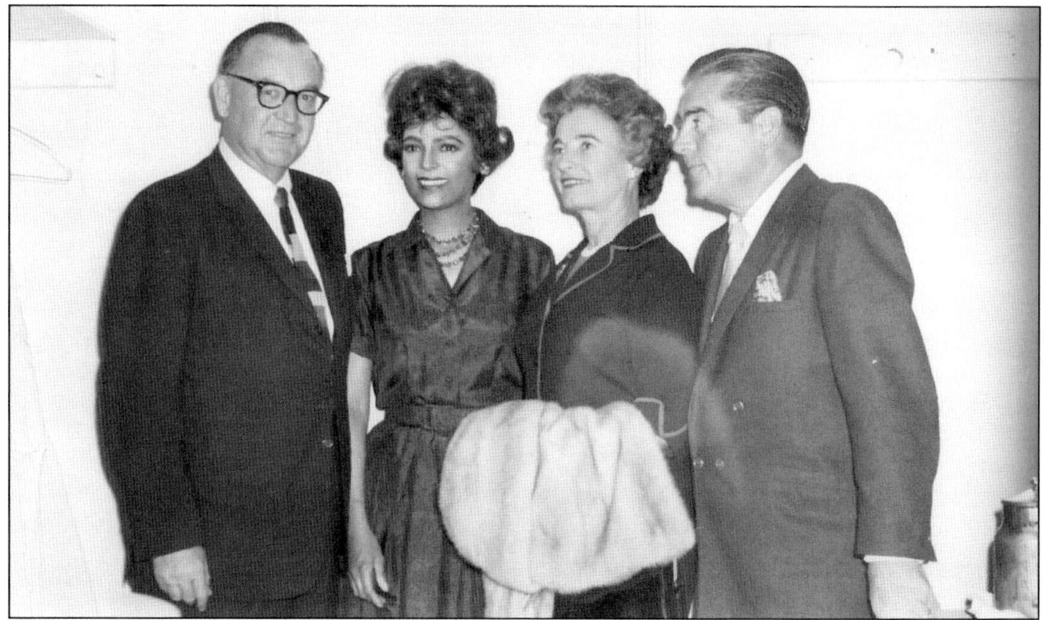

Pat Brown (left) was the 32nd governor of California and father of Jerry Brown, the 34th and 39th governor of California. Pat Brown's legacy includes the Fair Housing Act, the Fair Employment Act, the Master Plan for Higher Education of 1960, highway expansion, and the California Aqueduct. Bernice Layne Brown (second from right), childhood sweetheart and wife of Pat Brown, was the matriarch behind a devoted Democratic political family.

Four

GROUPS OF STARS AND CELEBRITIES

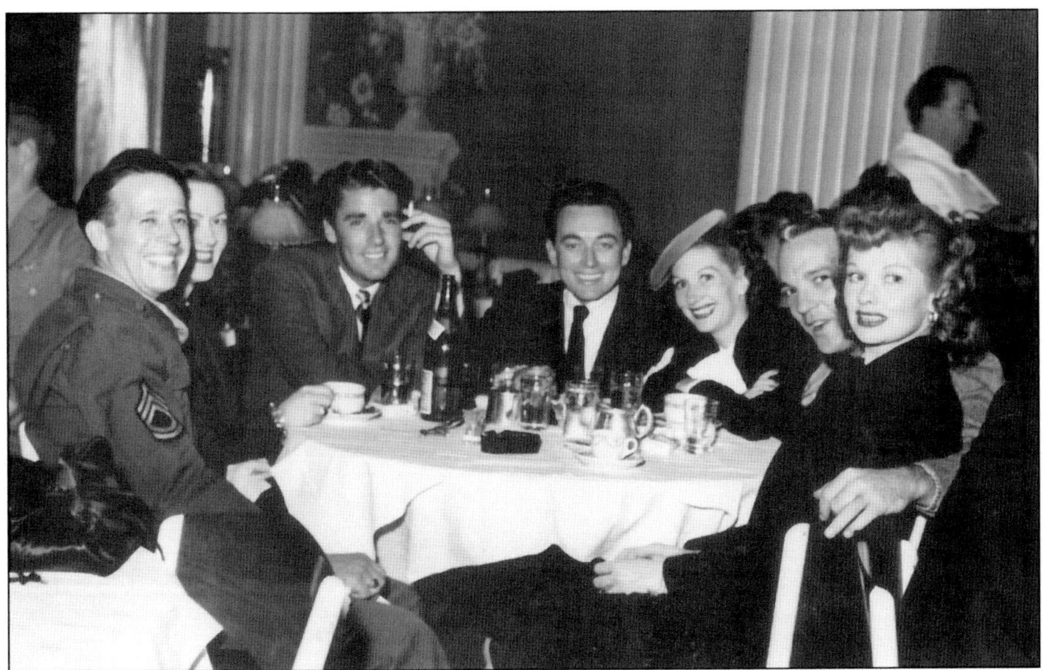

As seen on the cover of this book, Lucille Ball (far right) is the beloved comedic actress of the long-running *I Love Lucy* sitcom. Lucy's wacky antics week-to-week continue to delight new generations of viewers. Peter Lawford (third from left) was a film and television actor and producer. He was a member of the Rat Pack (including Frank Sinatra, Sammy Davis Jr., Dean Martin, and Joey Bishop) and appeared in Vegas and in two Rat Pack movies, *Ocean's 11* and *Sergeants 3*.

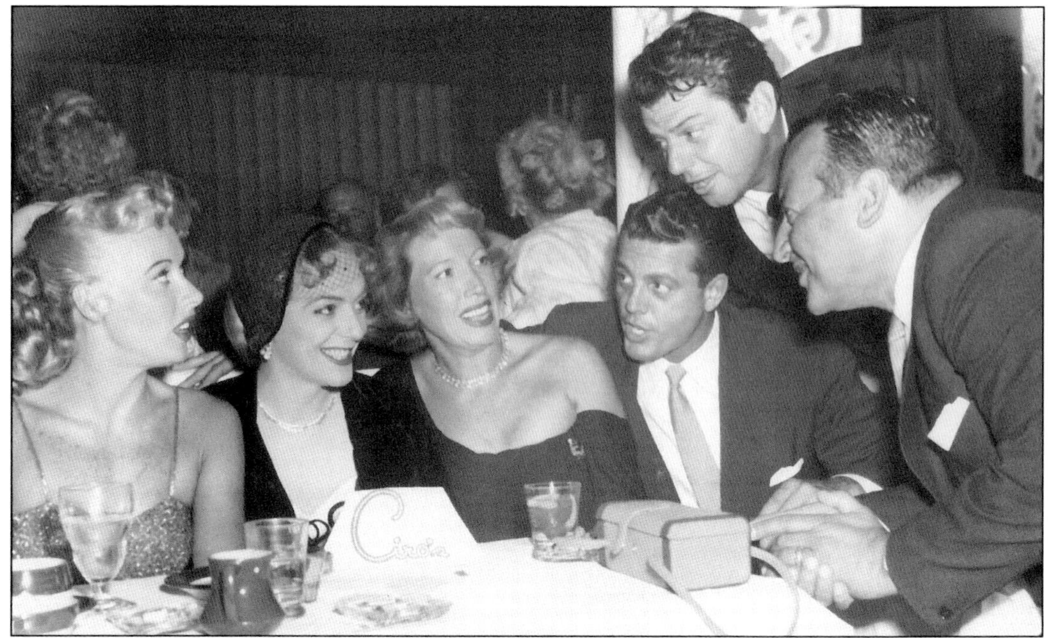

Christine Jorgensen (second from left) was an actress, singer, and nightclub entertainer who was the first widely known US citizen to undergo sex reassignment surgery. Michael St. Germain (third from right) was a socialite, Herman Hover (far right) was Ciro's owner, and John Carroll (second from right) was a successful actor (see page 47). Carroll and his casting director wife, Lucille, helped Marilyn Monroe financially and emotionally during a difficult time by inviting her to move in with them.

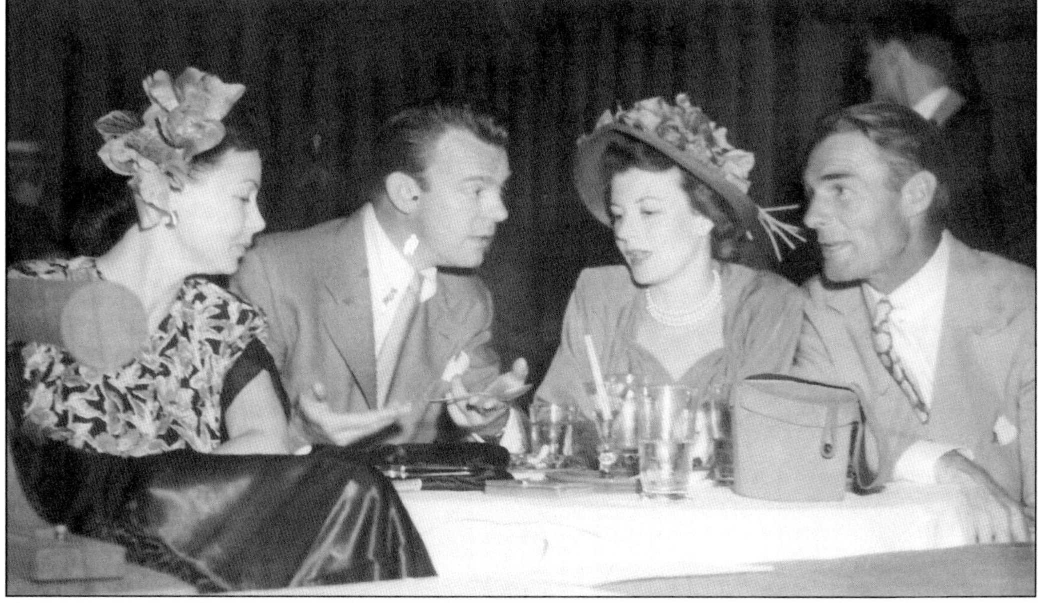

Actor Dennis O'Keefe (second from left) played in action productions, crime dramas, and comedies. He was the star of the sitcom *The Dennis O'Keefe Show*, which aired from 1959 to 1960. Randolph Scott (right) was a film actor who appeared in more than 100 movies, 60 of which are Westerns.

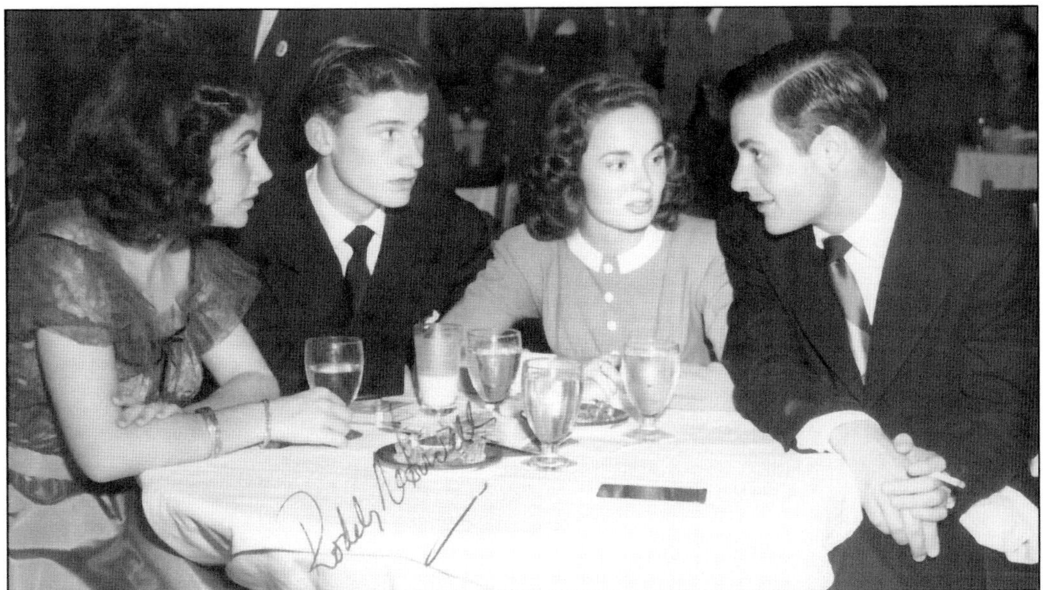

Elizabeth Taylor (left), legendary actress and tireless social activist, appeared in classic movies such as *Who's Afraid of Virginia Woolf?*, *National Velvet*, and *Cleopatra*. Roddy McDowall (second from left) was an actor best known for *Planet of the Apes*. Ann Blyth (second from right) was a singer and actress who appears in many musical movies. Richard Long (right) was a television and film actor, best known for television series *The Big Valley* and *Nanny and the Professor*.

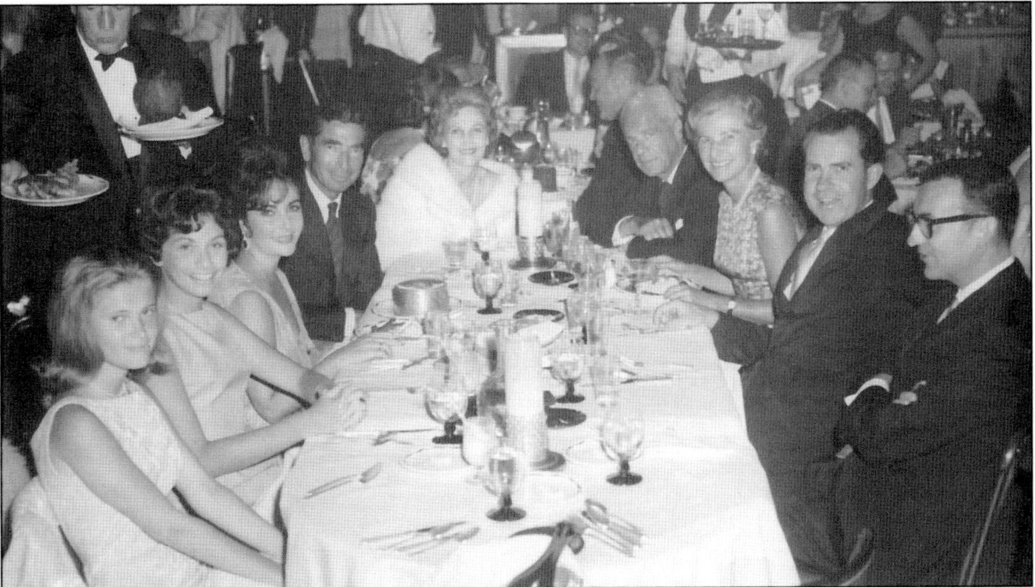

Tricia and Julie Nixon (front left) are seated next to Academy Award–winning actress Elizabeth Taylor (third from left). Former president Richard Nixon (second from right) was the 37th American president and the only president to resign from office. His legacy includes arms control agreements with the Soviet Union and the diplomatic opening of China. Former first lady Pat Nixon (third from right) promoted volunteerism, supported the development of recreational areas, and helped improve the lives of those with disabilities. Walter Wanger (fourth from right) was a film producer.

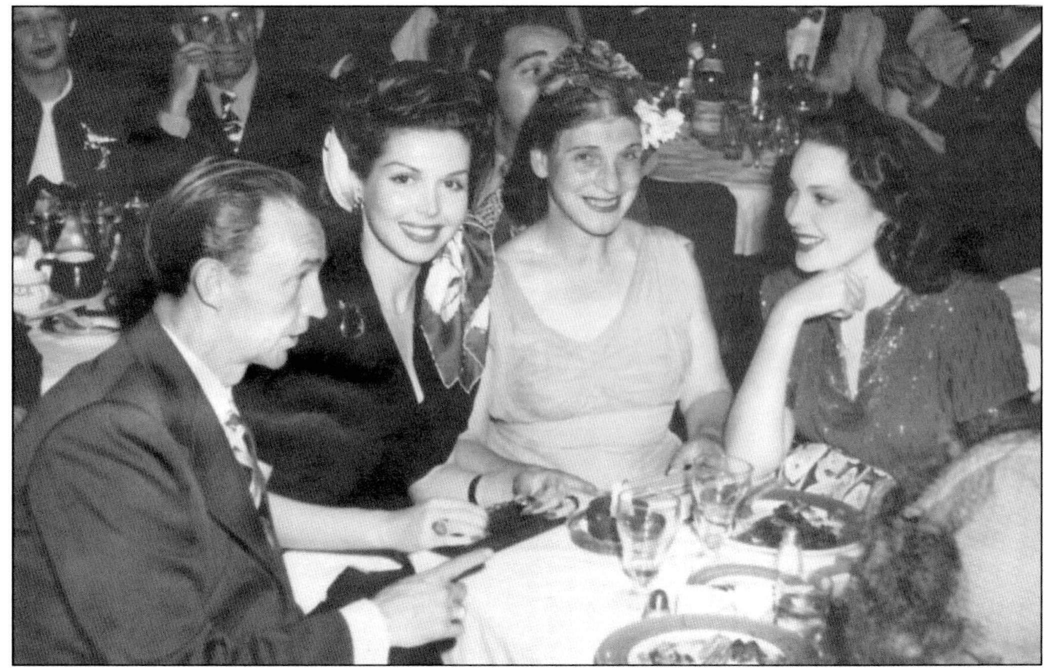

Ann Miller (second from left) was a film, television, and stage actress, singer, and dancer in musical films in the 1940s and 1950s. She appears in hits such as *Easter Parade*, *On the Town*, and *Kiss Me Kate*. She starred on Broadway in *Mame* and *Sugar Babies*. Miller was known for the speed at which she could tap dance. Linda Darnell (right) was a film actress who struggled with Hollywood life and disappeared from film by the 1950s. She died in a house fire at age 41. In the picture below, Ann Miller is at the far left, Linda Darnell is at back right, and Darnell's husband cinematographer Peverell Marley is in the back to the far right.

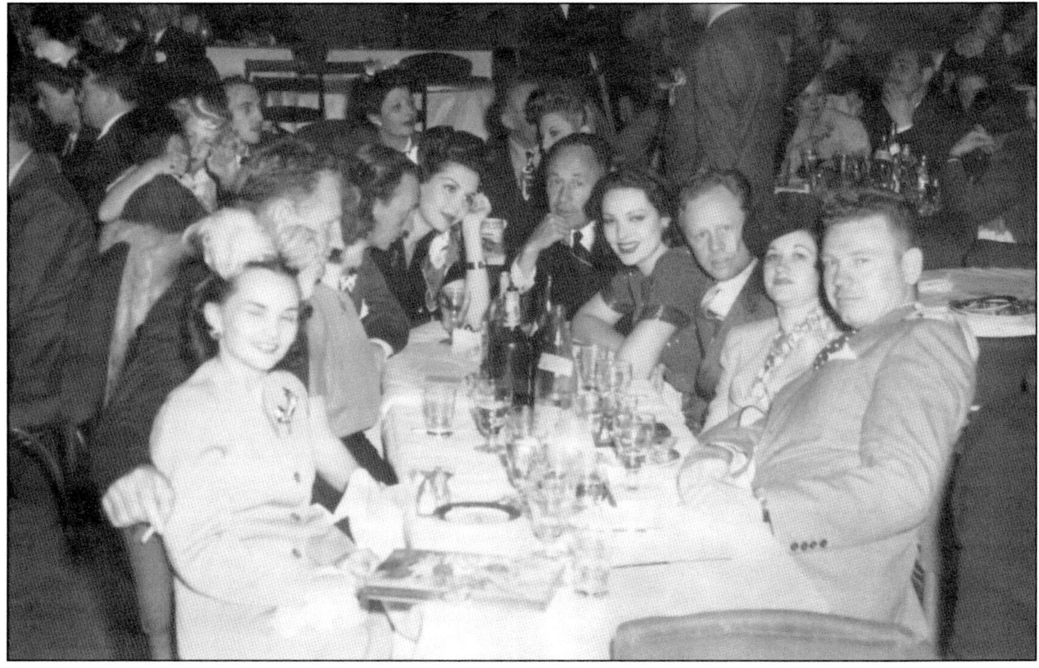

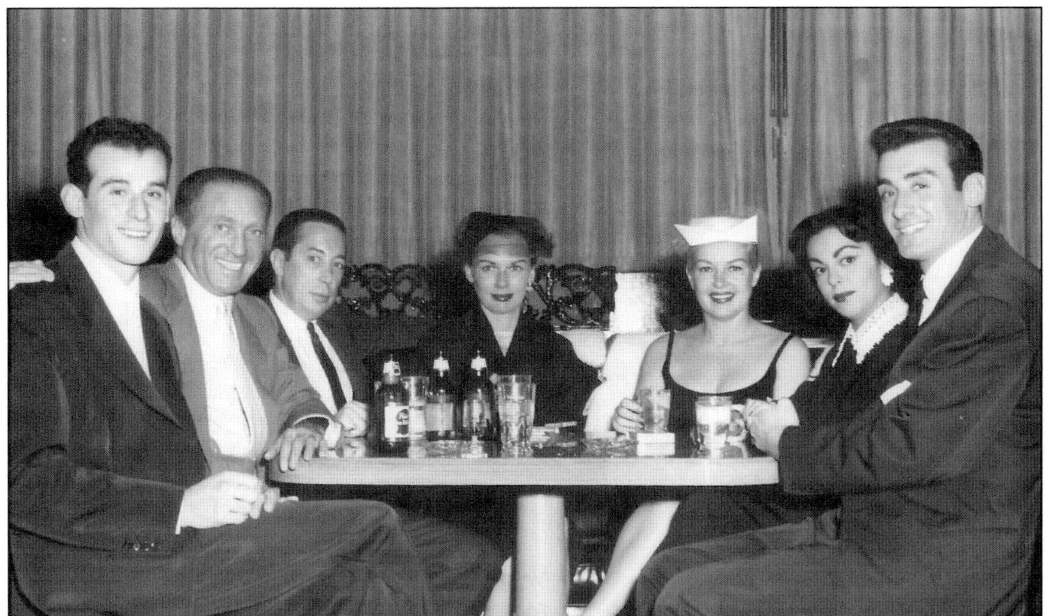

Comedian Harry Ritz (second from left) was part of a sibling trio comedy team who performed onstage from the mid-1920s until the late 1960s. Betty Grable (third from right) was an actress, singer, and dancer best known for her beautiful legs. Grable's studio took out an insurance policy for Grable's legs with Lloyd's of London for one million dollars.

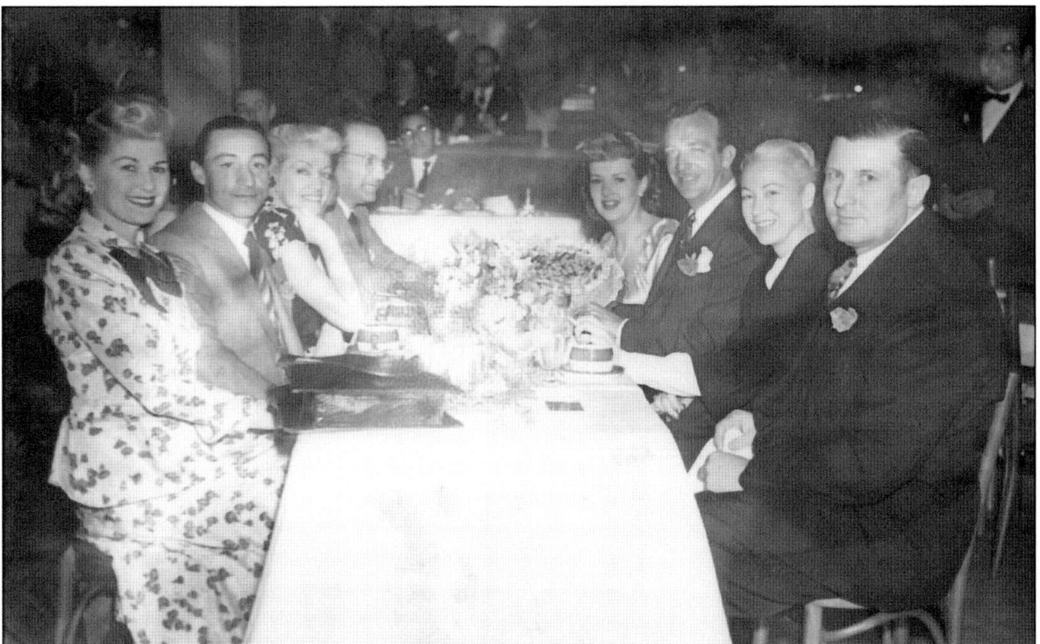

Eddie Arcaro (second from left) was an American horse jockey who had 4,779 career wins, including the Kentucky Derby five times, Belmont Stakes six times, Preakness Stakes six times, and Triple Crown twice. Betty Grable (back right) was the favorite pinup girl during World War II, number one box office draw in 1943, and top-paid entertainer in 1947. Grable's second husband, Harry James (back right), was an actor, swing bandleader, and trumpeter.

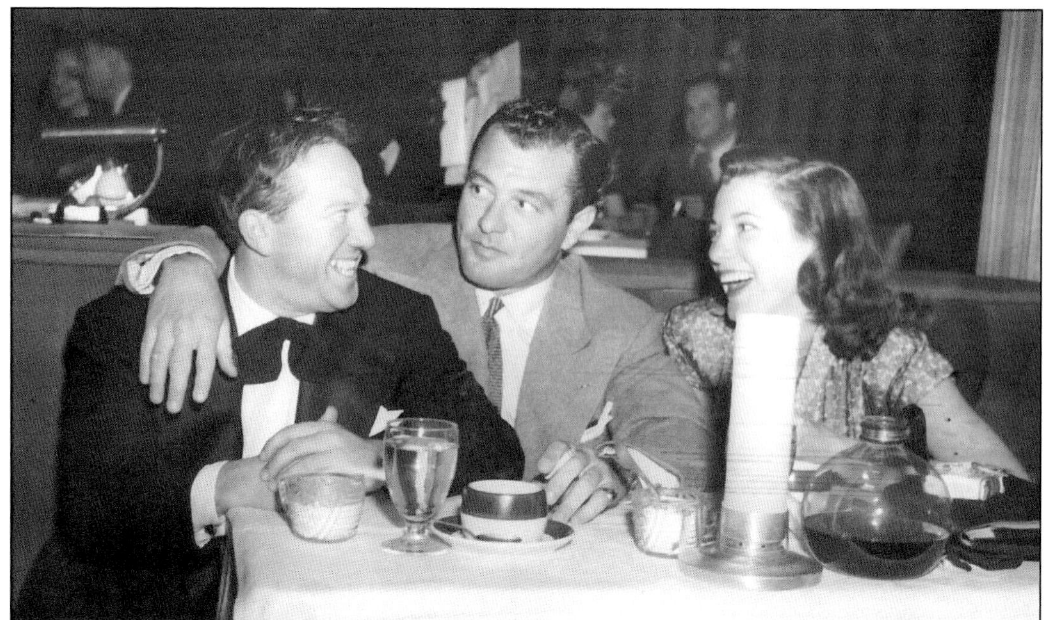

Jerry Lester (above, left; below, right) was a comedian, actor, and late-night show host who appeared on Broadway, radio, film, and television. Lester was the first entertainer to host a late-night comedy and music show on television, *Broadway Open House*. His show paved the way for *The Tonight Show*. Lester, a contracted Ciro's performer, settled a salary dispute against Ciro's owner Herman Hover due to a percentage reduction during a curfew period in Los Angeles, which resulted in a loss of revenue for Hover. Tony Martin, pictured above in the center, was a singer and an actor in 1940s and 1950s musicals. Martin had numerous hit records between the 1930s and 1960s. Lester is seen in the picture below on the right.

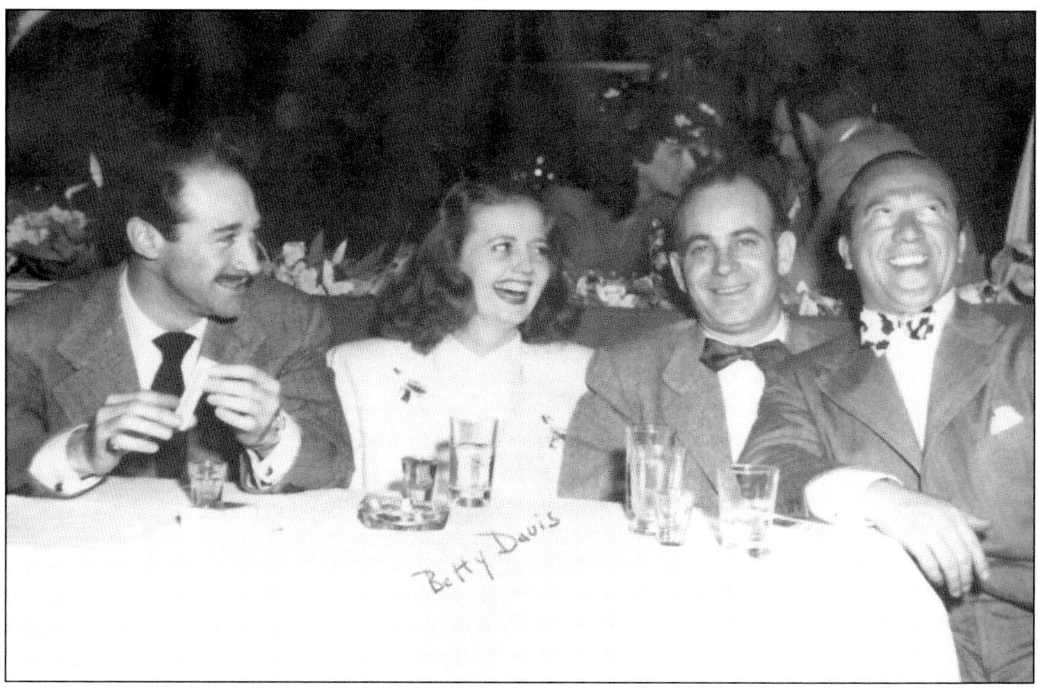

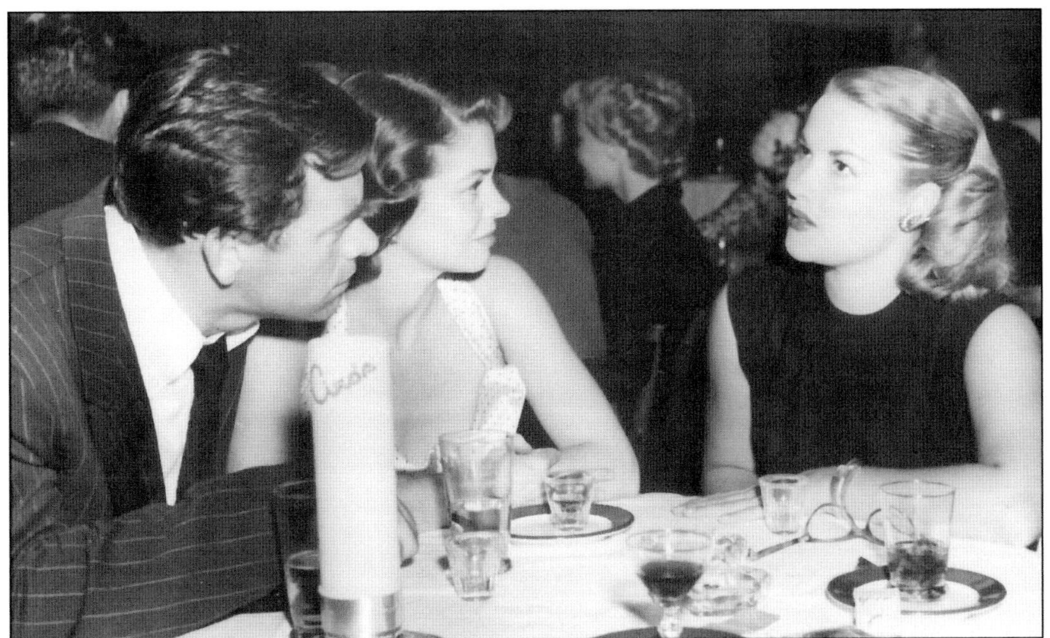

John Ireland was a Canadian-born actor and director who was married to television and film actress Joanne Dru (center). Ireland received an Academy Award nomination for his work in *All the King's Men*. Dru is also remembered for her role in *All the King's Men*. Patti Page (right) was a popular traditional pop singer in late 1940s and 1950s.

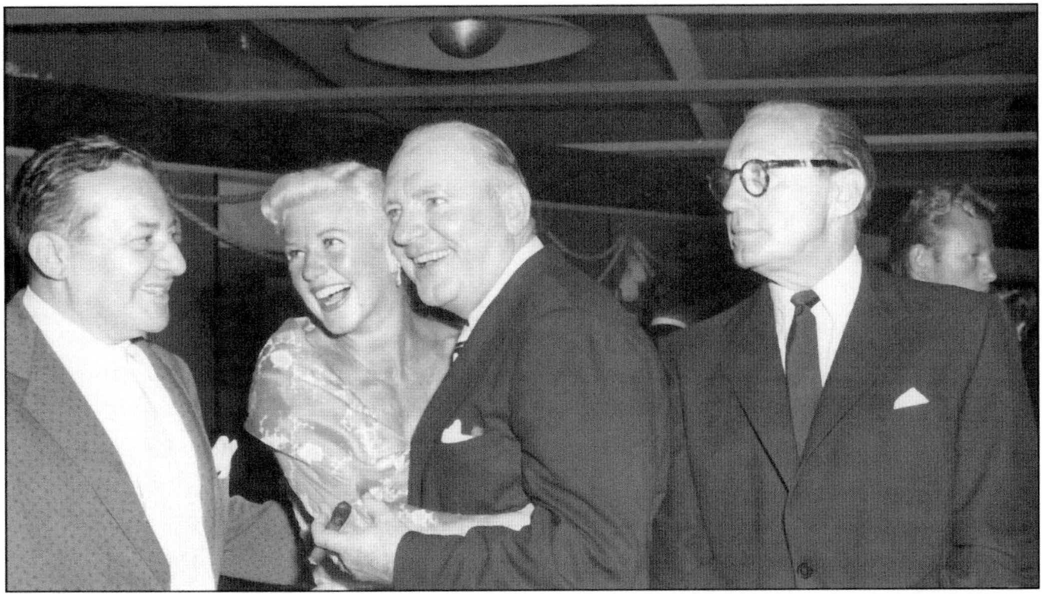

Ciro's nightclub owner Herman Hover (left) is pictured next to Academy Award–winning actress, dancer, and singer Ginger Rogers. Rogers appears with Fred Astaire in 10 movies. Actor Pat O'Brien (center) had more than 100 screen credits. Jack Benny (right) was a popular comedic entertainer who hosted radio and television programs from the 1930s until the 1960s. In the film *The Gay Divorcee*, Rogers sings "The Continental," which won an Academy Award for Best Original Song in 1934.

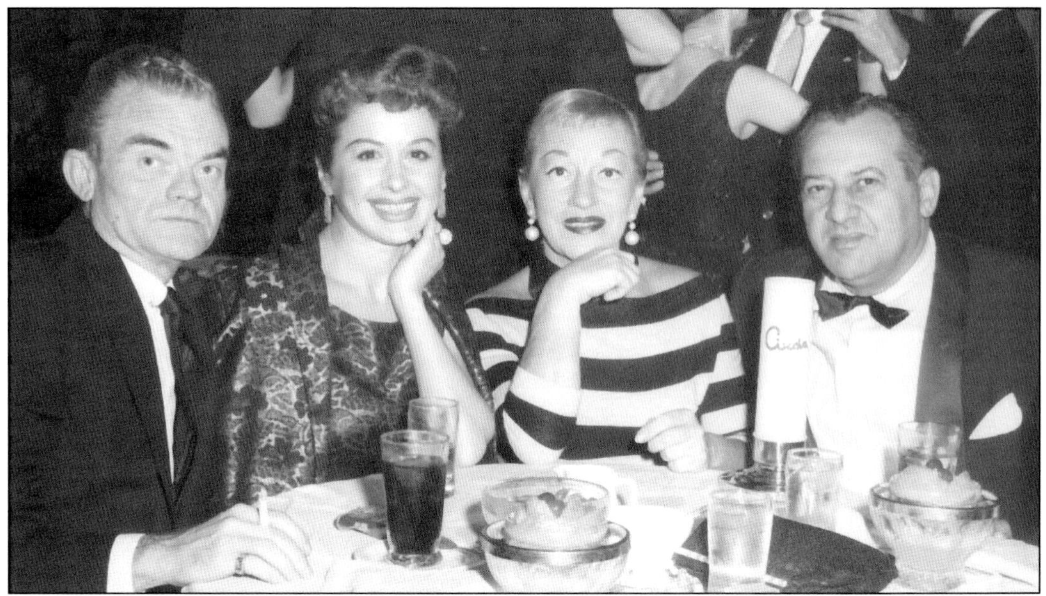

Spike Jones (left) was a musician and bandleader known for satirical arrangements of popular songs. Singer and actress Helen Grayco (second from left) was married to Jones and appeared on her husband's show, *The Spike Jones Show*, during the 1950s and 1960s. Kay Thompson (second from right) was an actress, comedienne, pianist, composer, dancer, clothing designer, and best-selling children's author of the Eloise series. The genial owner of Ciro's, Herman Hover (right), frequently visited with patrons.

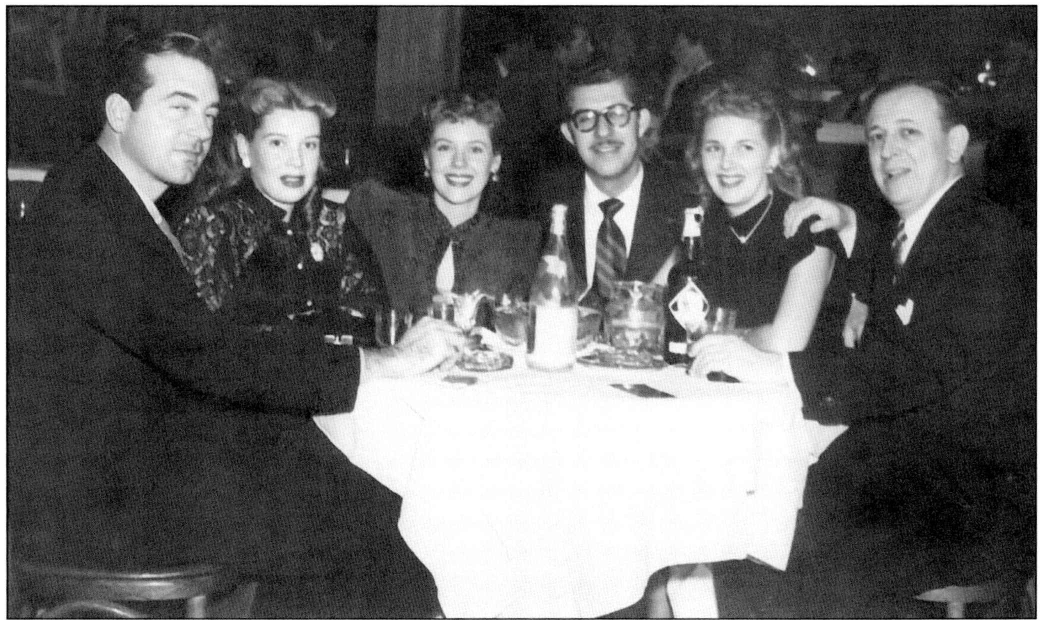

Actor John Payne (left) was known for crime story films and musicals. He is best remembered for Christmas classic *Miracle on 34th Street* and the television series *The Restless Gun*. Gloria DeHaven (far left) was a singer and MGM-contracted actress married to John Payne from 1944 to 1950. Marie McDonald (middle left) was an actress and singer nicknamed "The Body" who was married to Harry Karl (middle right), president of Karl's Shoe Stores.

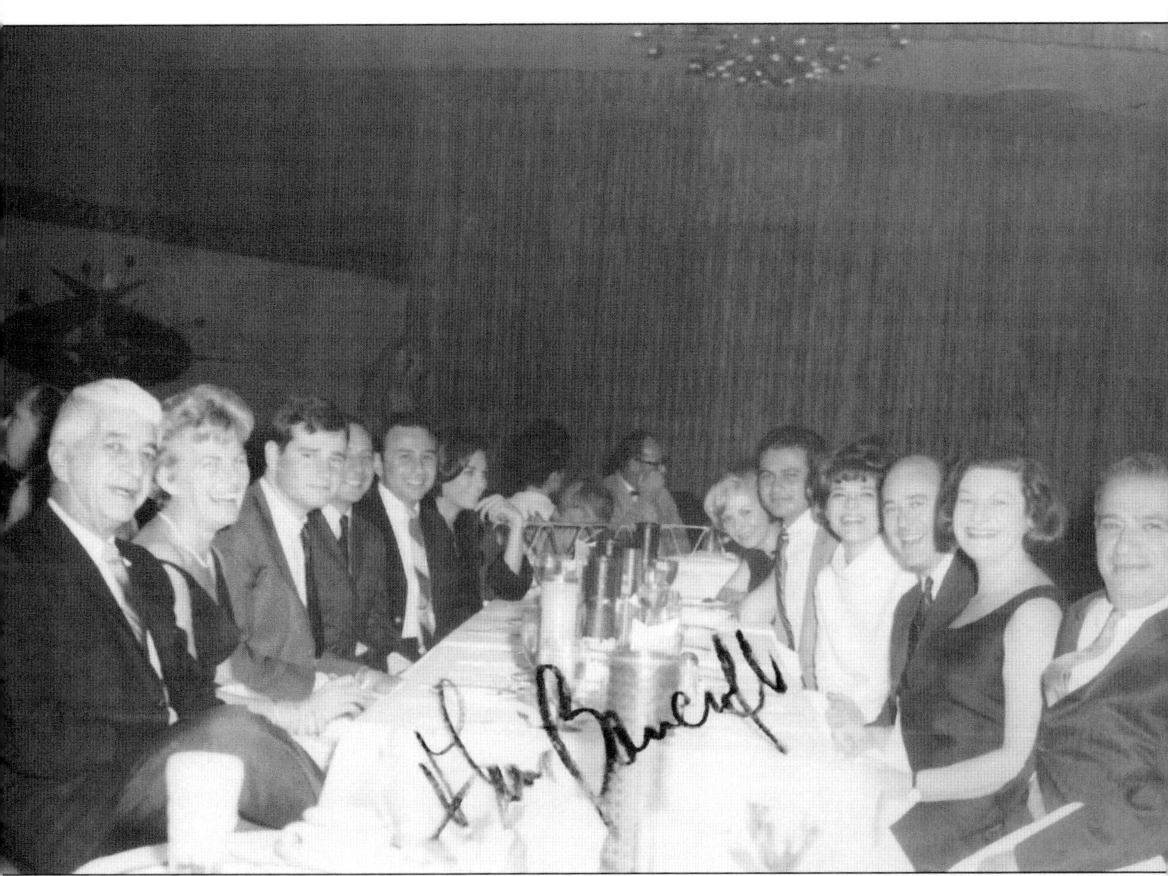

Rob Reiner (third from left) is an actor, director, producer, and activist. In the 1970s, he was known as "Meathead" in the sitcom *All in the Family*. He has produced numerous hit movies such as *Stand By Me*, *When Harry Met Sally*, *A Few Good Men*, *This Is Spinal Tap*, and *The Princess Bride*, to name a few. In 1997, Reiner and his wife founded a nonprofit organization that promotes early childhood development through educational videos hosted by celebrities. Reiner's mother, Estelle Reiner (second from right), was a singer and actress. His father, Carl Reiner (third from right), was a comedic icon, actor, director, producer, writer, and voice artist. Carl created *The Dick Van Dyke Show* and won 12 Emmys and one Grammy. Versatile actress Anne Bancroft (back far right) received an Academy Award, two Golden Globes, two Tonys, and two Emmys. Although she acquired many accolades and much success throughout her career, her best-known role is arguably Mrs. Robinson in the 1967 hit film *The Graduate*.

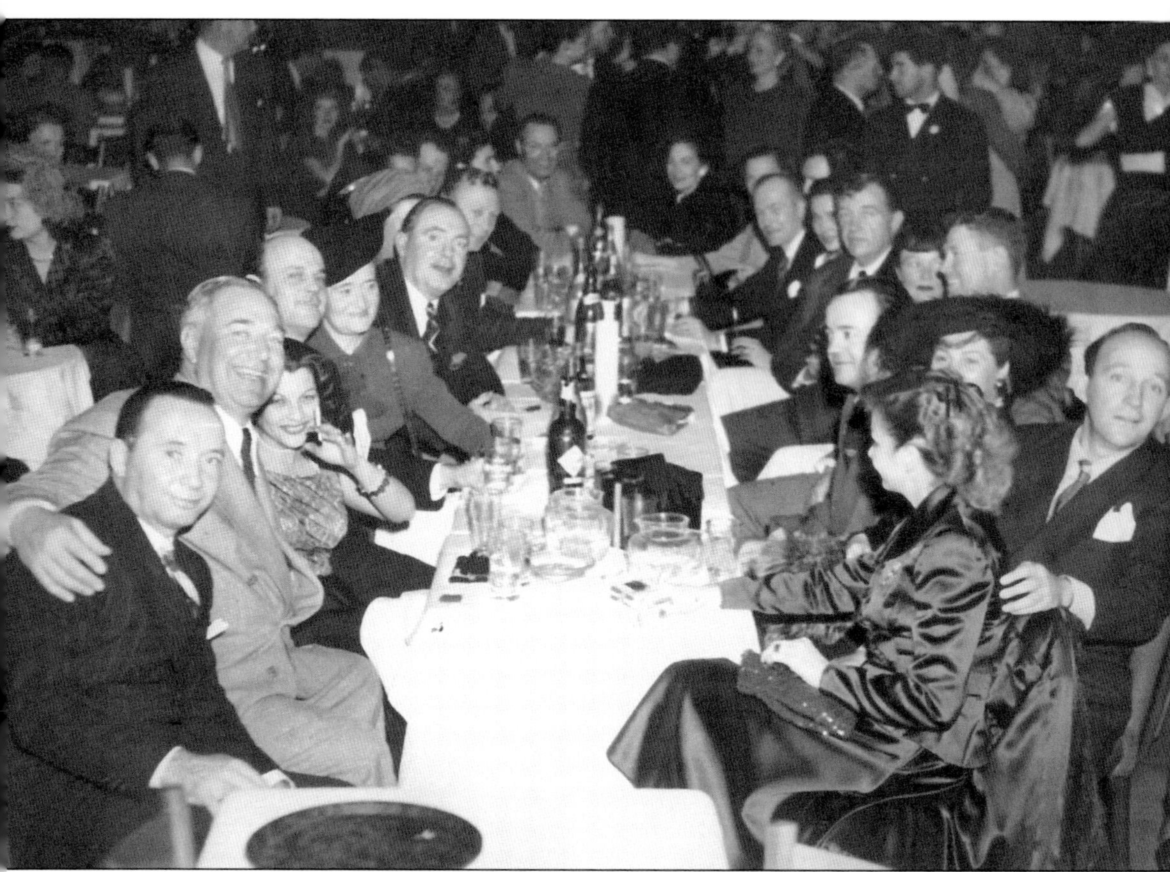

Film, stage, and television actor Pat O'Brien (sixth from left) appears with James Cagney in nine films and has over 100 screen credits. Some memorable films he stars in include *Knute Rockne, All American*; *Angels with Dirty Faces*; and *Some Like It Hot*. Character actor Andy Devine (seventh from right) appears in over 400 movies. He is the cowboy sidekick to Roy Rogers in 10 of Rogers' films. Jack Oakie (fifth from right) was known for his supporting role in *The Great Dictator*. Bing Crosby (second from right), with his rich baritone voice, was one of the best-selling singers of the 20th century. He topped the charts in record sales and radio ratings and became a box-office favorite as well. Some of Crosby's more popular films include *The Bells of St. Mary's*, *Holiday Inn*, *High Society*, and the holiday classic *White Christmas*. In 1944, he received a Best Actor Academy Award for his work as Father Chuck O'Malley in *Going My Way*. He received the Grammy Global Achievement Award in 1963. Crosby was active from 1926 until the year of his passing, 1977.

Five

COMEDIANS

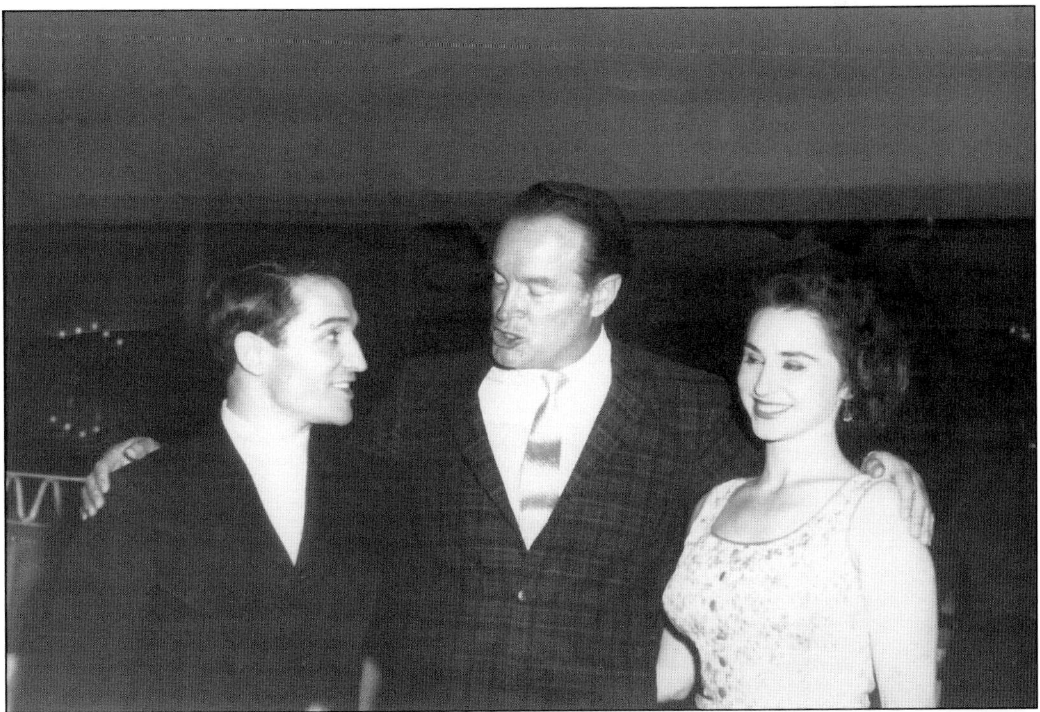

Bob Hope (center) was a multitalented actor, author, comedian, dancer, and singer who performed in vaudeville, film, television, and radio. Hope was active for nearly 80 years, appears in over 70 films, and hosted the Academy Awards 14 times. He entertained 11 presidents, from Franklin D. Roosevelt to Bill Clinton. Hope accrued 58 honorary degrees and also holds two records in the *Guinness Book of Records*. One record is for receiving over 2,000 awards and honors; the other for having the longest-running entertainment contract.

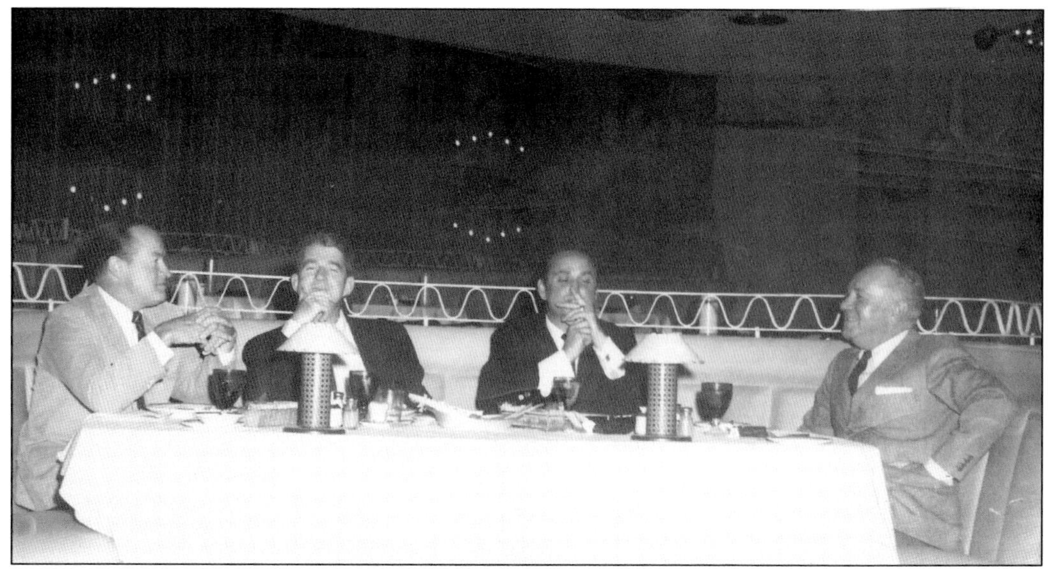

Bob Hope (above, left; below, center) was a beloved entertainer known for his cowardly, humorous roles in movies, often costarring with his friend, Bing Crosby. Hope was also known for his dedication to entertaining troops overseas. He headlined 57 tours in every war from World War II to the Gulf War. His deep respect for American troops propelled him to entertain and visit wounded soldiers. His self-imposed rule was to never let the wounded soldiers see him cry, which he only broke once. Hope has an airport, theaters, buildings, a military cargo plane and ship, streets, named after him—as well as a US postage stamp. It is estimated that Hope donated about $1 billion to charity over the years, including several acres of land in Rancho Mirage, California, for the Eisenhower Medical Center. He was quoted as saying, "If you haven't got charity in your heart, you have the worst kind of heart trouble."

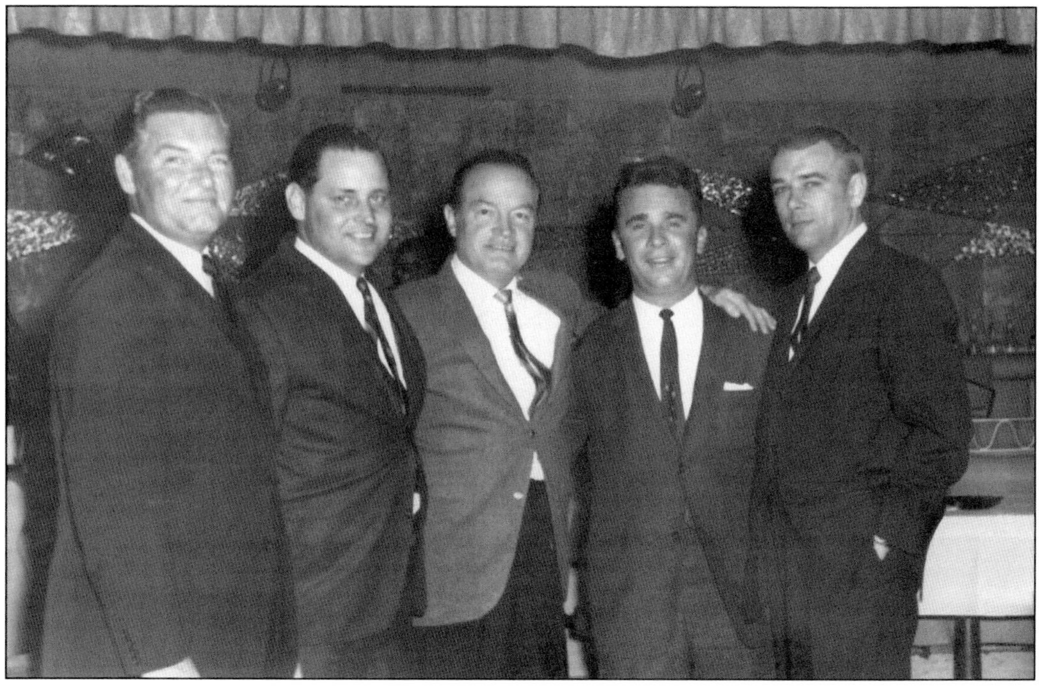

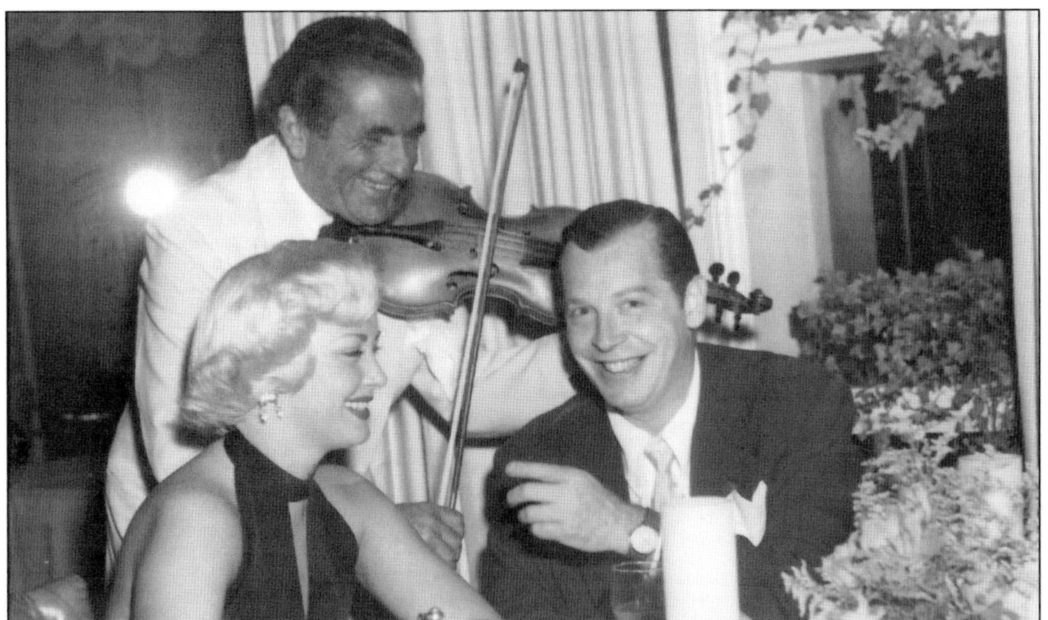

Milton Berle was a comedic actor known as "Uncle Miltie" and "Mr. Television" during television's heyday. He began working in the entertainment industry at age five. He was in silent films, vaudeville, television, film, and radio. He was the first major television star and was active from 1914 to 2000. He hosted television shows called *Texaco Star Theater* and *The Milton Berle Show*. Berle performed for various charity events, which helped raise millions of dollars.

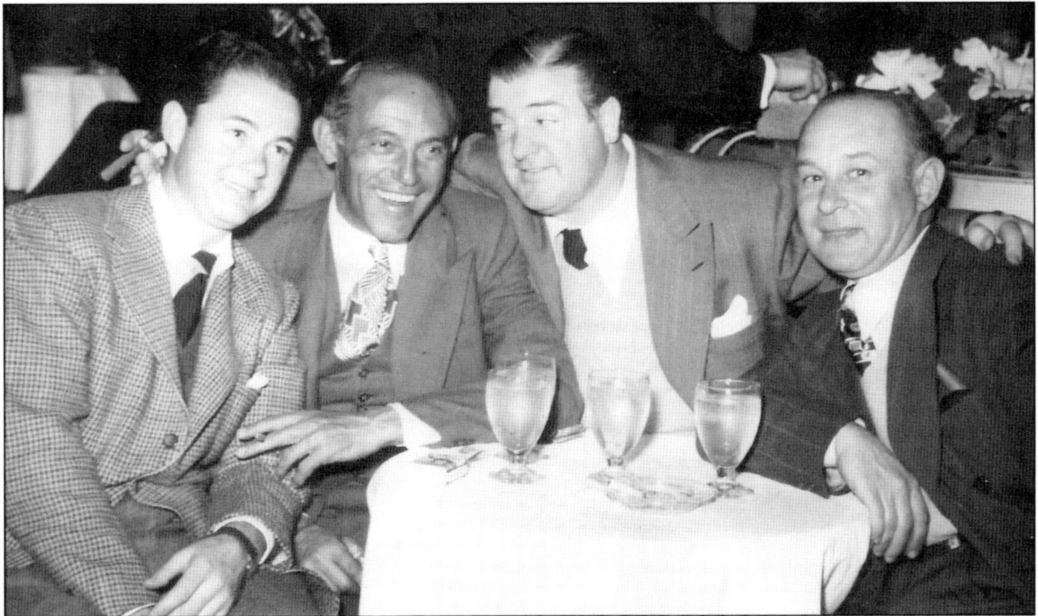

Actor and comedian Lou Costello (second from right) was best known as the funny guy in the comedic duo Abbott and Costello. The pair made 36 films together between 1940 and 1956, appearing on radio and television as well. Although the two had contractual conflicts regarding finances during their career, in the end, they parted amicably in 1957. Costello died of a heart attack in 1959, just three days shy of his 53rd birthday.

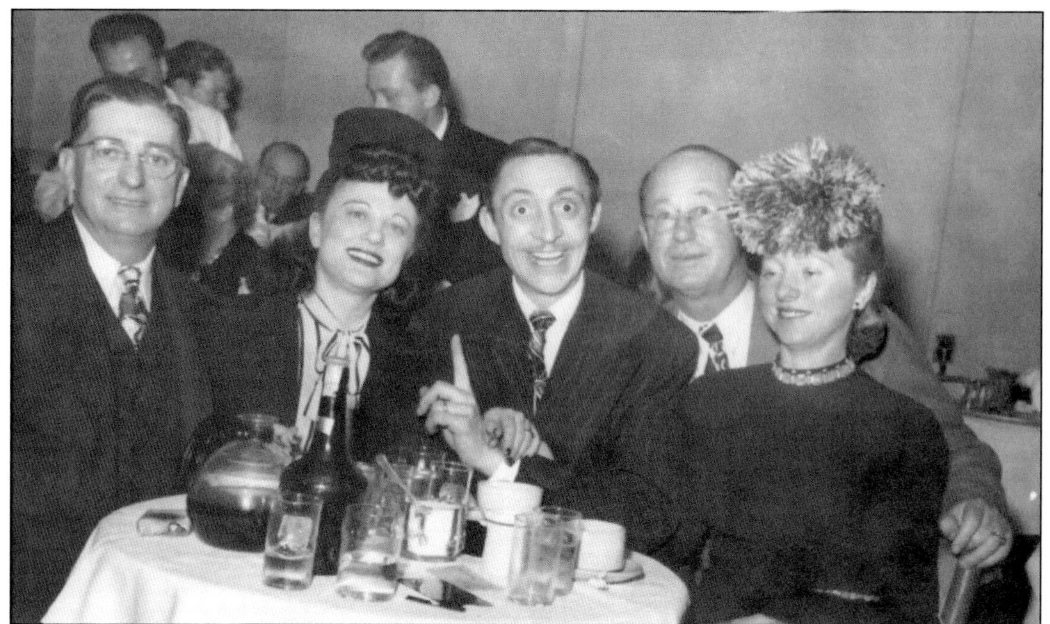

Mischa Auer (center) was a Russian-born American actor who appeared in numerous well-known films beginning in the late 1920s. He was often cast in zany comedic roles. A few of the comedies he appears in are *You Can't Take It With You*, *Destry Rides Again*, and *My Man Godfrey*. He received one Academy Award nomination, and he spoke six languages. He made movies in France and Italy prior to his death in 1967 at age 61.

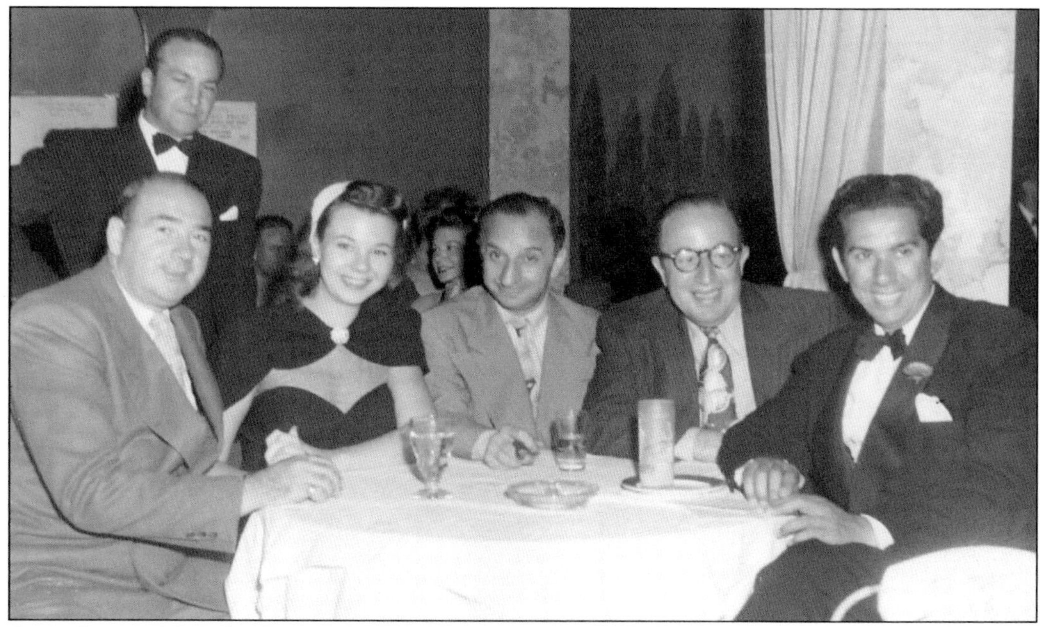

Comedian and bandleader Chaz Chase (center) was a vaudeville entertainer in the 1920s whose performances entailed eating various inedible objects such as cardboard, cigarettes, cigars, and matches. He appeared in some cameo performances in movies and then joined carnival shows for 20 years. In the 1950s, he appeared on variety shows and in nightclubs. Carmen Cavallaro (right) was one of the bandleaders at Ciro's nightclub.

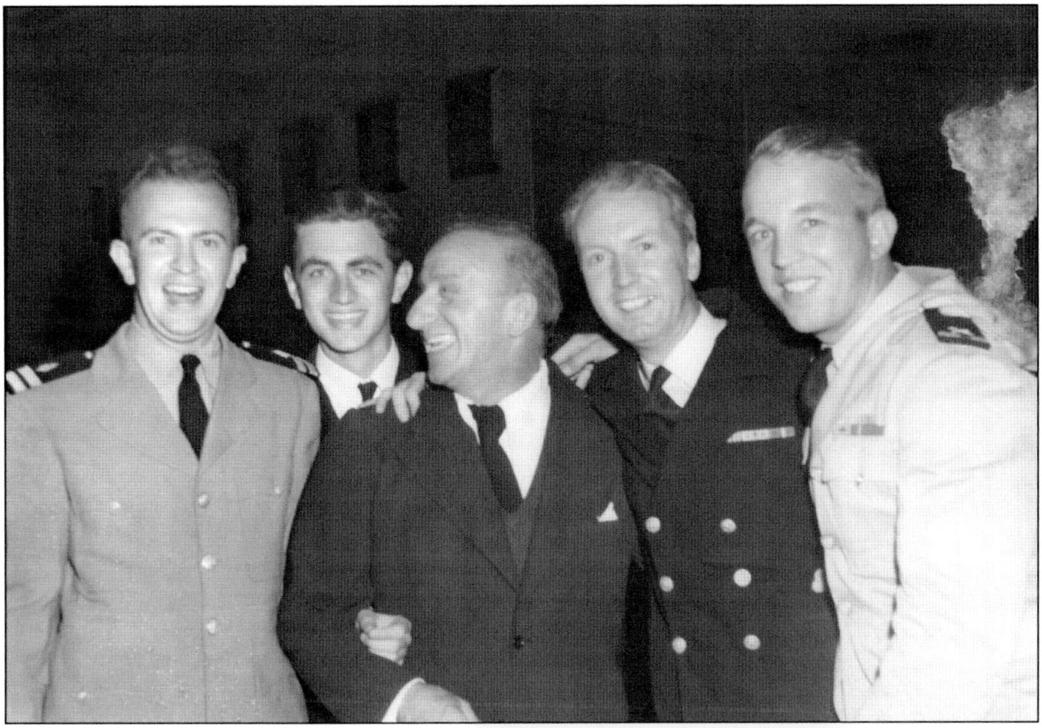

Jimmy Durante (above, center; right) was a comedian and jazz-influenced singer, actor, and pianist with a memorable voice and thick New York accent. Durante was a popular American personality from 1920 through the 1970s. His distinctive, gravelly voice and large nose were his trademarks. He referred to his nose as the Schnozzola; his nicknames were "The Great Schnozzola" or "The Schnoz."

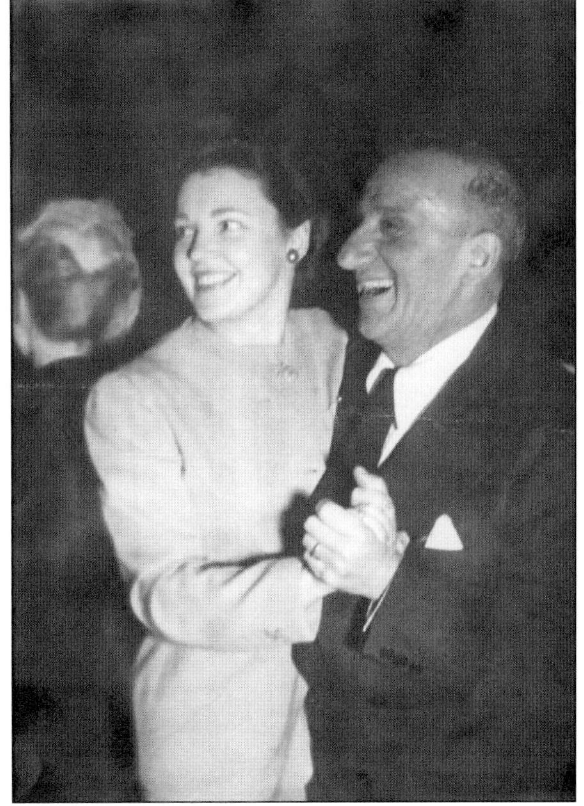

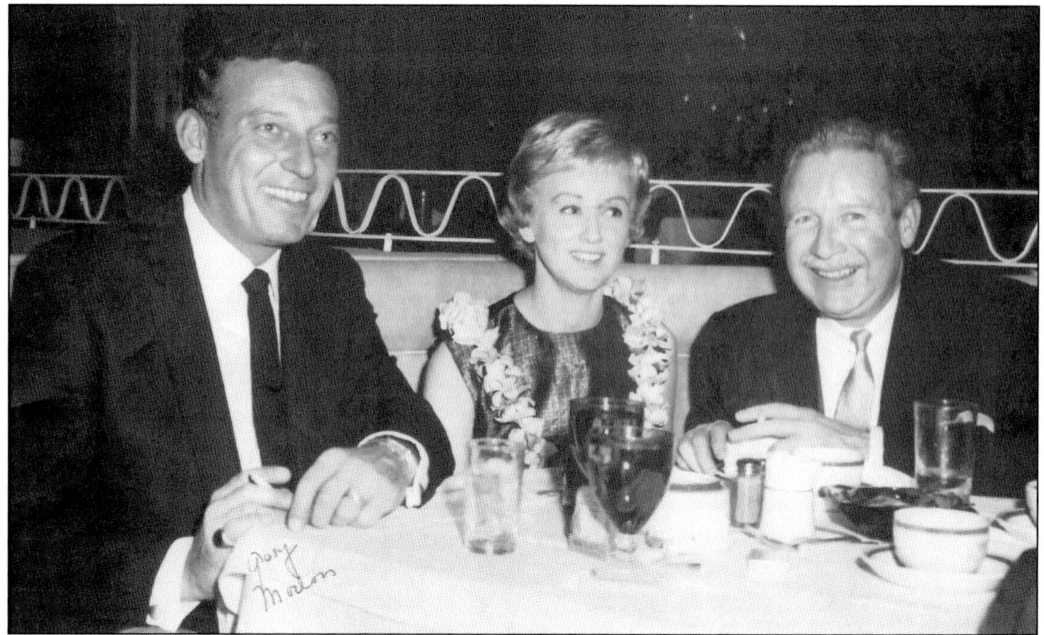

Gary Morton (left) was a stand-up comedian and the second husband of Lucille Ball. Morton helped manage Ball's career after they were married in 1961. He produced some of Ball's television series, played small parts in television and films, and even warmed up audiences prior to Ball's television show tapings. Morton also contributed to the formation of Lucille Ball Productions. Arthur O'Connell is pictured on the right.

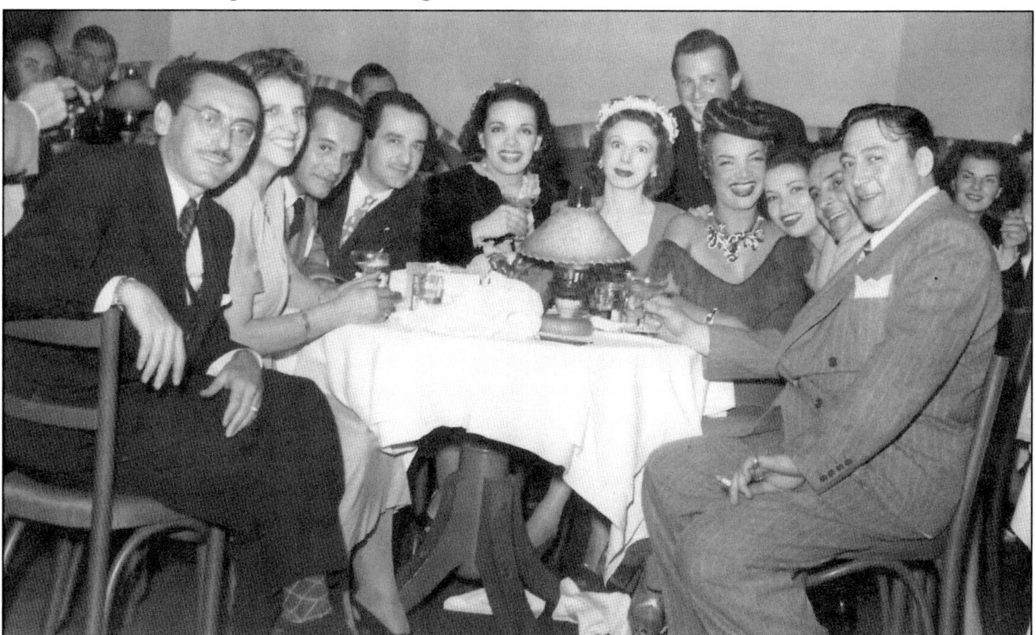

B.S. Pully (right) was a stage actor and nightclub comedian. He appeared in the original Broadway production of *Guys and Dolls* in the role of Big Jule. He appeared in over 1,000 performances and played the same role in the film version as well. He is also in the 1945 films *A Tree Grows in Brooklyn* and *Nob Hill*. Entertainer Carmen Miranda (fourth from right) performed regularly at Ciro's.

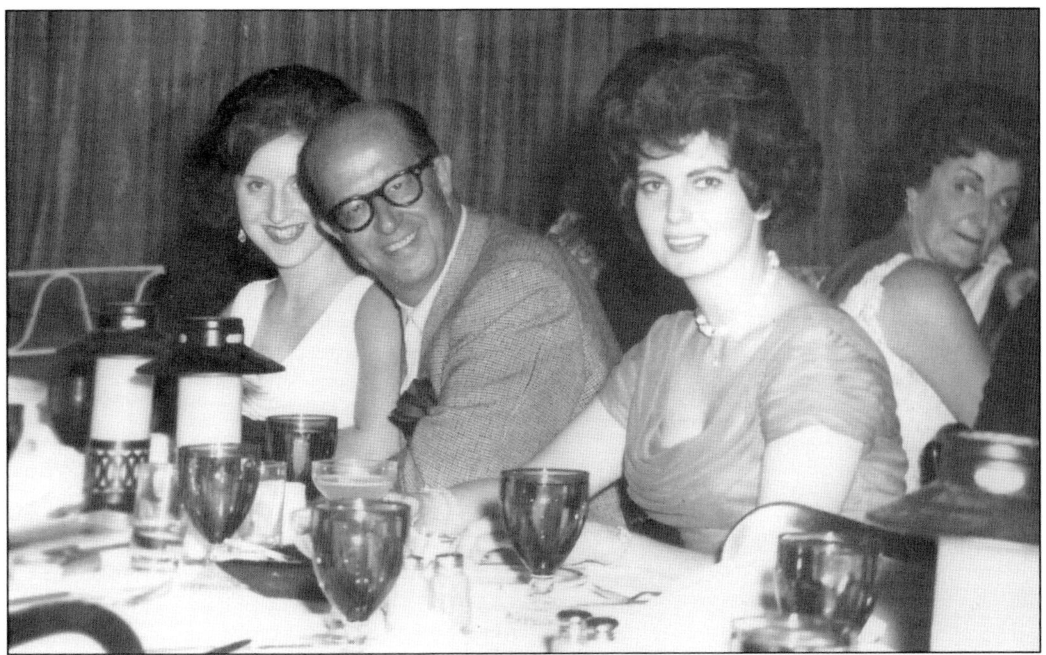

Phil Silvers was a comedian and actor in television, film, and stage. He is best known for *The Phil Silvers Show*, a 1950s sitcom set on a US Army post; Silvers plays Sergeant Bilko. Silvers enjoyed numerous successes on Broadway and received two Tony Awards, one for *Top Banana* in 1951 and one for *A Funny Thing Happened on the Way to the Forum* in 1971.

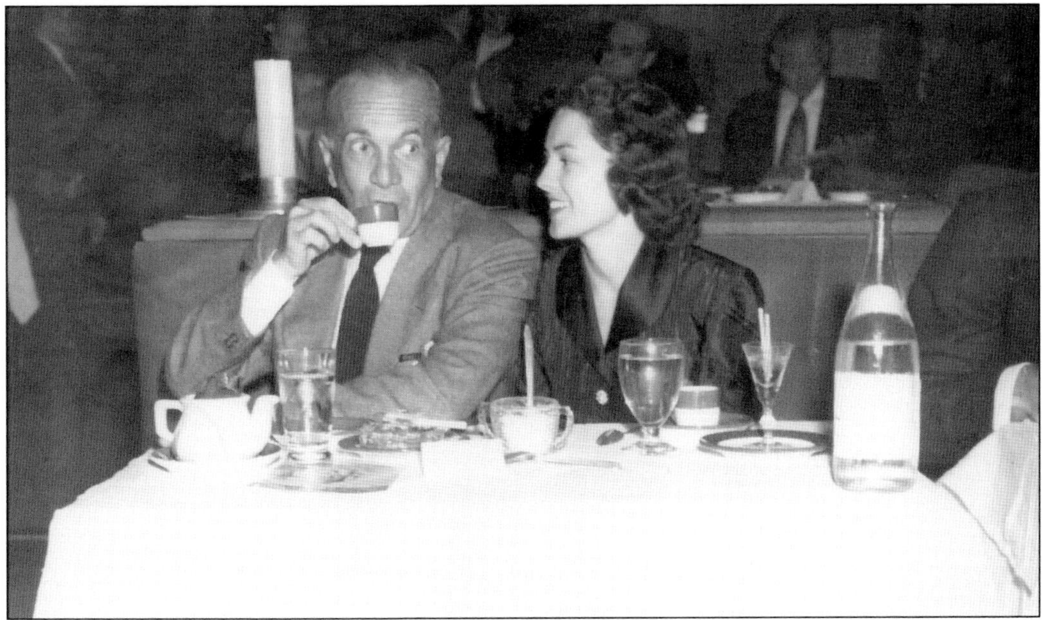

Al Jolson was a singer, actor, and comedian who appeared in vaudeville and on Broadway. He stars in the first talking movie, *The Jazz Singer*, released in 1927. Jolson is remembered for his blackface routine and for his long, successful Broadway career. He was the first star to perform for American troops after Pearl Harbor and one of the highest-paid entertainers in the 1930s. Many in the industry regard him as one of the greatest entertainers of all time.

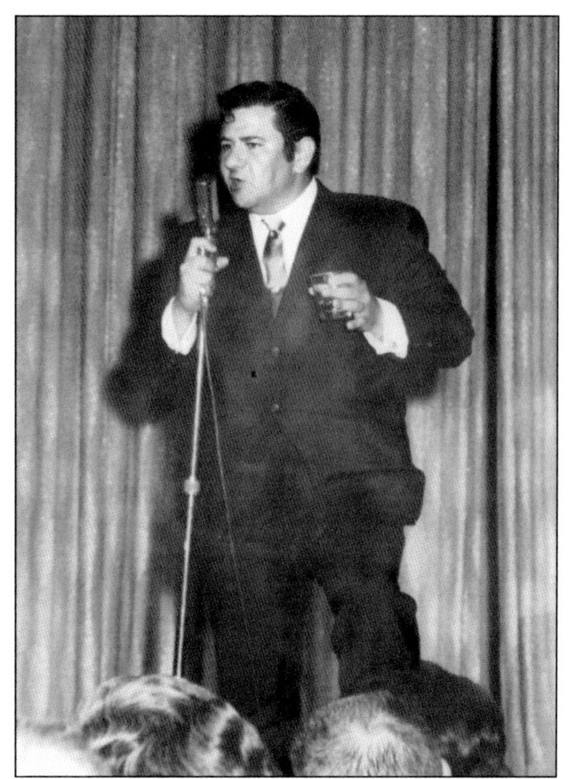

Buddy Hackett was mainly a nightclub comedian and a comedic actor who became a frequent guest on the Jack Paar, Arthur Godfrey, and Johnny Carson shows. He preferred nightclub performance more than film or television performance. He is best known for his work in *The Music Man* (1962), *It's a Mad, Mad, Mad, Mad World* (1963), *The Love Bug* (1968), and *The Little Mermaid* (1989).

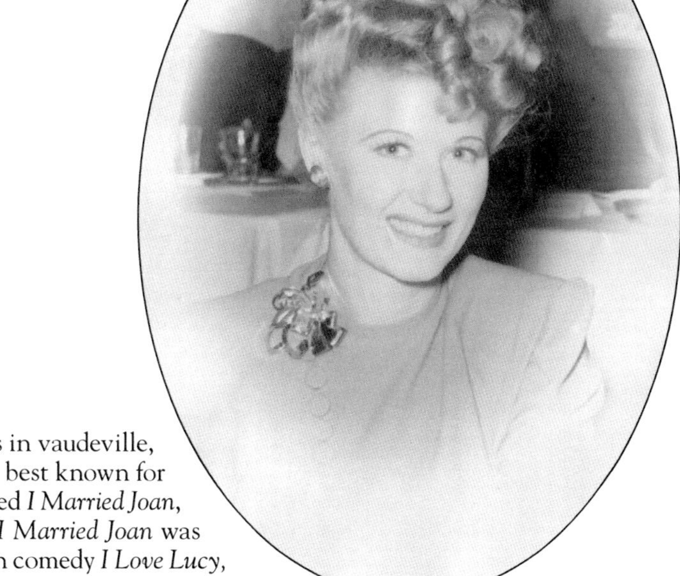

Joan Davis was a comedic actress in vaudeville, film, television, and radio. She is best known for the television sitcom on NBC titled *I Married Joan*, which aired from 1952 to 1955. *I Married Joan* was NBC's rebuttal to the hit situation comedy *I Love Lucy*, which began airing the previous year in 1951 on CBS.

Wayne Newton (left) is a singer, entertainer and one of the best-known Las Vegas acts of all time. His nicknames include "Mr. Las Vegas," "The Midnight Idol," and "Mr. Entertainment." His most popular song is "Danke Schoen." Jack Benny was a comedian, television, film, and stage actor who is considered one of the leading entertainers of the 20th century. Benny helped give Newton his start by giving him the opportunity to open for his show.

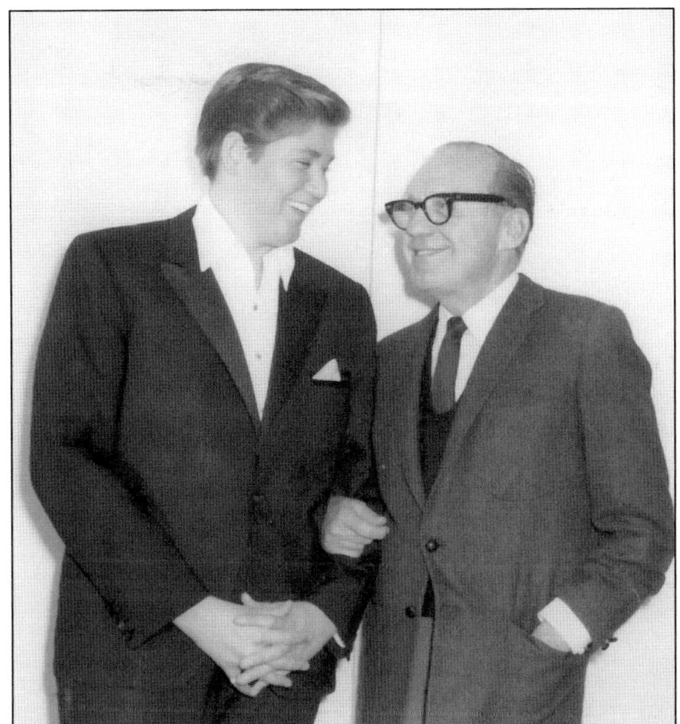

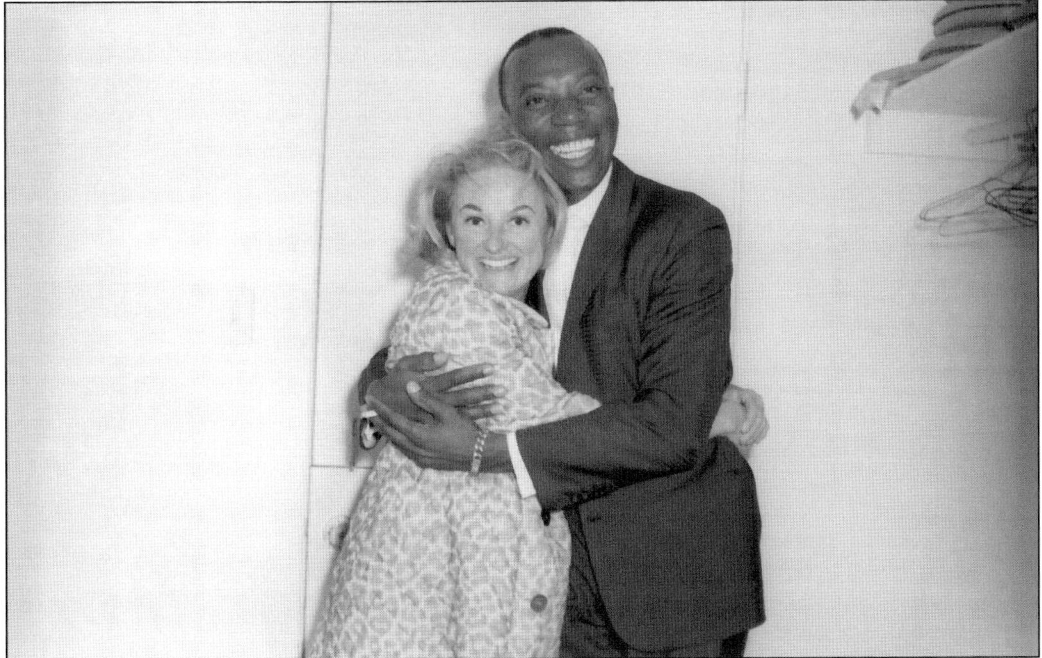

Phyllis Diller was a housewife who transformed herself into the world's first female stand-up comedian. Diller was also an actress, singer, dancer, and voice artist. She was best known for her eccentric clothes, wild hairdo, and her long cigarette holder. Her cackle of a laugh was unforgettable, and her self-effacing one-liners were uniquely hers. She performed in nightclubs and in Las Vegas regularly. The man in the photograph is unidentified.

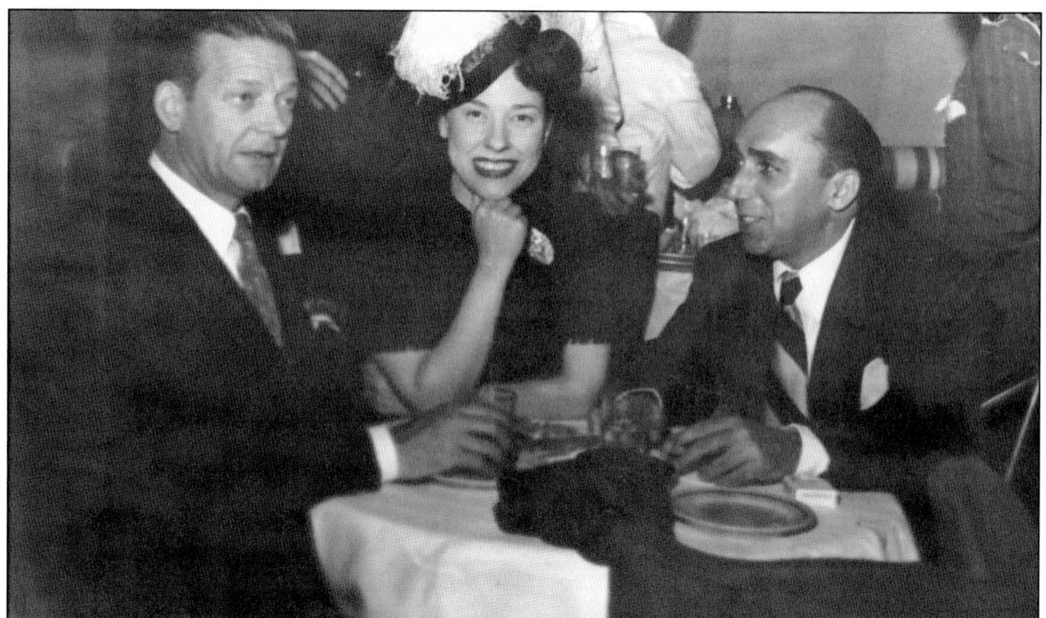

Judy Canova was a singer, comedienne, and actress who began her career in vaudeville alongside her brother and sister. Her success extended from vaudeville and nightclubs to radio and Broadway to television and film. Canova performed on her own radio show called *The Judy Canova Show*, where she delighted audiences for 12 years with her country bumpkin antics. Canova often played the yodeling country hillbilly part in her various radio, stage, and film performances.

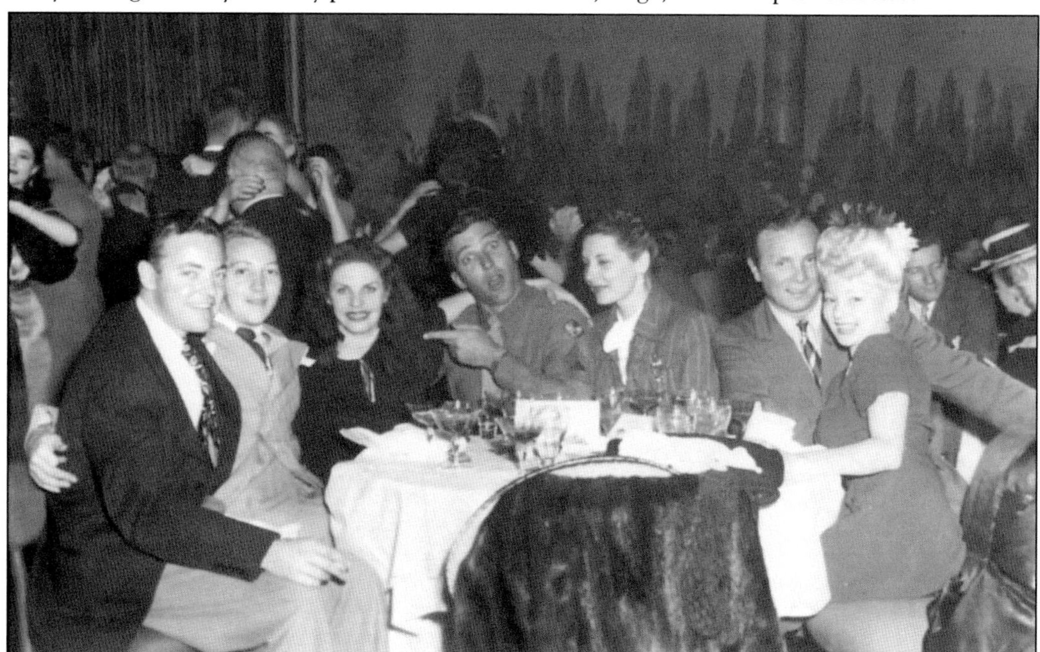

Comedic actress and singer Martha Raye (third from left) was nicknamed "Colonel Maggie" for the numerous USO tours she did during World War II, the Korean War, and the Vietnam War. She received the Jean Hersholt Humanitarian Award in 1969 for her tireless volunteer efforts and service to American troops. She performed in movies, in television, and on Broadway.

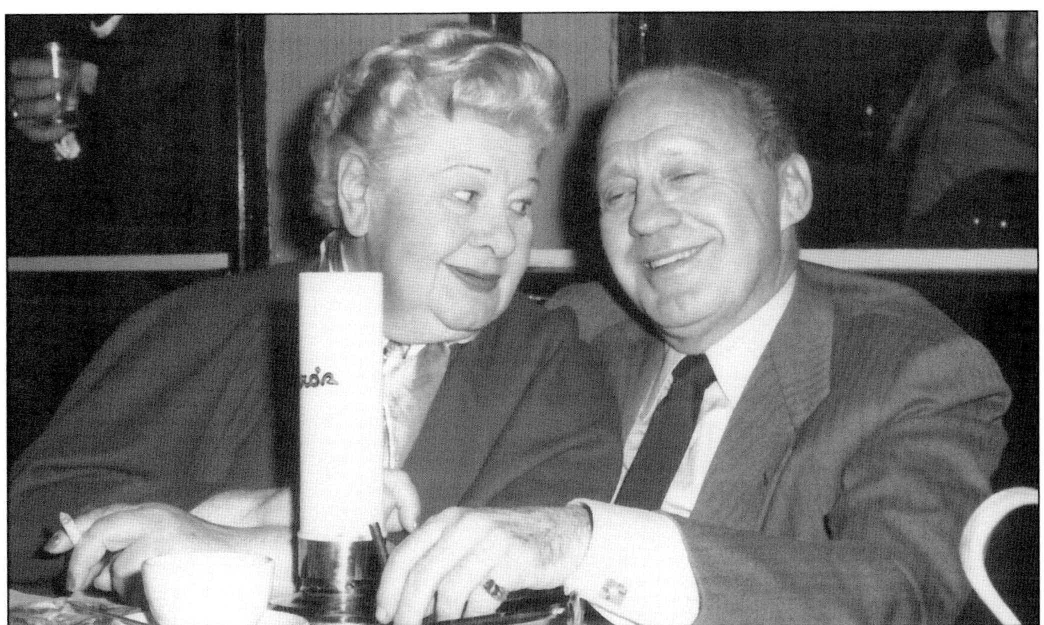

Sophie Tucker (above, left; below, right) was a Ukrainian-born American comedienne, actress, singer, and radio personality who became known as the "Last of the Red Hot Mamas." Tucker thrived on live stage audiences. She performed in vaudeville and clubs and on film and Broadway. She was also on numerous television variety and talk shows. Her signature song was "Some of These Days." Jack Benny (above, right) was a comedian and actor who appeared in vaudeville and on radio, television, film, and stage. His successful radio and television programs were popular from the 1930s through the 1970s. He was known for his impeccable timing, pregnant pauses, and single comical expressions. Tucker and Benny are considered to be the among the leading entertainers of the 20th century. Marie Wilson (below, left) was a television, film, and radio actress who is best remembered from radio and television situation comedy as Irma Peterson on *My Friend Irma*.

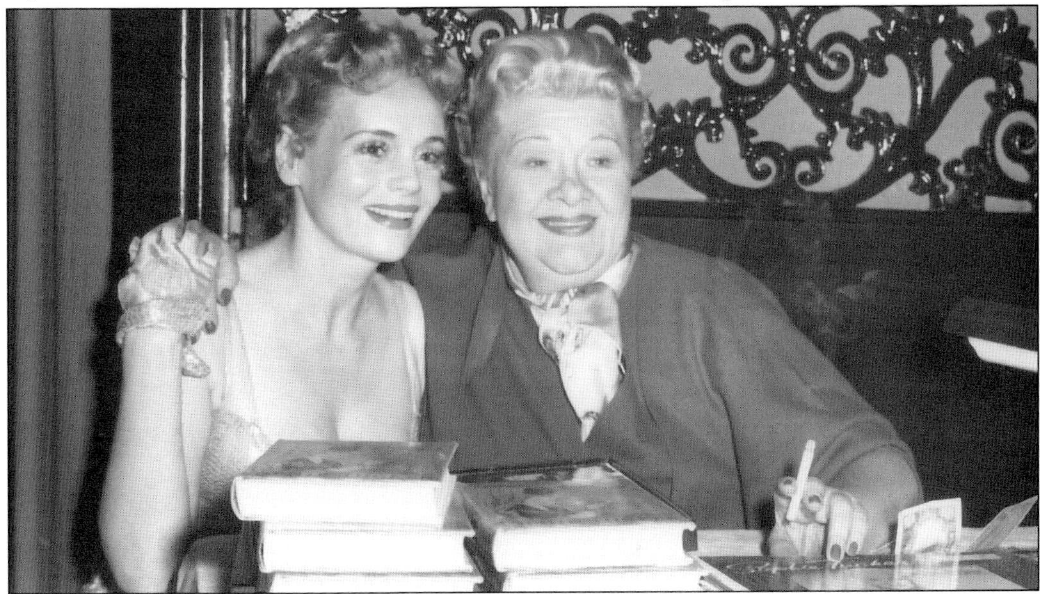

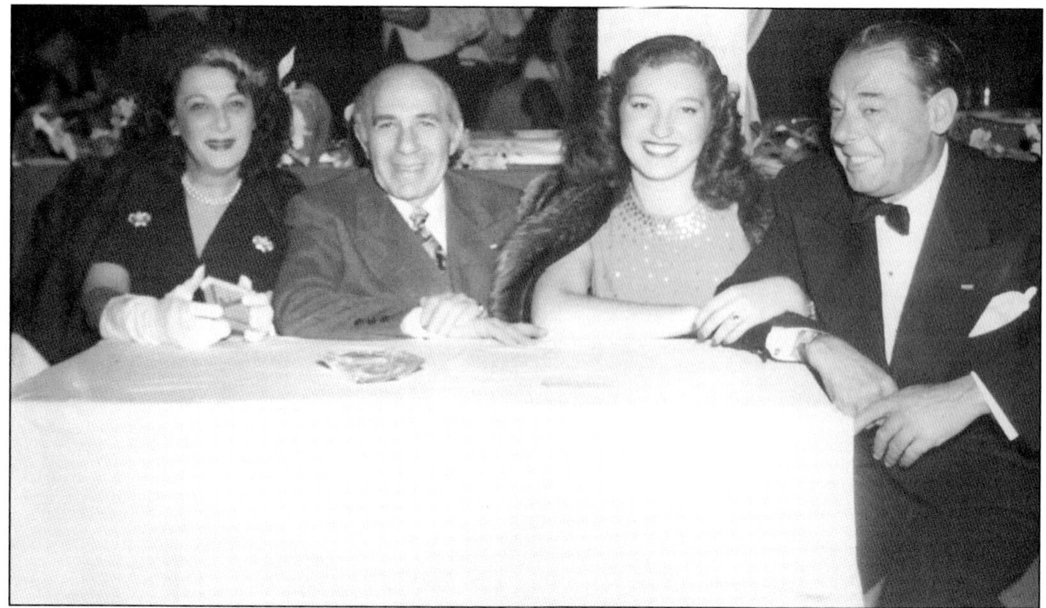

Comedian and singer Joe E. Lewis (above, right; below, left) was assaulted in 1927 by Al Capone's lieutenant Jack "Machine Gun" McGurn, who mutilated Lewis's throat and tongue due to his refusal to renew a contract to perform at a nightclub partially owned by McGurn. It is reported that Capone was displeased with the assault, as he was fond of Lewis. Consequently, Capone gave Lewis thousands of dollars to aid him in recovery. It took Lewis a few years to learn to speak again, but ultimately he recovered and resumed his career. Frank Sinatra signed his longtime friend Lewis to his record label, Reprise Records. Lewis toured with USO shows and was in several movies, on talk shows, and on game shows.

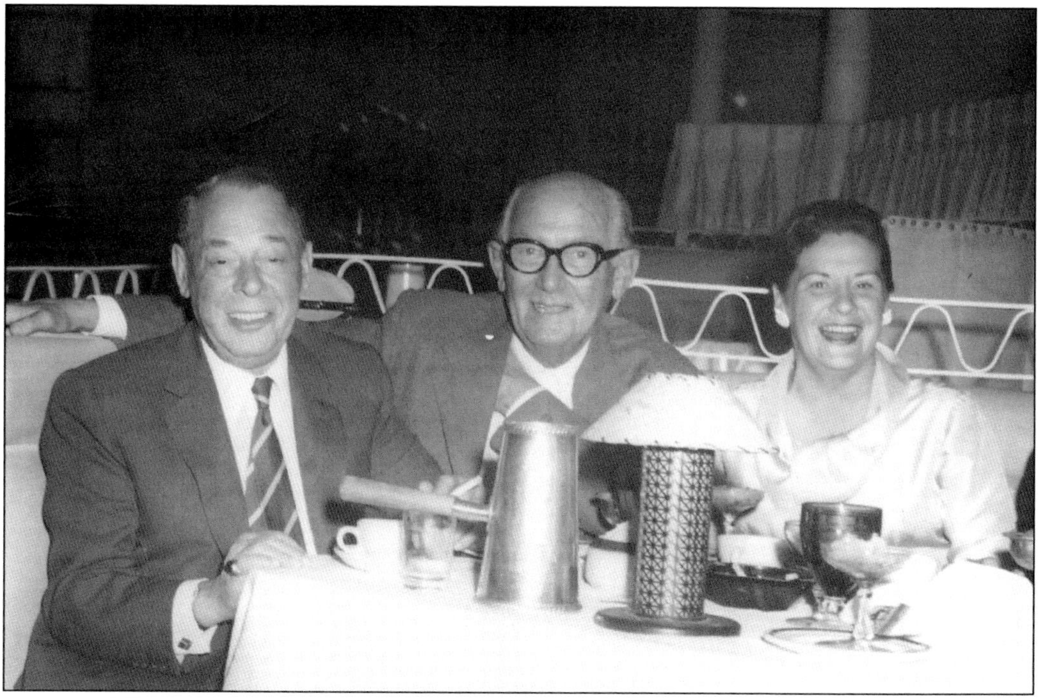

Six

Bandleaders, Singers, and Musicians

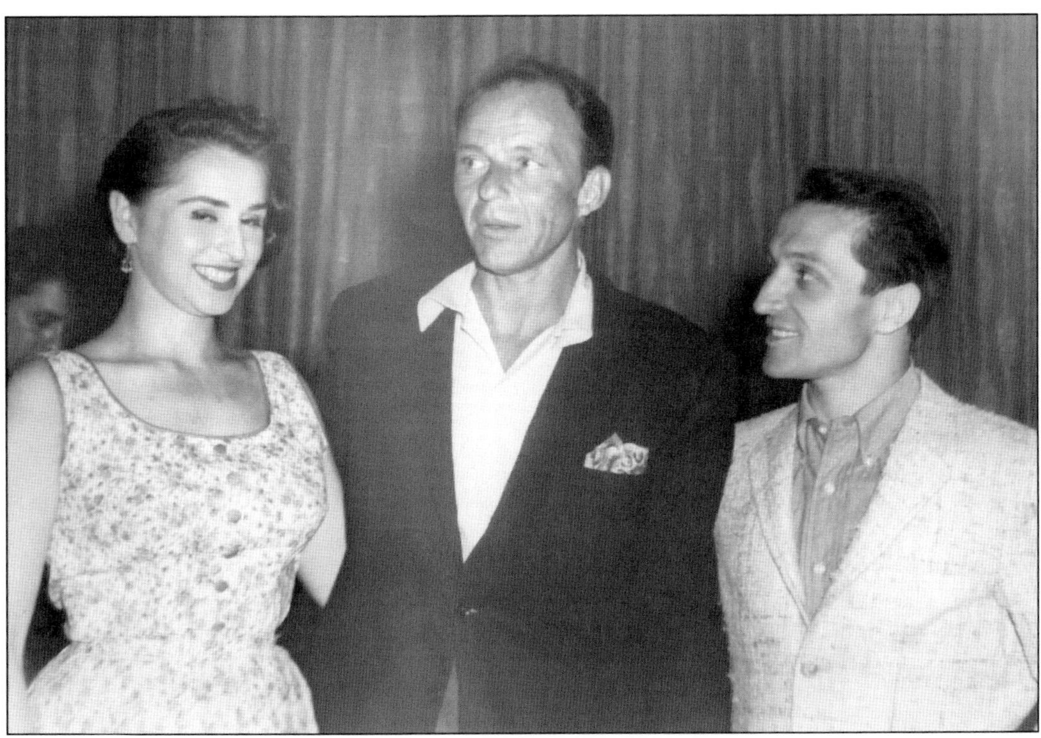

Frank Sinatra (center), "Ol' Blue Eyes," was an American icon and believed by many to be one of the greatest and most influential singers of all time. He sold over 150 million records worldwide. His most popular songs include "My Way," "Luck Be a Lady," "Mack the Knife," "Come Fly with Me," "Strangers in the Night," and "New York, New York." He was an actor, director, producer, and humanitarian. He was also the leader of the Rat Pack, which included famous actors who appeared together onstage and in movies such as *Ocean's 11* and *Sergeants 3*. He received numerous awards and accolades over his career, including Golden Globes, Academy Awards, and multiple Grammys. He received three honorary degrees, a Presidential Medal of Freedom, and a Congressional Gold Medal. He was a Kennedy Center Honoree and has a commemorative stamp in his honor.

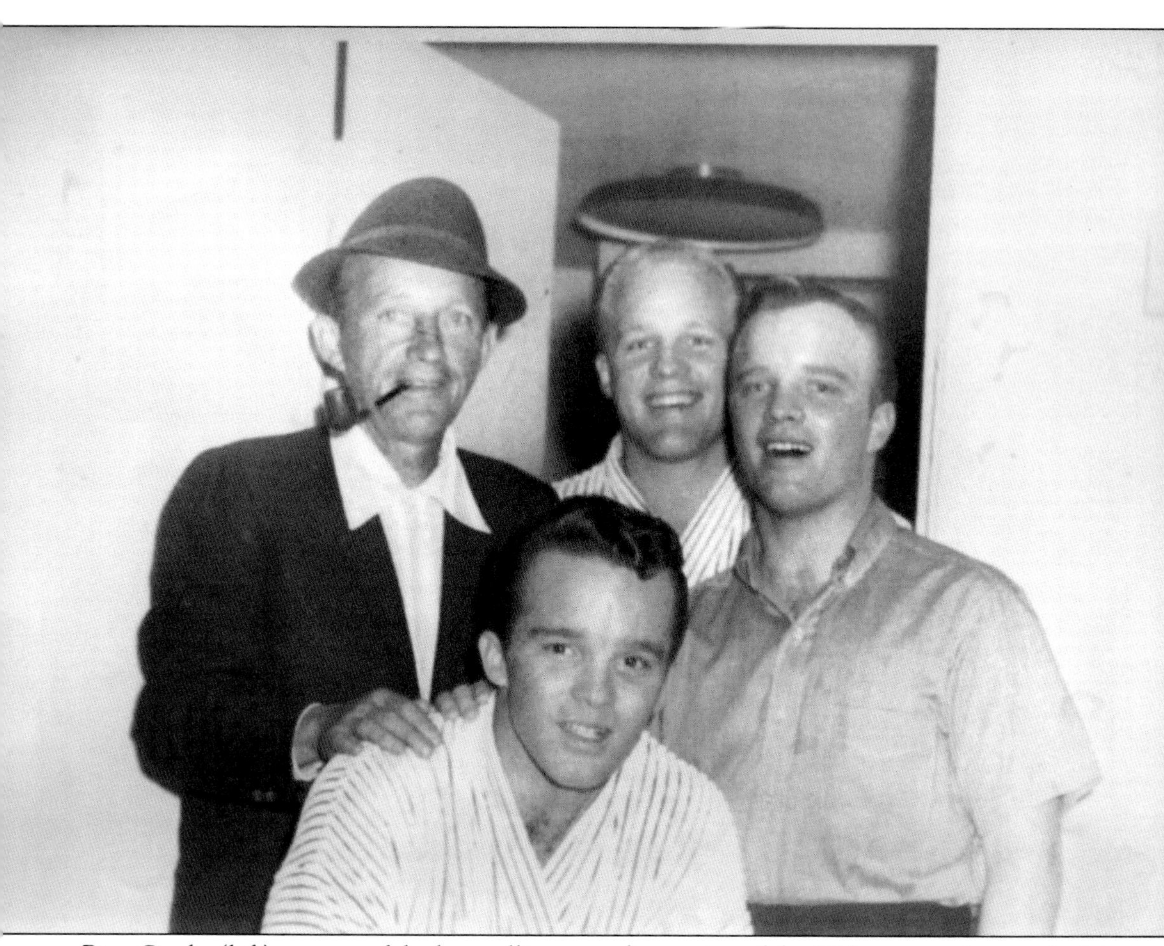

Bing Crosby (left) was one of the best-selling recording artists of the 20th century, known for his trademark bass-baritone voice. In the 1930s to 1950s, the multitalented Crosby led in gross movie sales, radio ratings, and record sales. He was active for more than 50 years. His most popular song, "White Christmas," hit radio waves on December 1941 and continues to be a holiday favorite each year, along with the movie musical he starred in of the same title, *White Christmas*. Bing won an Academy Award for Best Actor in 1944 for *Going My Way* and the Hollywood Foreign Press Association's Cecil B. DeMille award in 1960. Bing is pictured here with three of his four sons—the Crosby Boys, from left to right, Lindsay, Phillip, and Dennis—from his first wife, Dixie Lee, who was a jazz singer and actress. The Crosby Boys were a harmonizing singing group.

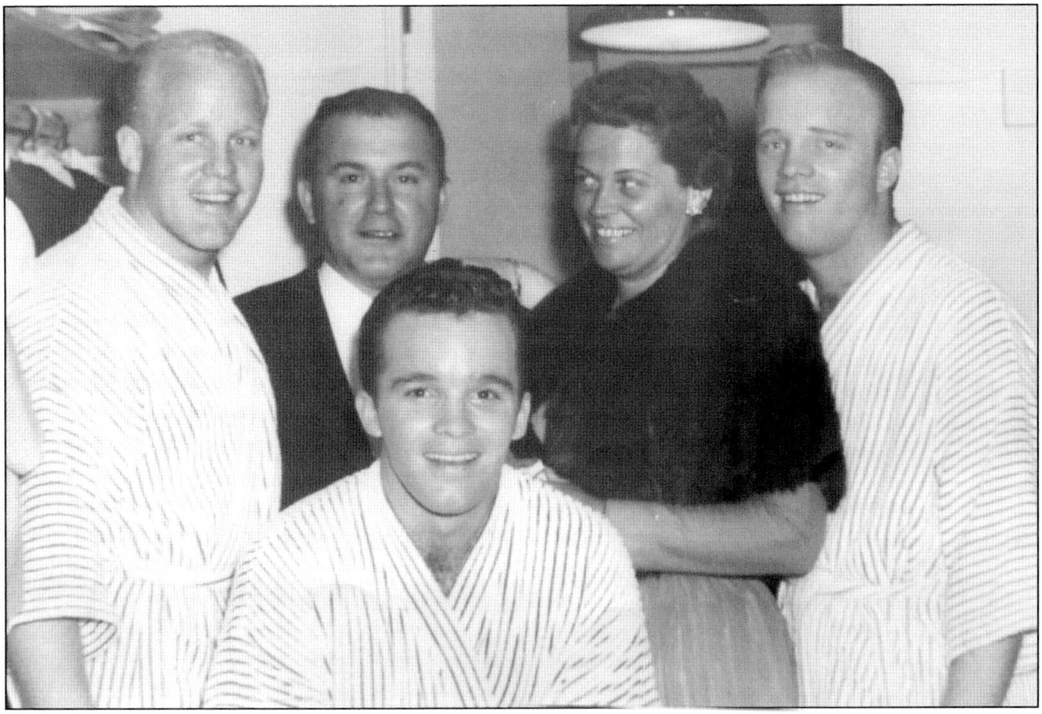

The Crosby Boys—Phillip (both, left), Dennis (both, right), and Lindsay (above, front; below, back row, center)—were a vocal harmony group who performed together during the 1950s and 1960s in nightclubs, in Las Vegas, on the *Ed Sullivan Show*, and on their father's *The Bing Crosby Show*. Phillip and Dennis were twins, and Lindsay was the youngest of Bing's four sons from his first wife, Dixie. Lindsay committed suicide in 1989 at age 51 and Dennis followed suit, taking his life two years later in 1991 at age 56.

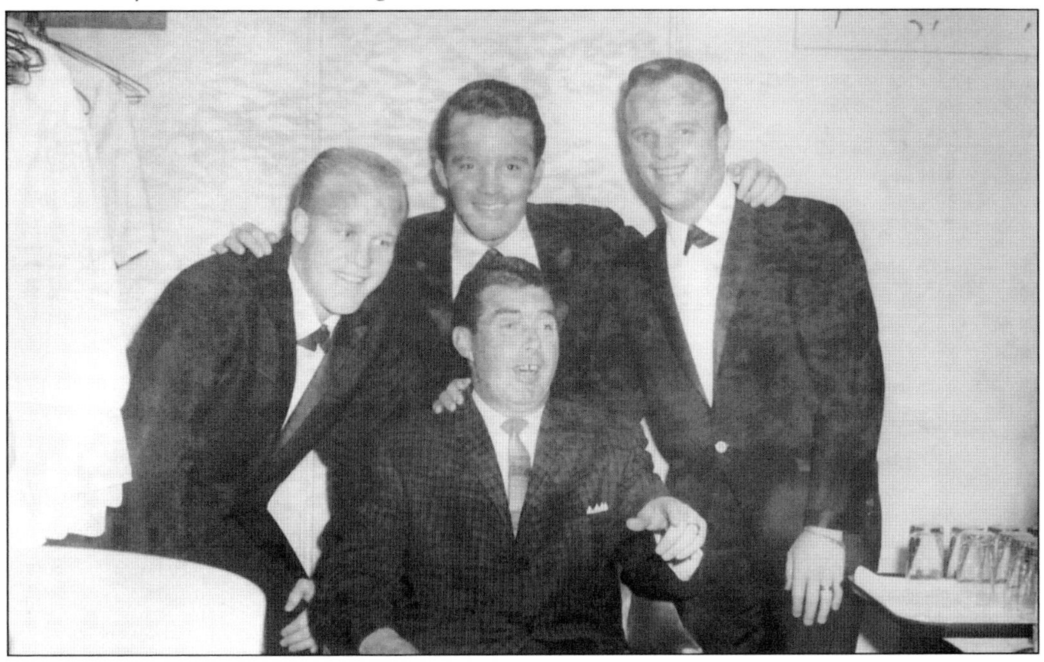

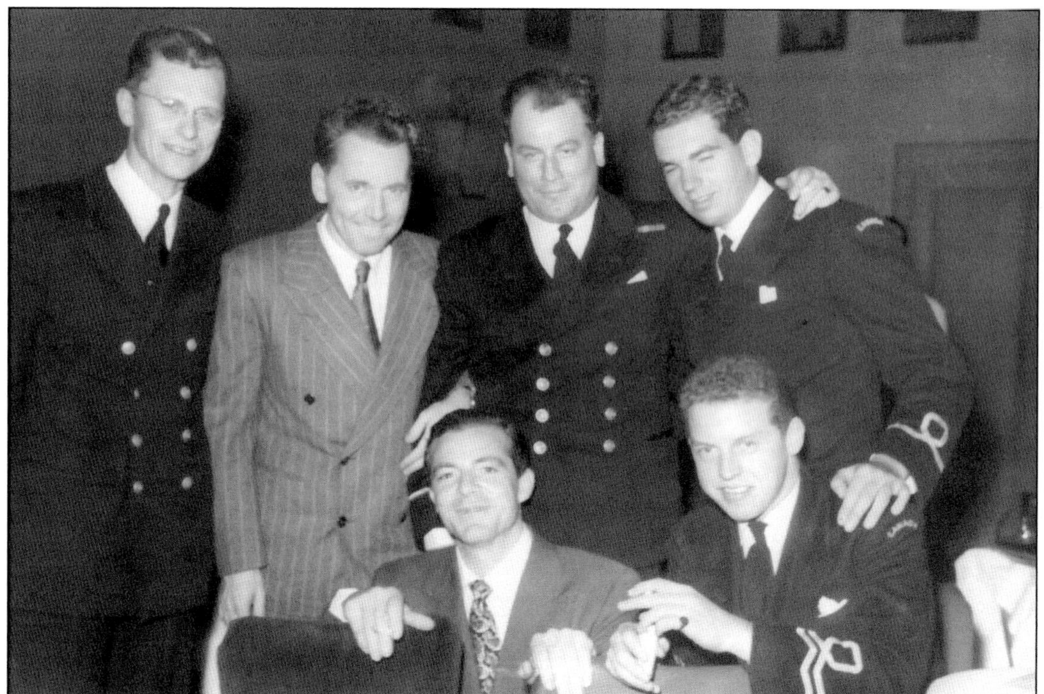

Dana Andrews (first row, left) was a major film actor in the 1940s and 1950s. His most well-known role was as veteran Fred Derry in the 1946 film *The Best Years of Our Lives*. Andrews struggled with alcoholism, which affected his career, and by the mid-1950s, he was mainly performing in B movies. He got his alcoholism under control by the 1970s and, in his later years, became a spokesperson on the disease for the Department of Transportation.

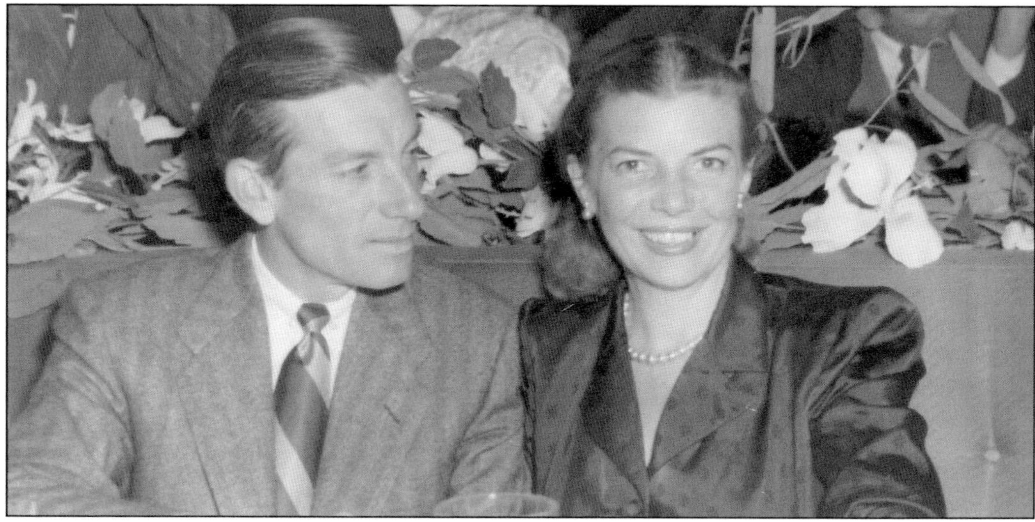

Hoagy Carmichael, pictured with his first wife, Ruth Meinardi, was a singer, composer, bandleader, pianist, and actor. Carmichael composed four of the most recorded songs in America: "Georgia on My Mind," "Heart and Soul," "Stardust," and "The Nearness of You." Carmichael's music has been rerecorded by incredible artists, such as Ray Charles, Norah Jones, and Barbra Streisand. In 1952, Carmichael won an Oscar for *Here Comes the Groom*'s "In the Cool, Cool, Cool of the Evening" as Best Original Song. He appeared in 14 films and hosted musical radio programs as well.

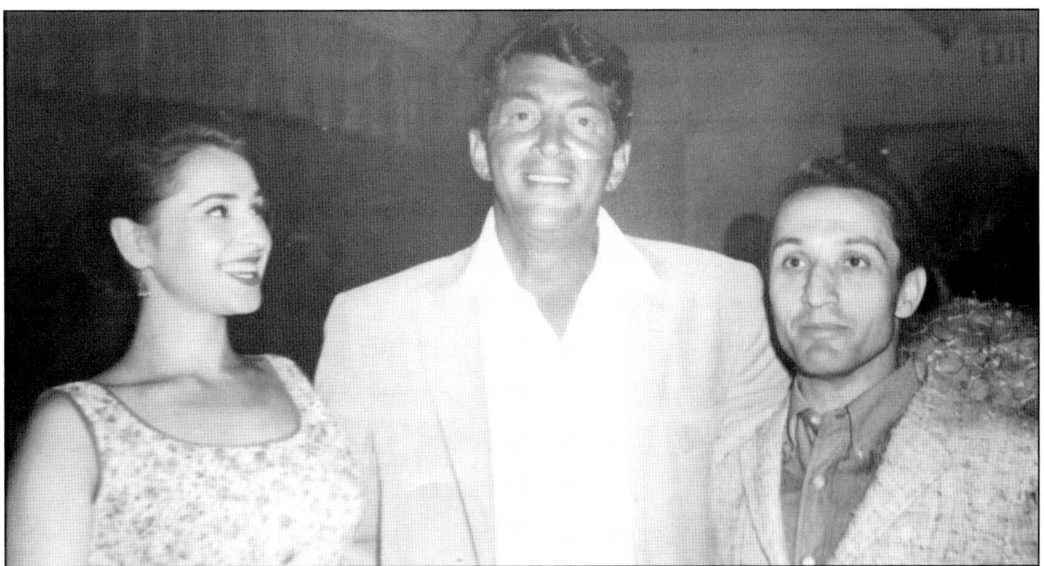

Dean Martin (above, center; below, left) was an American entertaining icon of the 20th century. He was a successful comedian, actor, television star, musician, singer, nightclub performer, producer, and member of the Rat Pack. He hosted a variety show from 1965 to 1974 and the wildly popular *Dean Martin Celebrity Roasts* from 1974 to 1985. Martin's signature song was "Everybody Loves Somebody." Patti Page (below, center) was one of the best-selling pop singers of 1950s, selling over 100 million albums during her 60-year music career. "Tennessee Waltz" is considered her signature song. Dick Stabile (below, right) was an accomplished and popular jazz saxophonist and bandleader for Dean Martin and Jerry Lewis. Stabile played with Tommy Dorsey's band as well and was the orchestra leader for Dean Martin on many of his recordings.

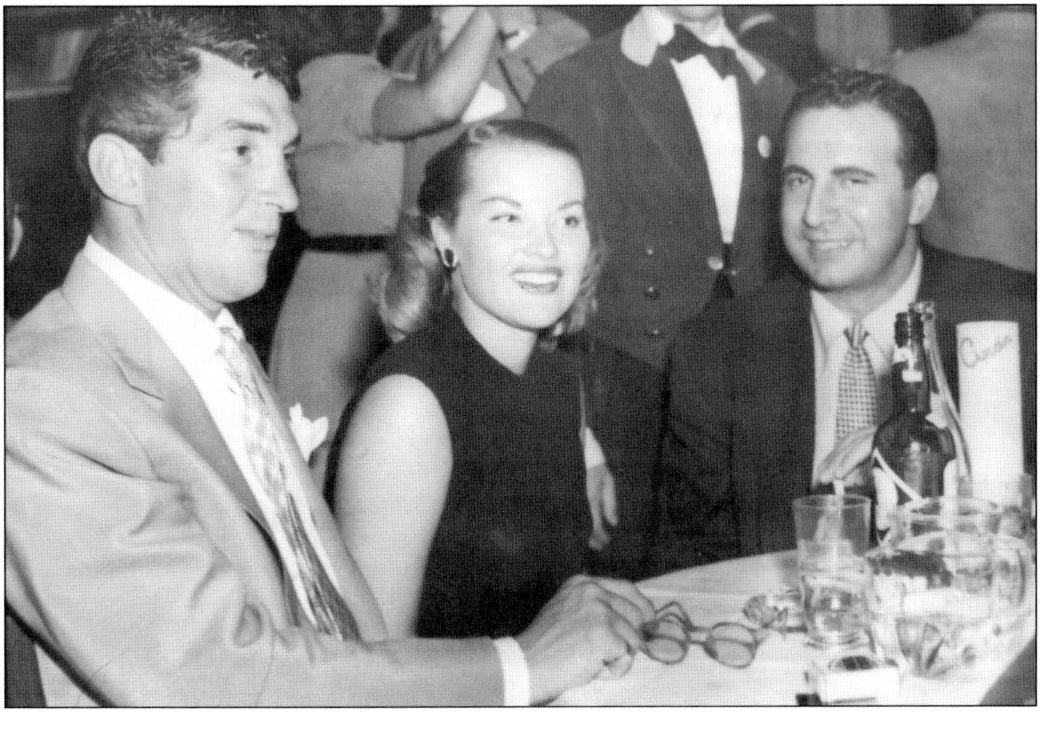

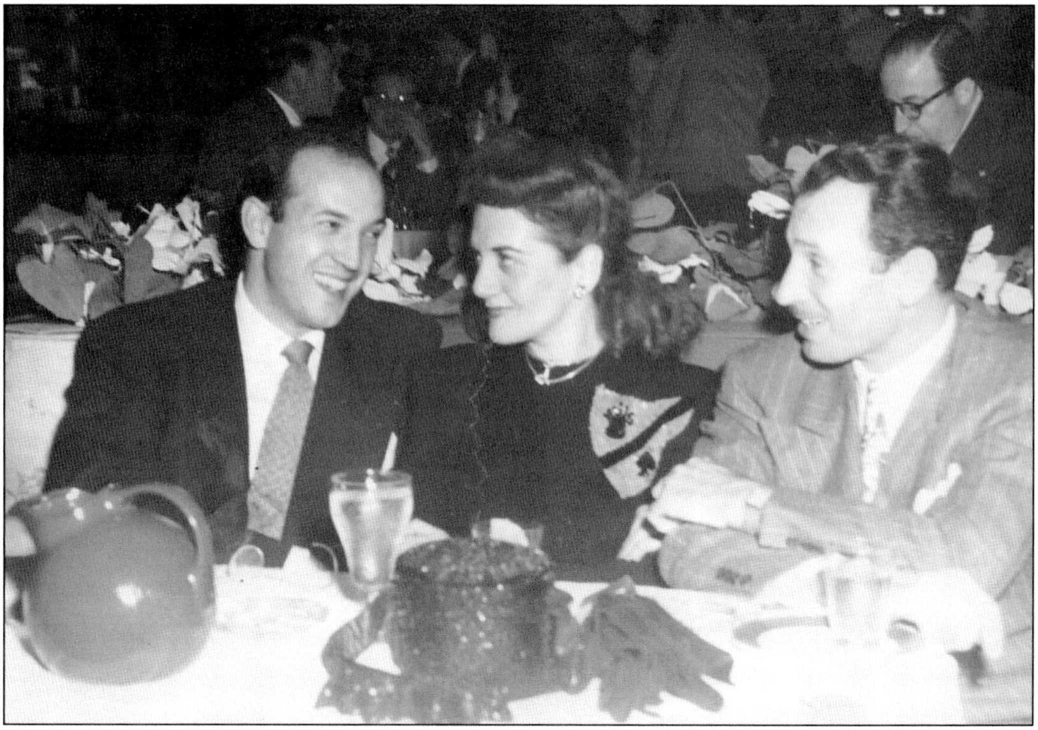

LaVerne Andrews was one of the Andrews Sisters, a highly successful and famously close harmonizing sister act that sold over 75 million records. The Andrews Sisters began performing in the early 1930s. "Boogie Woogie Bugle Boy" is among one of their most popular songs. The group disbanded when LaVerne, who was the eldest of the sisters, died of lung cancer in 1967 at age 55.

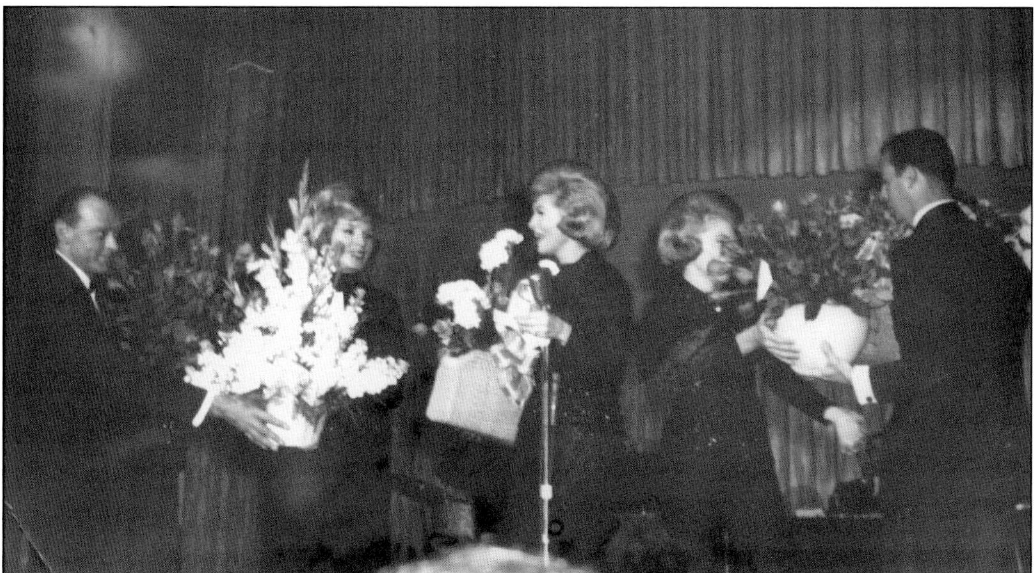

The McGuire Sisters were a popular singing trio comprised of three sisters—Christine, Dorothy, and Phyllis—who sang traditional pop music. Their most popular songs were "Sincerely" and "Sugartime." They were active from 1952 to 1968. After their music career faded, they opened McGuire's Irish Pub in Florida. In 1986, they came out of retirement and performed at various engagements.

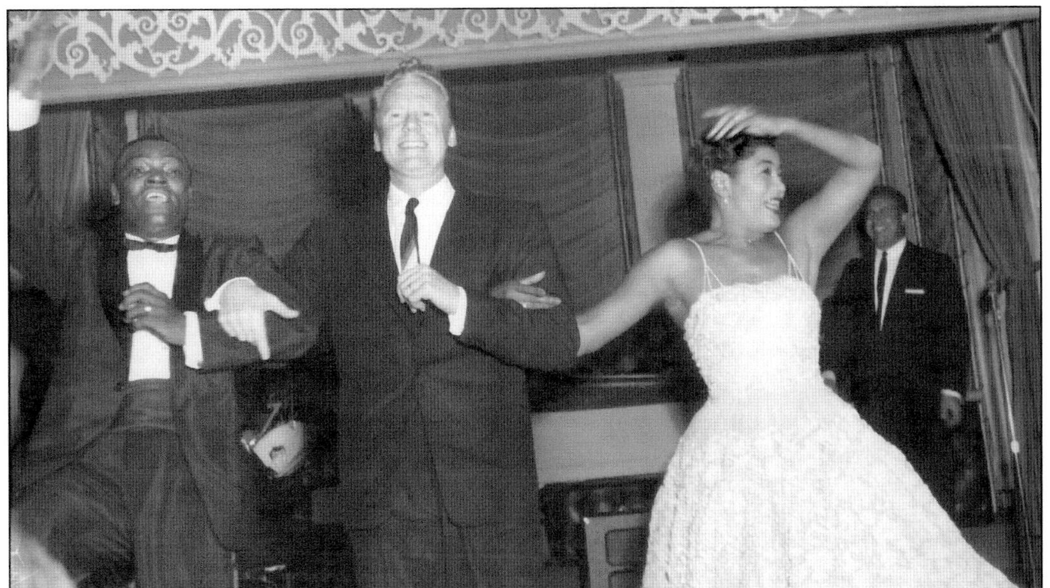

Bill Bailey (left) was a tap dancer and brother to singer and actress Pearl Bailey (right). Bill was recorded on film as the first person to do the moonwalk (dance step) in the 1940s, which he called the "backslide." Van Johnson (center) was a Hollywood movie star who was often cast in roles as the boy next door due to his wholesome looks.

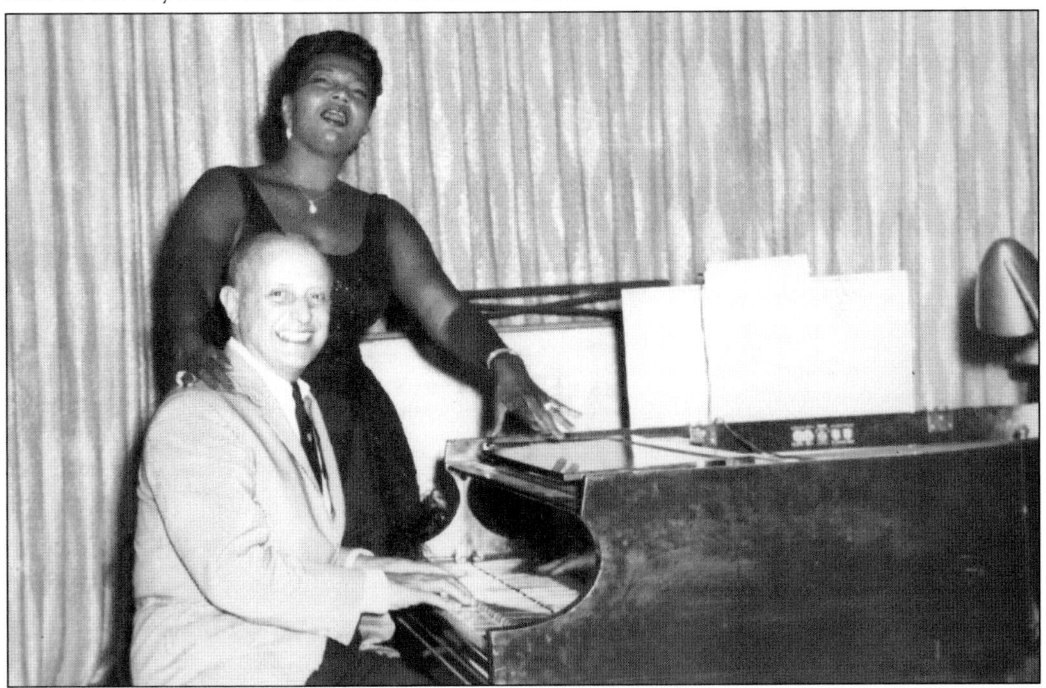

Pearl Bailey (right) was a television, stage, and movie actress as well as a singer, composer, songwriter, and dancer. She appeared in vaudeville, nightclubs, and movies and on Broadway and television. She stars in *St. Louis Blues*, a film with Nat King Cole. She won a Tony Award in 1968 for the lead role in an all-black production of *Hello, Dolly!* and won a Daytime Emmy in 1986 for *Cindy Eller: A Modern Fairy Tale*.

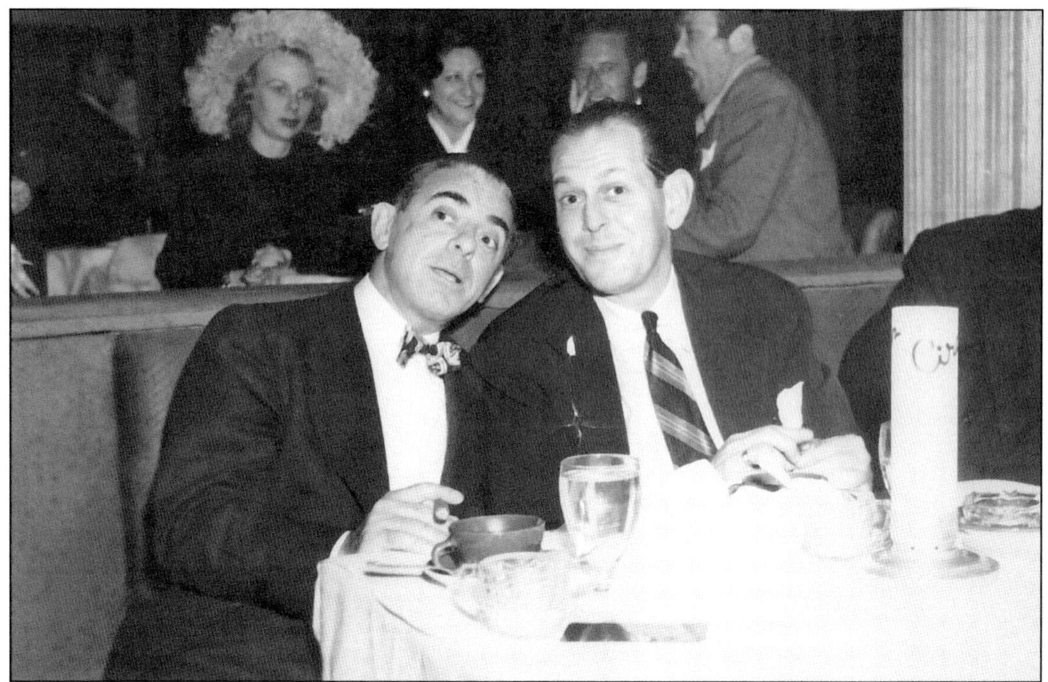

Eddie Cantor (left) was a comedian, actor, singer, songwriter, author, and dancer. Cantor appeared on Broadway and radio and in television and film. On his top-rated radio broadcast, he would often share amusing personal experiences or anecdotes about his wife and five daughters, which were not always appreciated by his children. He was a devoted humanitarian who is credited with naming the March of Dimes charity.

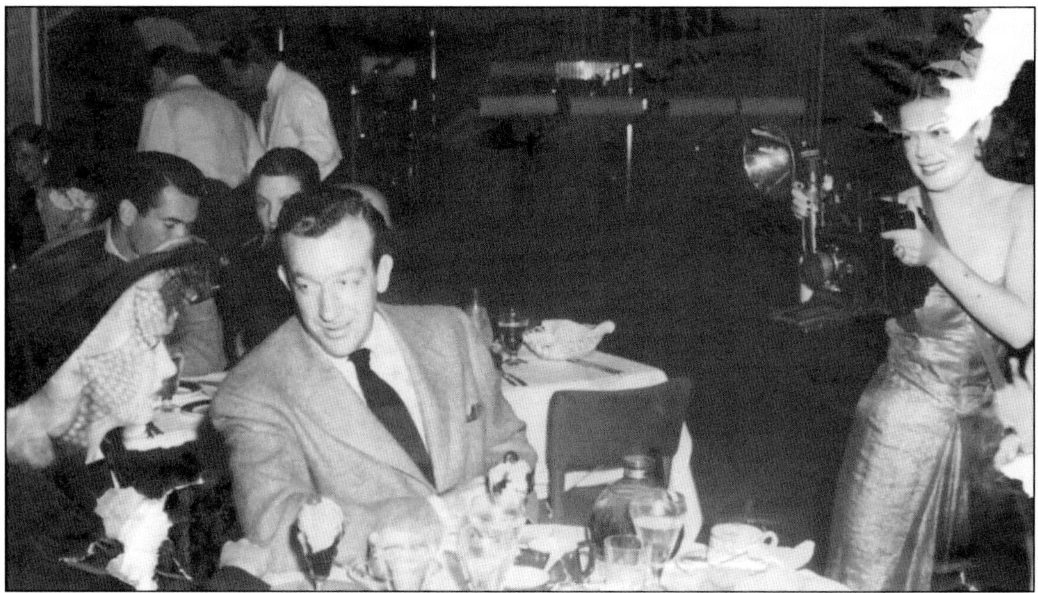

Harry James was a musician and bandleader for big band and swing music as well as an actor. He was a role model for up-and-coming trumpet players due to his excellent tone and technical proficiency. He played with Frank Sinatra, Benny Goodman, Buddy Rich, Ben Pollack, and Louie Bellson. James was active from 1933 until his death in 1983.

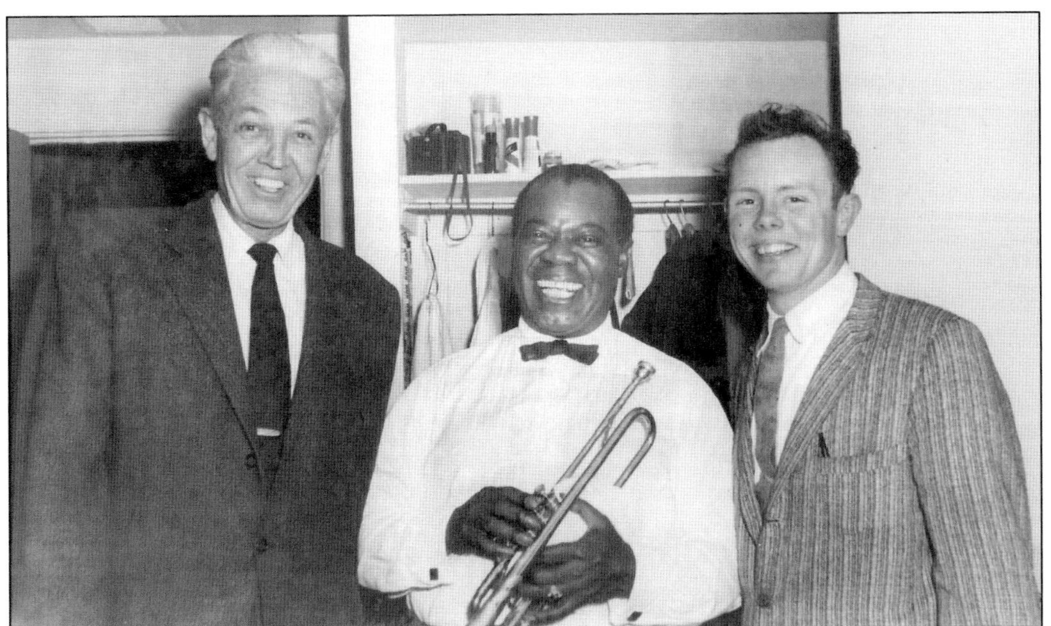

Louis Armstrong (center) was a charismatic jazz trumpeter and singer with a distinctive gritty voice, an infectious grin, and a happy disposition that put others at ease. He appeared on Broadway and in nightclubs and popularized swing music with his unique ability to improvise in jazz both musically and lyrically. He was known for songs such as "La Vie en rose," "Mack the Knife," "Ain't Misbehavin'," "Hello, Dolly!," and "It's a Wonderful World." In 1995, a commemorative stamp was issued in his honor.

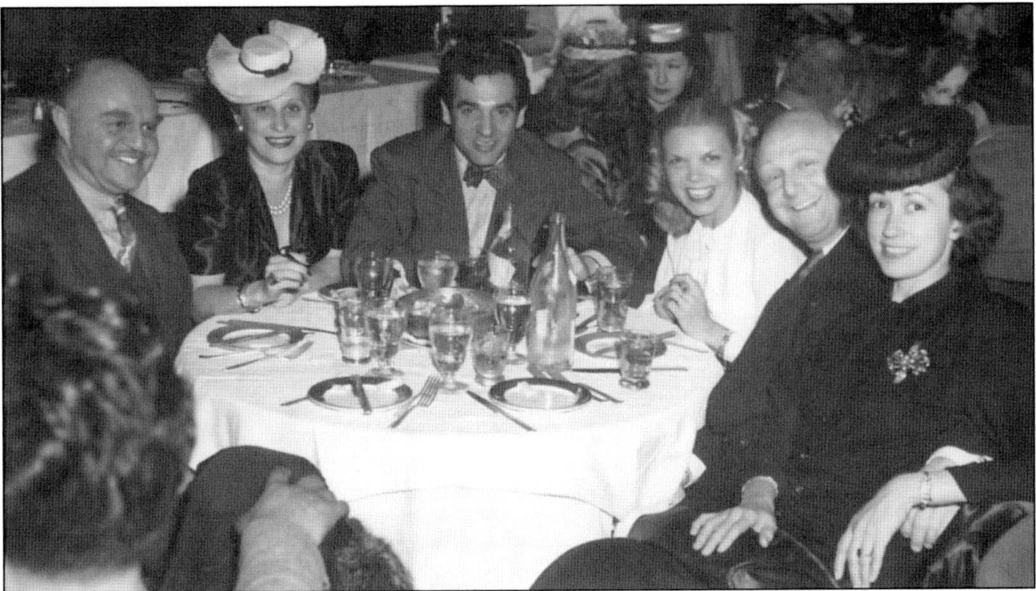

Gene Krupa (center) was a popular drummer during the big band era. He was also a composer and bandleader. Krupa worked with bandleader greats such as Glenn Miller and Benny Goodman. His flamboyant and energetic showmanship and style made him an audience favorite. He did cameo appearances in a few films such as *Ball of Fire*, *The Best Years of Our Lives*, *The Glenn Miller Story*, and *The Benny Goodman Story*.

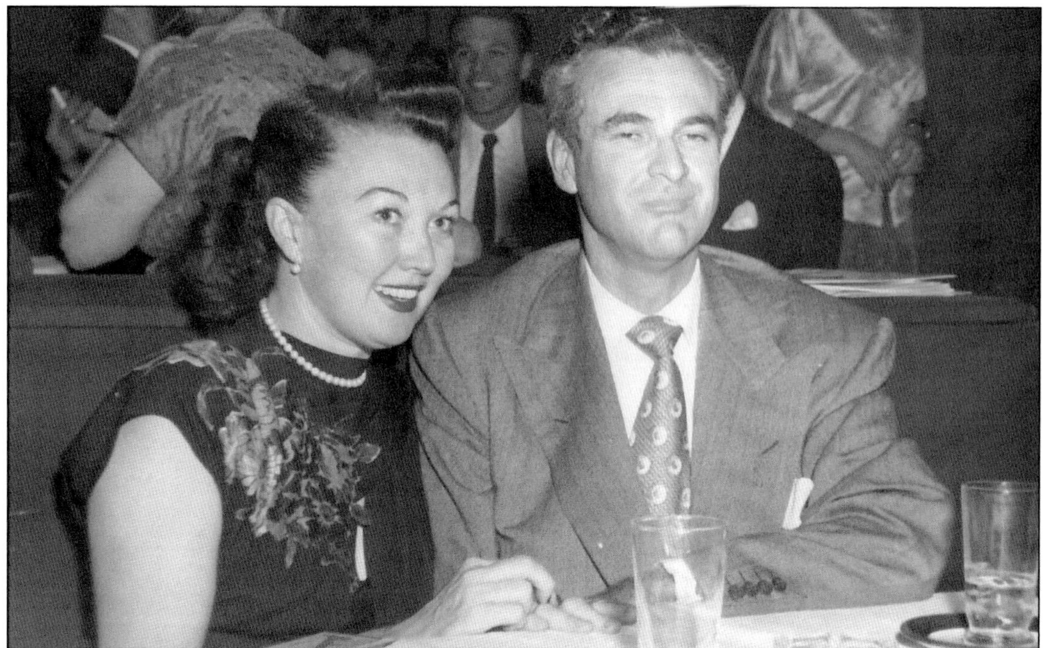

Ginny Simms was a singer during the big band era and a contracted actress with MGM. She appears in 11 movies, which include *Here We Go Again*, *Broadway Rhythm*, and *Night and Day*. She was married three times, to Hyatt Hotels founder Hyatt Von Dehn, Bob Calhoun, and Don Eastvold. In 1951, she hosted a Los Angeles television show featuring talented military personnel.

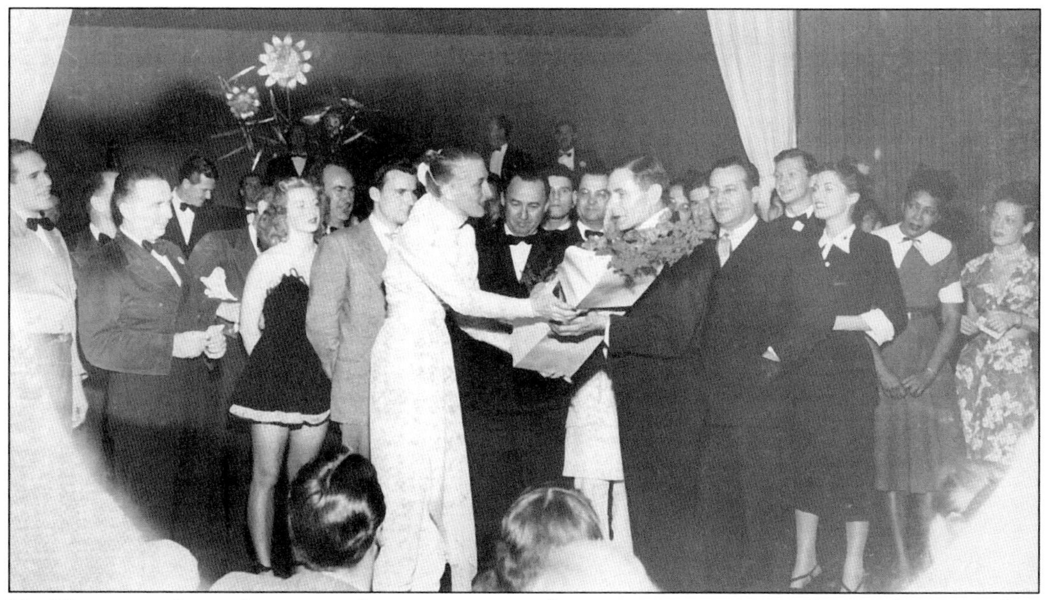

Kay Thompson (center) was an author, pianist, comedienne, singer, composer, dancer, choreographer, coach, actress, and clothing designer. By age 16, Kay was performing with the St. Louis Symphony. In the 1940s, she was hired as a composer, arranger, and vocal coach for MGM stars such as Judy Garland, Frank Sinatra, Lena Horne, and Gene Kelly. In 1947, she opened at Ciro's with a singing and comedy act she created. In the 1950s, she generated the beloved, best-selling Eloise children's book series.

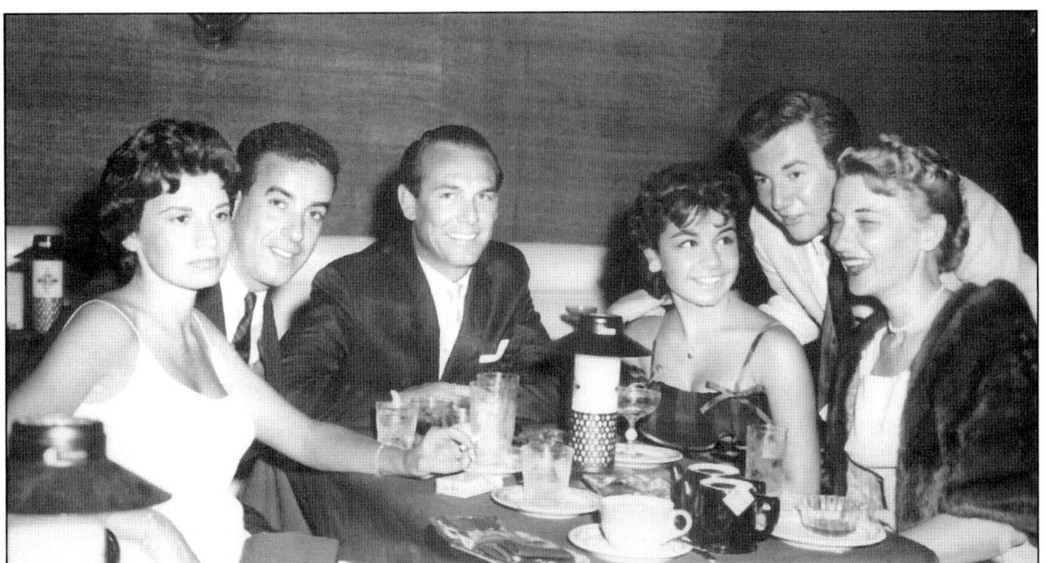

Annette Funicello (third from right) was a singer and actress who began as a child star in 1955 as a Mouseketeer on *The Mickey Mouse Club.* As a teenager, she had pop singles and acted in Beach Party genre movies alongside Frankie Avalon. Bobby Darin (second from right) was a singer, songwriter, and actor. Some of the well-known songs he wrote and recorded include "Dream Lover" and "Splish Splash." He received a Golden Globe for his work in the film *Come September.*

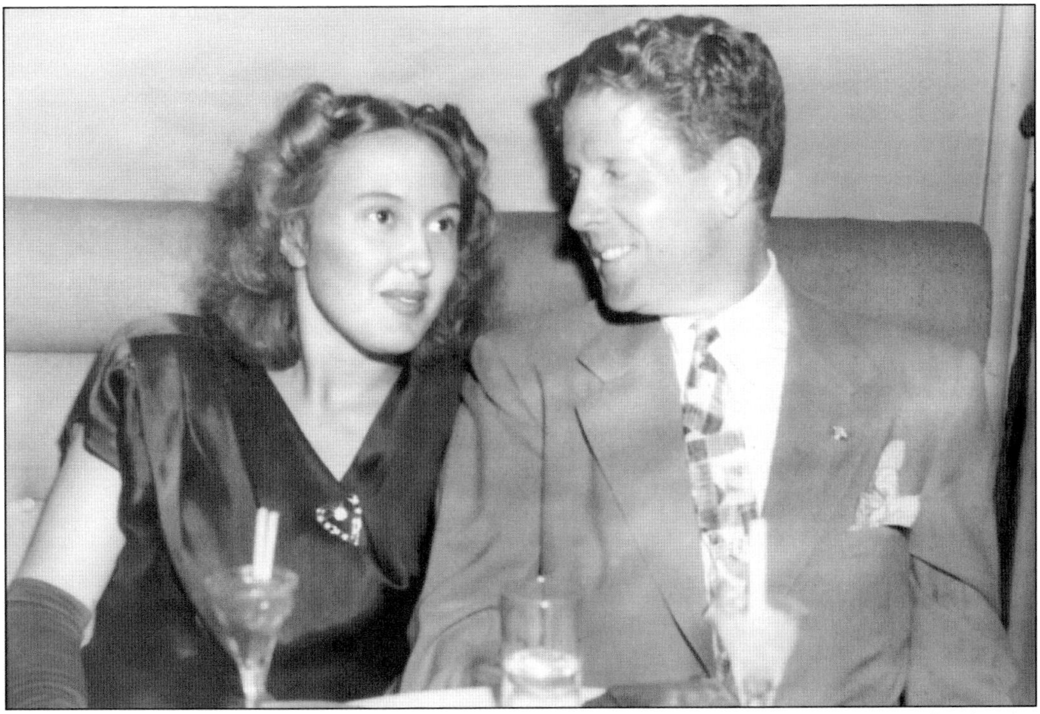

Rudy Vallée was a singer, songwriter, bandleader, actor, and teen pop star. As a bandleader, he introduced songs that became popular, such as "I'm Just a Vagabond Lover," "As Time Goes By," and "Goodnight, Sweetheart." In the 1920s through the 1930s, he had a hit radio show, *The Fleischmann's Yeast Hour.* He appeared on Broadway and television and in nightclubs and movies.

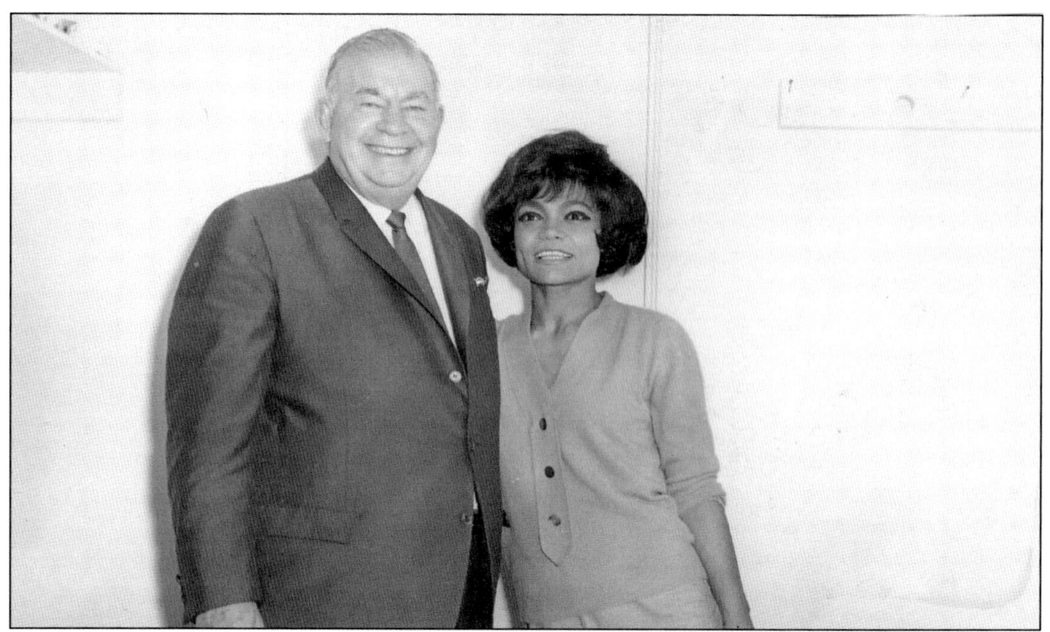

Eartha Kitt was a singer, dancer, cabaret star, actress, and activist. She is well-known for her role as Catwoman in the 1960s *Batman* television series. Kitt earned three Emmys during her career and was nominated twice for Broadway's Tony Award. In 1968, while at the White House, she made antiwar comments that affected her career. She consequently moved to Paris, learned French, and performed overseas for about a decade.

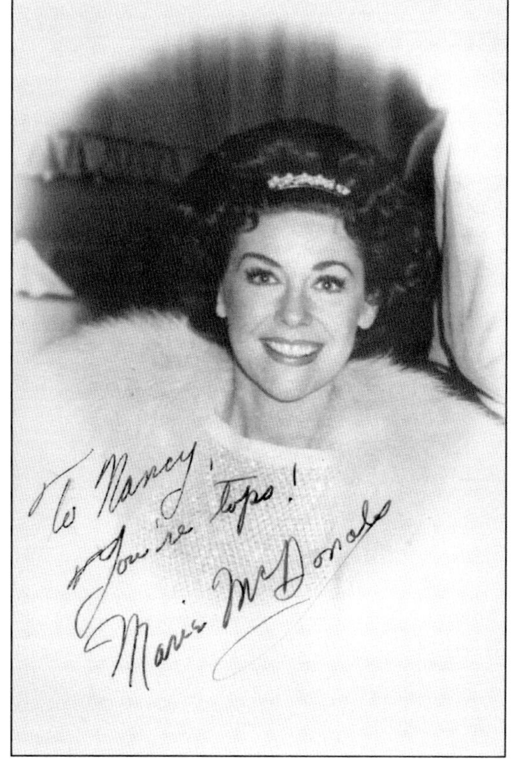

Marie McDonald was an actress, singer, and popular 1940s pinup girl known as "The Body." She costars with Gene Kelly in *Living in a Big Way*. McDonald had numerous personal problems in her short life, including health problems, substance abuse, several failed marriages, multiple miscarriages, sex scandals, and numerous run-ins with the law. She died in 1965 at age 42 due to a drug overdose.

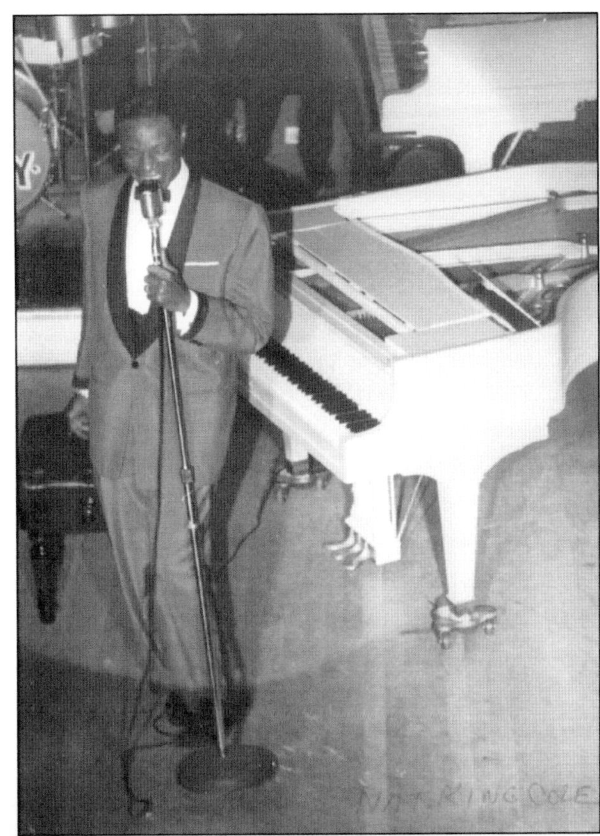

Nat King Cole was a jazz pianist and singer who performed during the big band era. He had a smooth baritone voice and created numerous hit songs, a few of which are "Unforgettable," "Mona Lisa," and "Route 66." He was the first African American to host a variety television show, called *The Nat King Cole Show*. Cole was a heavy chain-smoker and died of lung cancer in 1965 at age 45.

Desi Arnaz was a Cuban-born musician, house bandleader at Ciro's in 1941, actor, producer, and business executive who was best known as Ricky Ricardo in one of the most successful sitcoms of all time, *I Love Lucy*. He was married to his female counterpart, Lucille Ball, from 1940 to 1960. Arnaz was hired by a Latin music bandleader, Xavier Cugat, then formed his own Latin band and was known for popularizing conga drums in America. He met Ball on the set of the 1940 movie *Too Many Girls*.

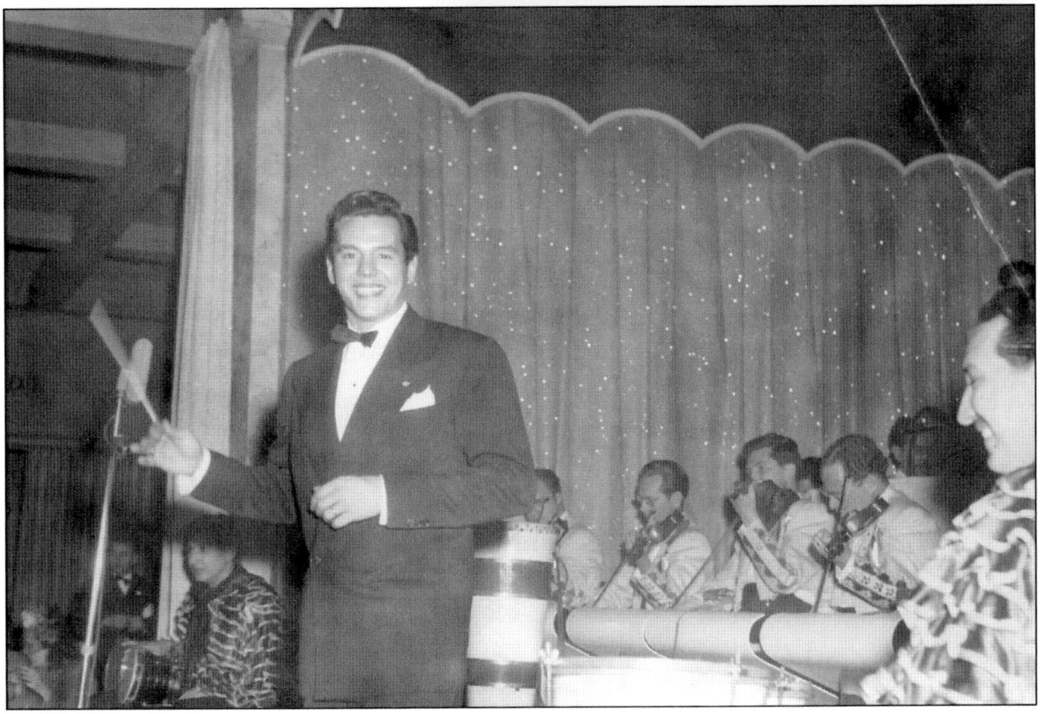

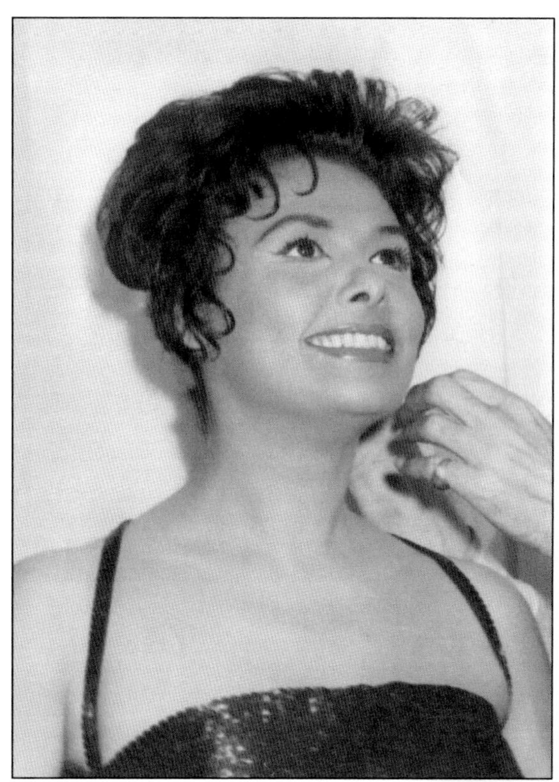

Lena Horne was a singer, dancer, and actress on stage, film, and television; she was also a civil rights activist. Horne began working in entertainment at age 16 as a dancer and was later a singer at the Harlem Cotton Club. In 1943, she starred in two all-black musicals, *Cabin in the Sky* and *Stormy Weather.* She was an active Democrat who worked with Eleanor Roosevelt regarding anti-lynching laws. Horne frequented the White House during the Kennedy administration.

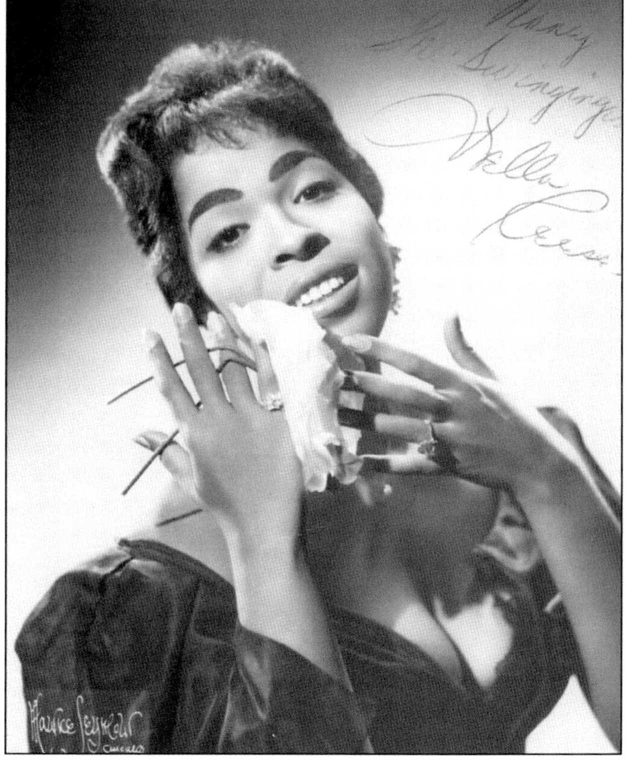

Della Reese is a singer and actress who has appeared on various television shows, including *Sanford and Son, Picket Fences,* and her own television talk show that she hosted from 1969 to 1970. Reese is an ordained minister and was nominated for a gospel music Grammy in 1987. She starred in and created the theme song for the 1990s hit television drama *Touched by an Angel* and officiated at her costar Roma Downey's wedding in 2007.

Johnny Mathis is a pop singer who has had 16 gold albums, six platinum albums, and two multiplatinum albums. Mathis has been inducted into the Grammy Hall of Fame three times for singles "Misty," "Chances Are," and "Not for Me to Say." In 2003, Mathis received a Lifetime Achievement Award from the National Academy of Recording Arts and Sciences for his contributions as an outstanding recording artist. The other man pictured below is unidentified.

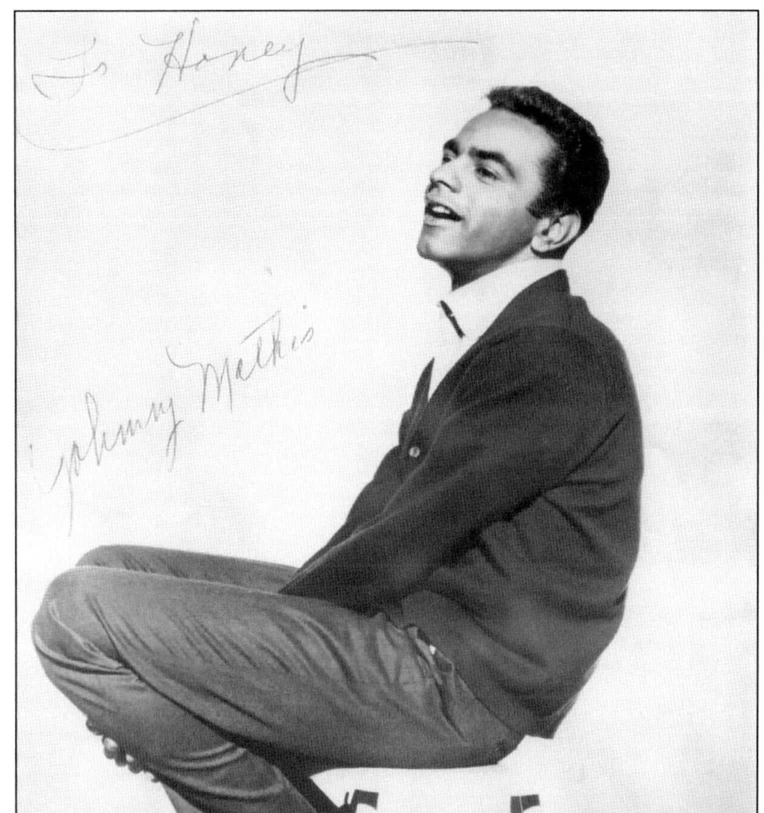

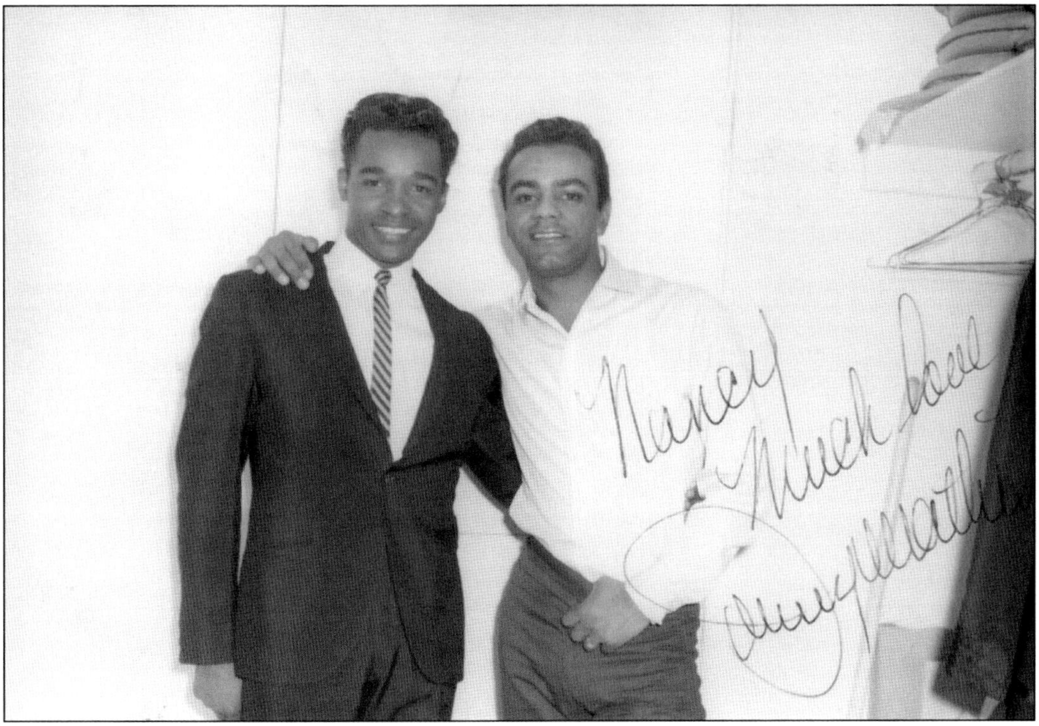

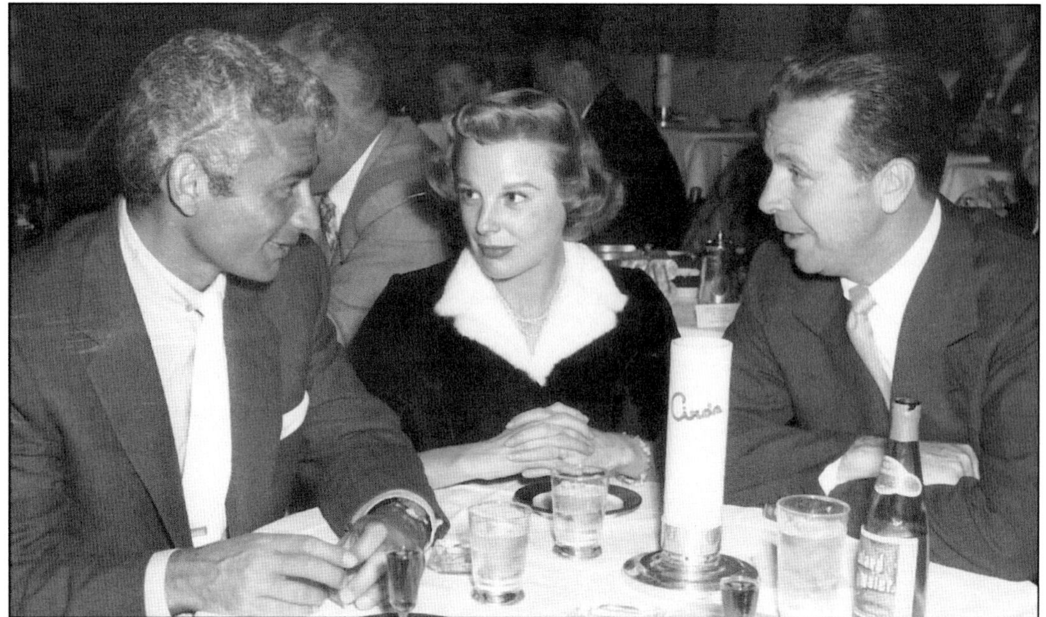

Jeff Chandler (left) was an actor and singer. He was nominated in 1951 for Best Supporting Actor for his work in *Broken Arrow*. June Allyson was a stage and film dancer, singer, and actress who had a "girl-next-door" look that endeared her to audiences. She won a Golden Globe for her work in *Too Young to Kiss*. Dick Powell (right) was a singer, actor, producer, director, and studio head. Powell and Allyson were married from 1945 until his death in 1963.

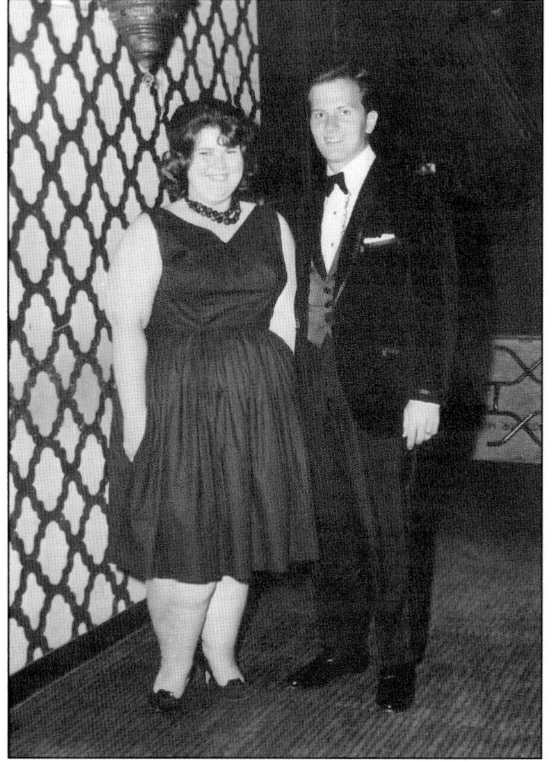

Pat Boone is a singer, actor, and writer who sold over 45 million albums during the 1950s and 1960s. He hosted 115 episodes of a variety television show titled *The Pat Boone Chevy Showroom*. Boone has had many hit songs, including "Moody River," "Speedy Gonzales," and "Bernardine." In 1959, he starred in the film *Journey to the Center of the Earth*. Boone is a television personality, motivational speaker, political commentator, gospel singer, and the father of singer Debby Boone.

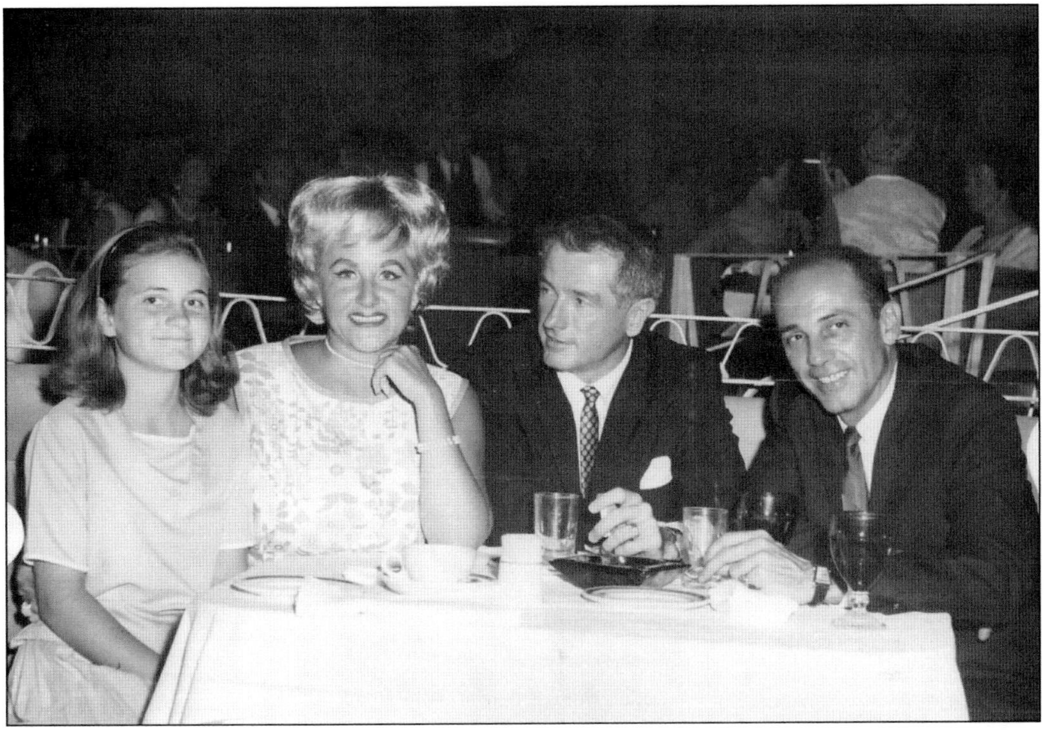

Margaret Whiting (above, second from left; at right) was a pop, jazz, and country music singer widely known during the 1940s and 1950s. From the 1940s to the 1970s, she had 40 singles to hit the Billboard charts. A few of these hits include "A Tree in the Meadow," "Moonlight in Vermont," "Now is the Hour," and her duet with Johnny Mercer, "Baby, It's Cold Outside." She frequented televisions variety shows and talk shows and starred alongside her sister Barbara in the biographical sitcom *Those Whiting Girls*. She performed on USO tours during World War II and the Korean War. Margaret continued performing in nightclubs through the 1990s. She was active for nearly 60 years.

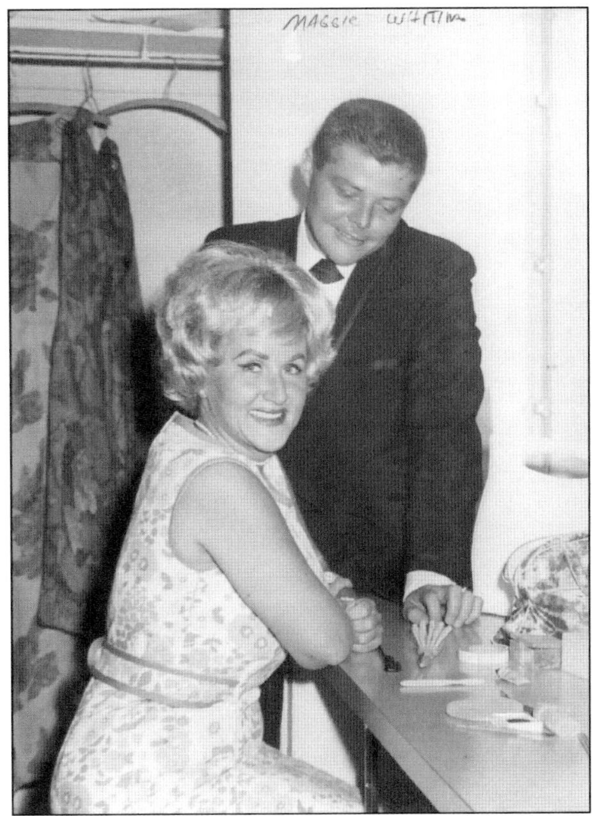

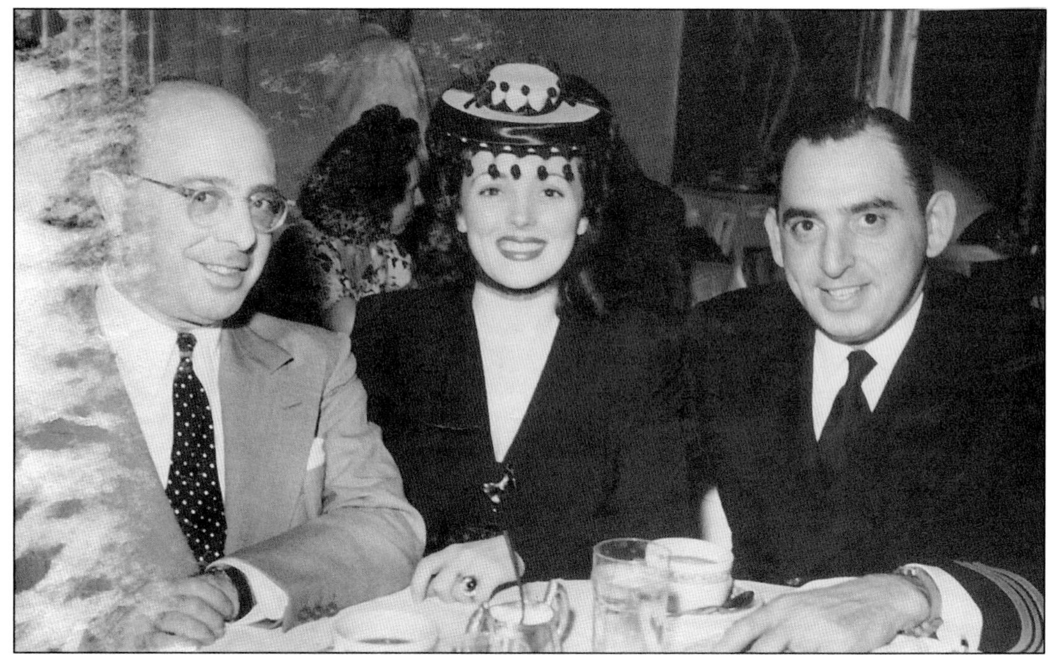

Lina Romay (center) was an English and Spanish singer, dancer, and actress. In 1940, Romay became the lead female vocalist for Xavier Cugat's band. Cugat wrote several ballads for her, and she is featured with the band in movies such as *You Were Never Lovelier* and *Bathing Beauty*. A few of her most popular performance numbers include "Alma Llanera," "Babalu," and "Guadalajara."

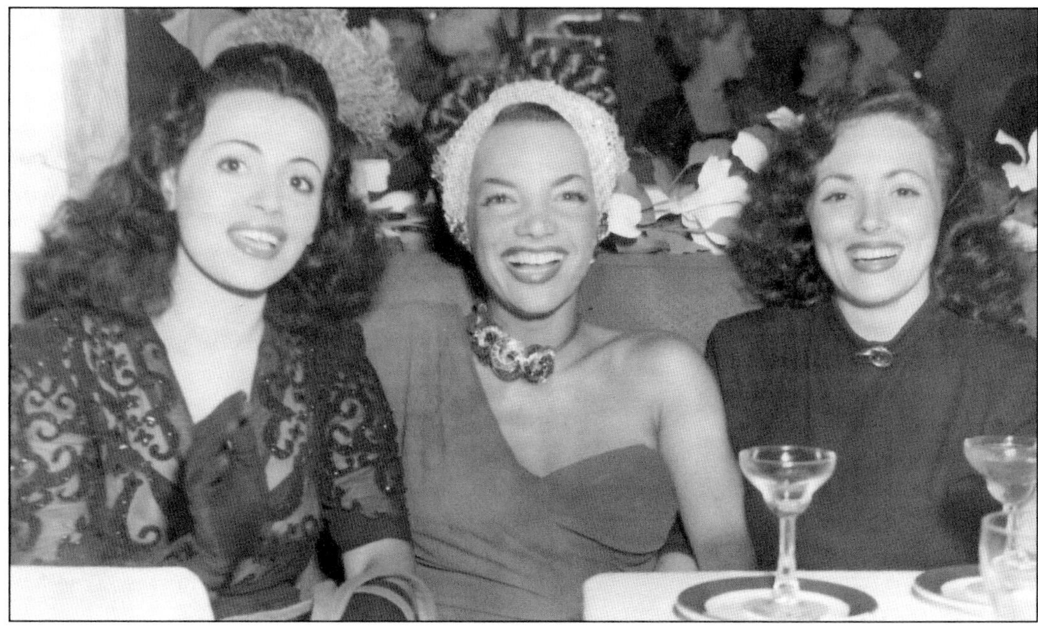

Aurora Miranda (left) was a Brazilian entertainer best remembered for the movie *The Three Caballeros*. Her sister Carmen Miranda (center) was a Brazilian samba singer, dancer, and film and Broadway actress. She was popular in nightclubs from the 1930s to 1950s. Lina Romay (right) was a Mexican American actress, dancer, and singer who performed with bandleader Xavier Cugat. She appeared on the Bing Crosby, Bob Hope, and Jack Benny radio shows as well.

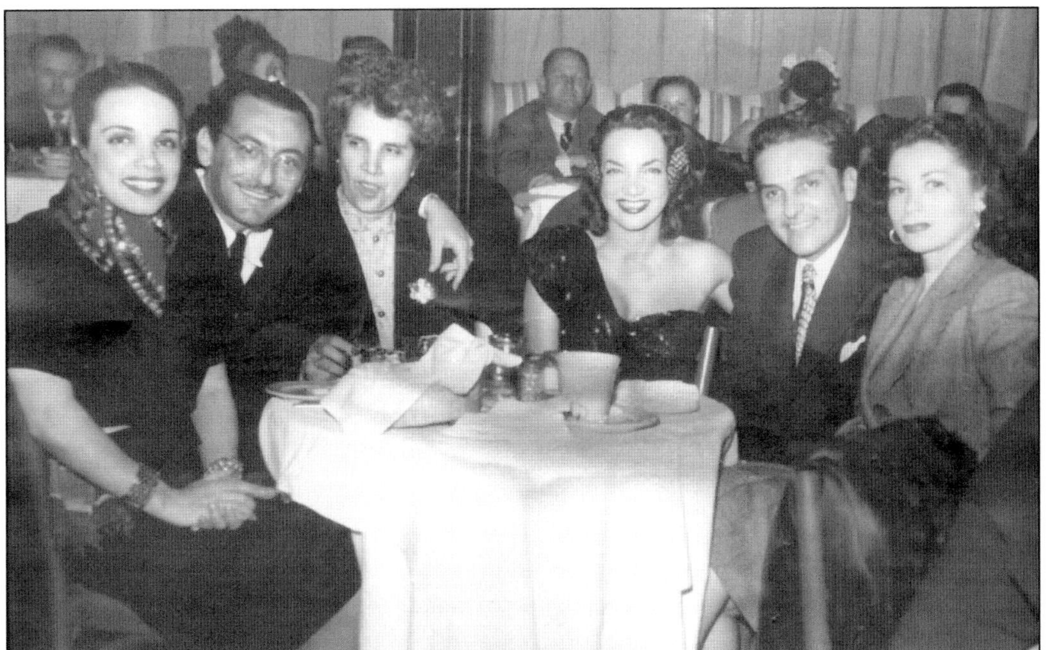

Carmen Miranda (center) popularized Brazilian samba music in America, appeared on numerous television variety shows, and was known for her trademark fruit hat and exotic clothing. She appears in 14 films, including *The Gang's All Here* and *Down Argentine Way*. Miranda's life was cut short when she died from a heart attack in 1955 at the age of 46.

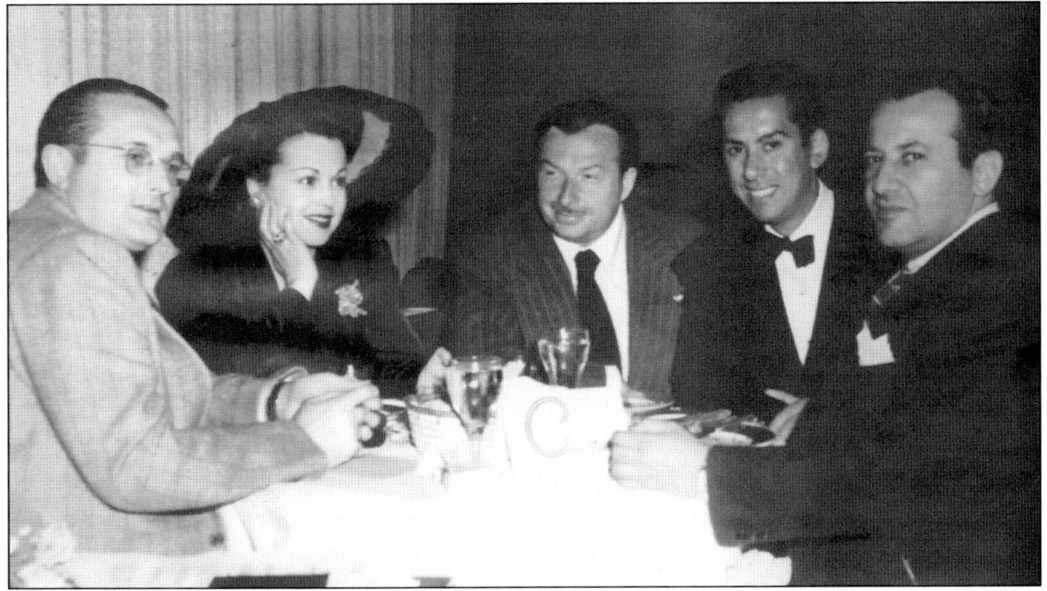

Tommy Dorsey (left), known as "The Sentimental Gentleman of Swing," was a bandleader, composer, trumpeter, and trombonist during the big band era. A few of his best remembered songs are "It's Always You," "Song of India," and "Marie." Film actress Pat Dane (second from left) was Dorsey's second wife. Dorsey died in 1956 at age 51 due to asphyxiation. Bandleader Xavier Cugat (center) and orchestra leader and pianist Carmen Cavallaro (second from right), along with owner Herman Hover (right), were all important fixtures at Ciro's.

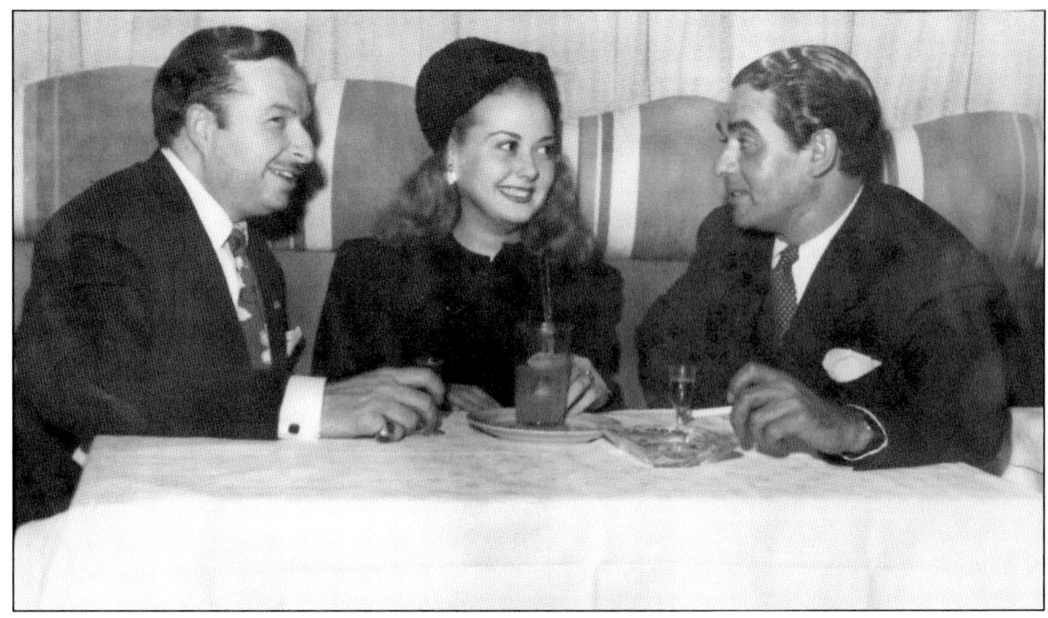

Bandleader Xavier Cugat (left) was nicknamed the "Rumba King." He was born in Spain, moved to Cuba during his formative years, was a trained violinist, moved to Los Angeles, and worked at the *Los Angeles Times* as a cartoonist. He got his big break as bandleader in 1928 at the Cocoanut Grove nightclub in Hollywood. He was a successful businessman and resident orchestra leader at the Waldorf Astoria in New York before and after World War II. He traveled back and forth between New York and Los Angeles, working as a bandleader. He was instrumental in bringing Latin music to the American public. Cugat and his band appeared in several musicals in the 1940s. He was married five times, including one marriage to entertainer Charo. The singer pictured below is unidentified.

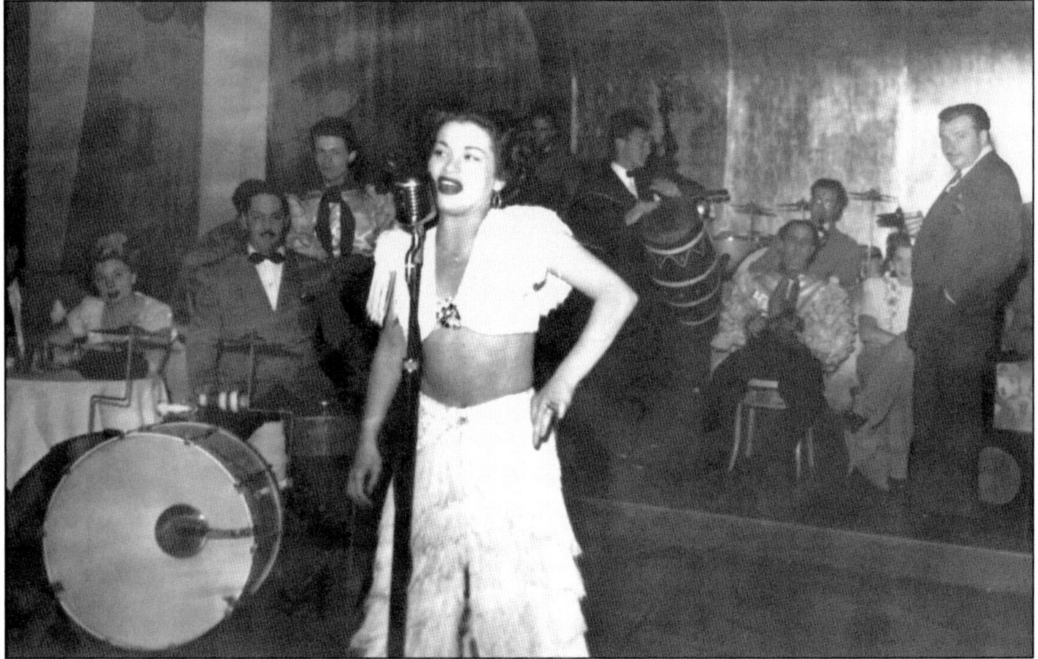

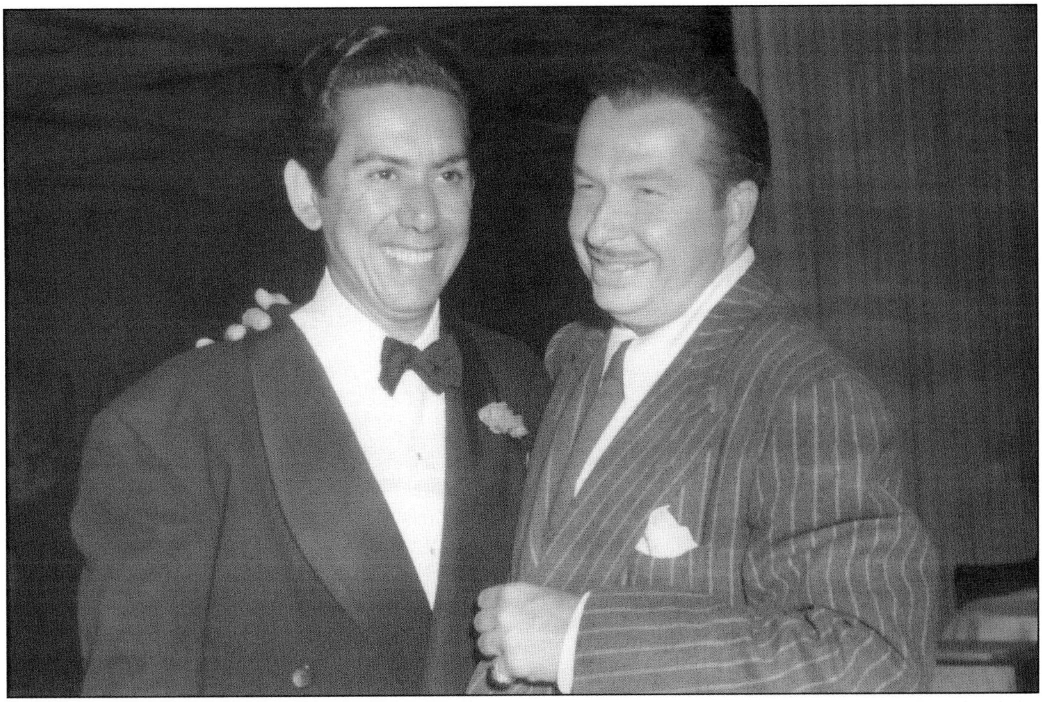

Carmen Cavallaro (left) was a pianist, composer, and conductor. A soloist in films and nightclubs and on radio and television, he became well known in the 1940s on *The Sheaffer Parade* radio program as the orchestra leader. He made many records; a couple of his most popular songs are "Masquerade Waltz" and "While the Night Wind Sings." Cavallaro's best-selling recording was *Chopin's Polonaise*. Cavallaro appears, playing himself, in movies such as *Hollywood Canteen*, *Diamond Horseshoe*, *Out of This World*, and *The Time, the Place and the Girl*. Cavallaro was the pianist who performed the music for *The Eddy Duchin Story* starring Tyrone Power.

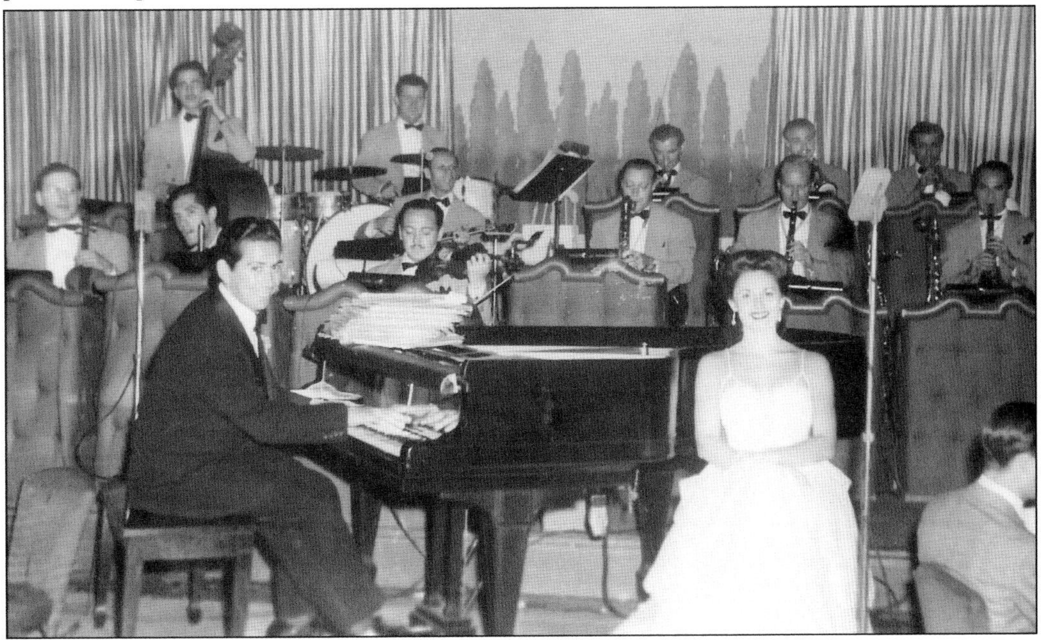

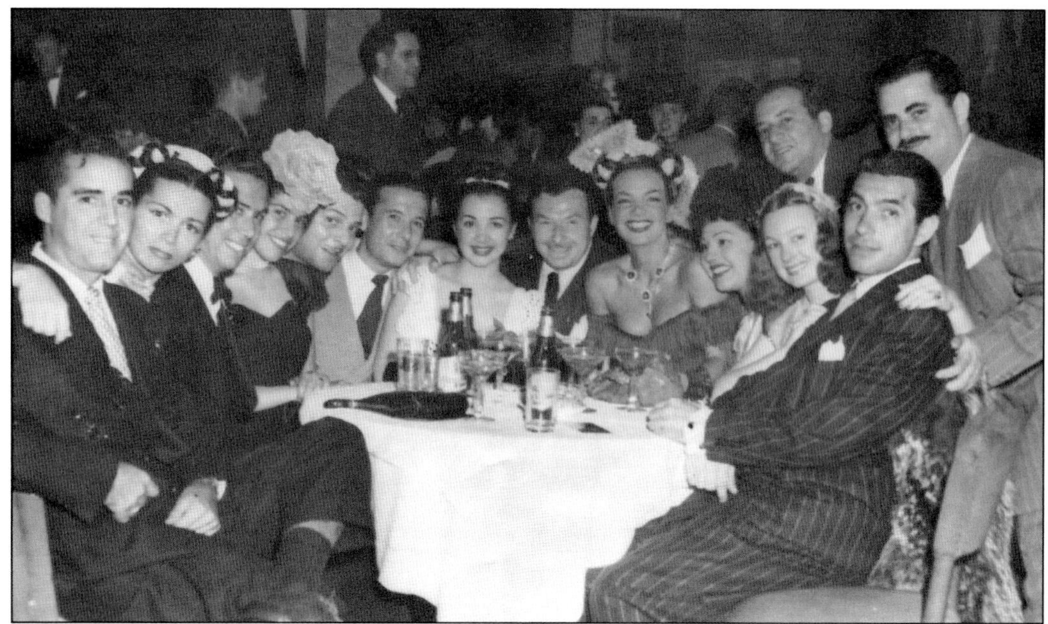

The above photograph includes Carmen Cavallaro (third from left; also below, front left), John Carroll (fifth from left), Xavier Cugat (center), Carmen Miranda (fourth from right), and Herman Hover (far back right), who appear to be relaxing between acts at this overcrowded table at Ciro's. This group of entertainers delighted audiences with their skilled Latin-flavored and big band dance music that erupted in popularity during the 1940s and 1950s. Ciro's came alive due to these performers who brought an excitement and showmanship worthy of the expense of a night out on the town. Flowing alcohol, cigarettes, a good meal, dancing, an exciting show, and possibly spotting a star or two were all a part of the experience during a night at Ciro's.

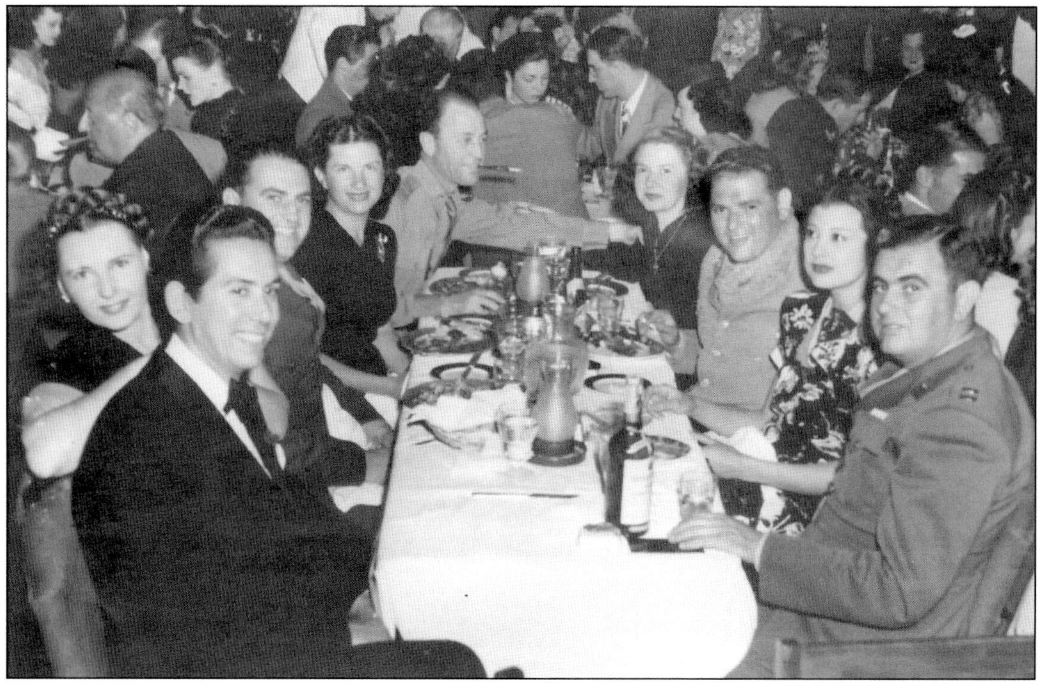

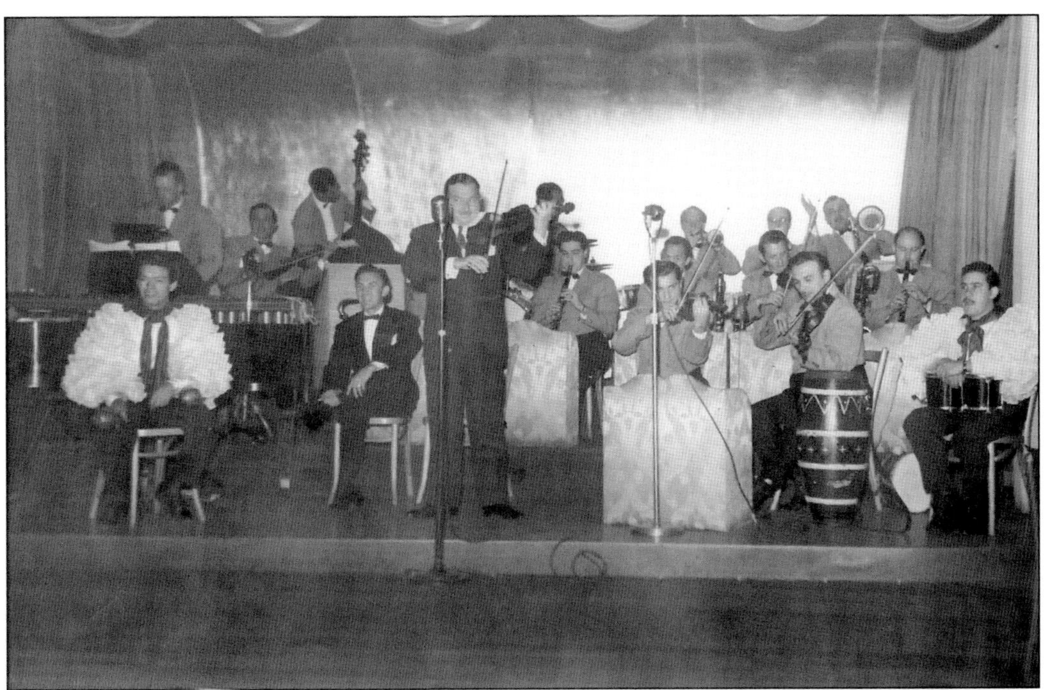

Xavier Cugat's band delighted audiences with the music of the day. The lighting cast a perfect glow on the patrons, who dressed in their evening best. The dance floor, purposely built a little too small, felt packed quickly and increased the odds of rubbing shoulders with someone famous or at least well-known. The mood created by the music and the lighting was romantic, exciting, and relaxing, where worries could be forgotten for at least a few hours.

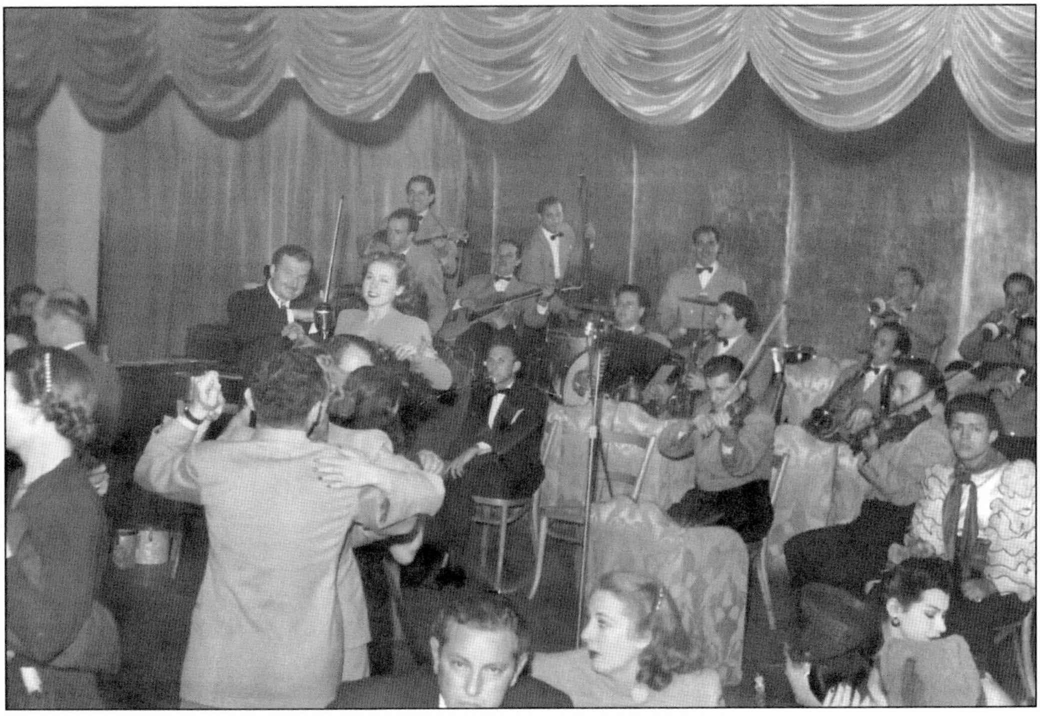

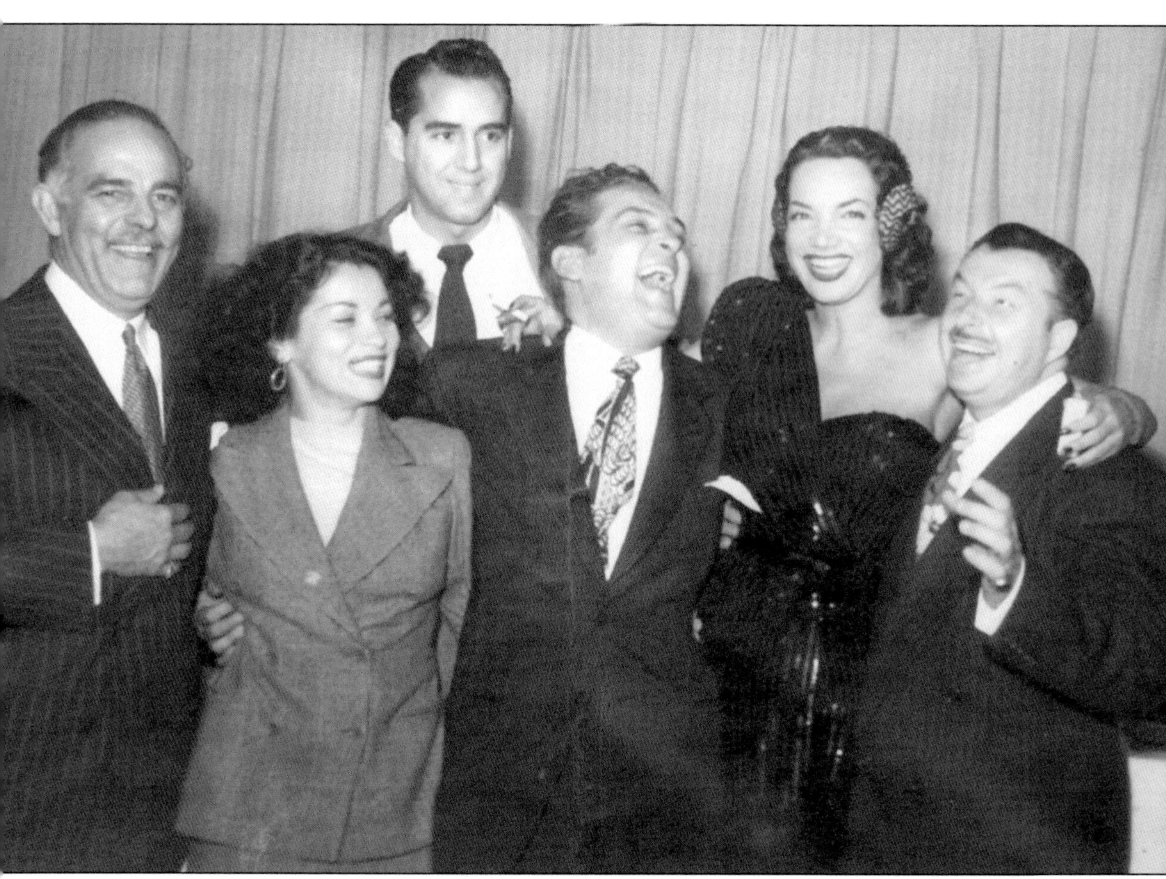

This photograph exemplifies the feel of the nightclub and era, with jovial entertainers Carmen Miranda and Xavier Cugat (right) with friends at Ciro's. Owner Herman Hover worked hard to create a memorable experience for all the patrons who frequented or visited Ciro's, by remembering the likes and dislikes of returnees. He also created an enjoyable working environment for the entertainers and staff. The mood was light, formal yet comfortable, and service-oriented. Great memories were made, life was celebrated, and glamour and glitz ruled the club.

Seven

Memories and Memorabilia

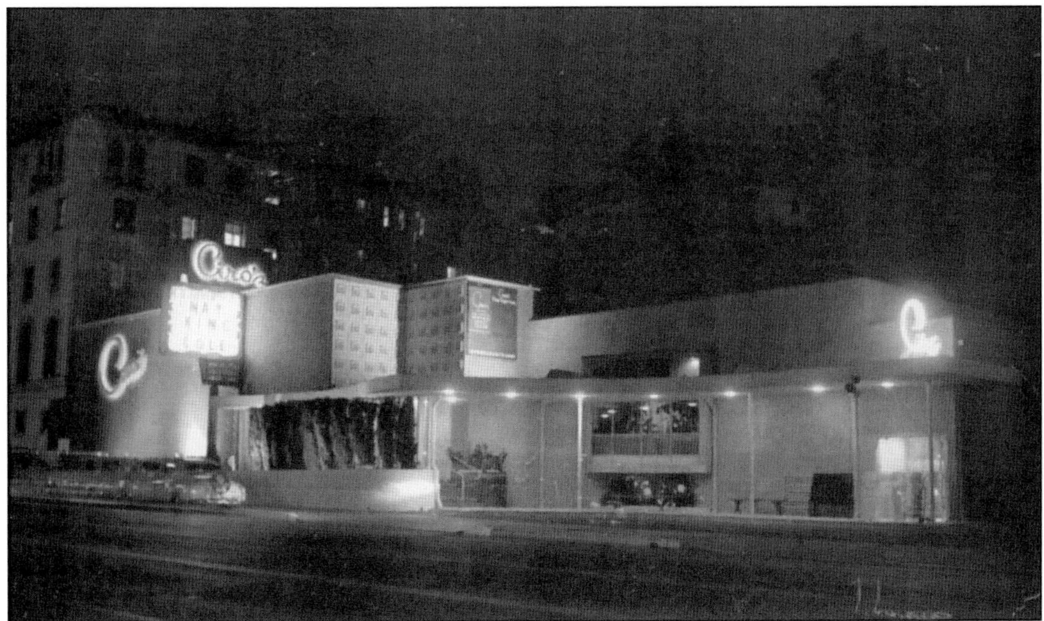

This postcard provides a nighttime view of the exterior of Hollywood's famous Ciro's nightclub located on the Sunset Strip. The well-lit marquee announces Nat King Cole as the current headliner. Postcards were one of the souvenirs patrons could purchase to send home to their friends and family or put in a scrapbook as a memory of a special night out. Ciro's had a few neon signs on its building that brightly lit up the Hollywood night sky in order to draw customers into the club. Inside the club, the baroque interior felt rich and luxurious, while the unadorned exterior appeared plain and simple at best.

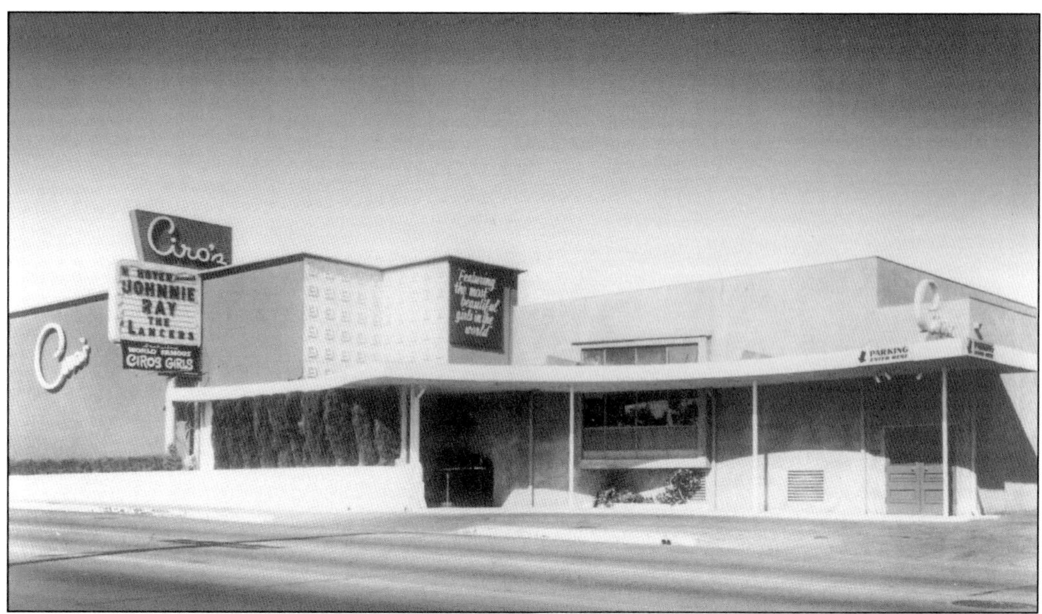

The above picture shows a view of Ciro's nightclub with the surrounding apartments removed from the image. This picture may have been altered for promotional purposes. The postcard below provides a closer view of Ciro's during the daytime, with a stylish 1954 Cadillac Series 62 accentuated in the foreground as a symbol of class and luxury. The marquee announces an All Comedy Show and the Continentals. The smaller marquee boasts "Best Dance Music in Town" with Dick Stabile's orchestra and Bobby Ramos's Latin band as the featured music. Stabile, a top saxophone player of the day, conducted, arranged, composed and played for many of the world's greatest performers, like Frank Sinatra, Dean Martin and Jerry Lewis, Sammy Davis Jr., Nat King Cole, and Bob Hope. Stabile's orchestra would play dance music in between shows, which typically began at 10:00 p.m. and midnight.

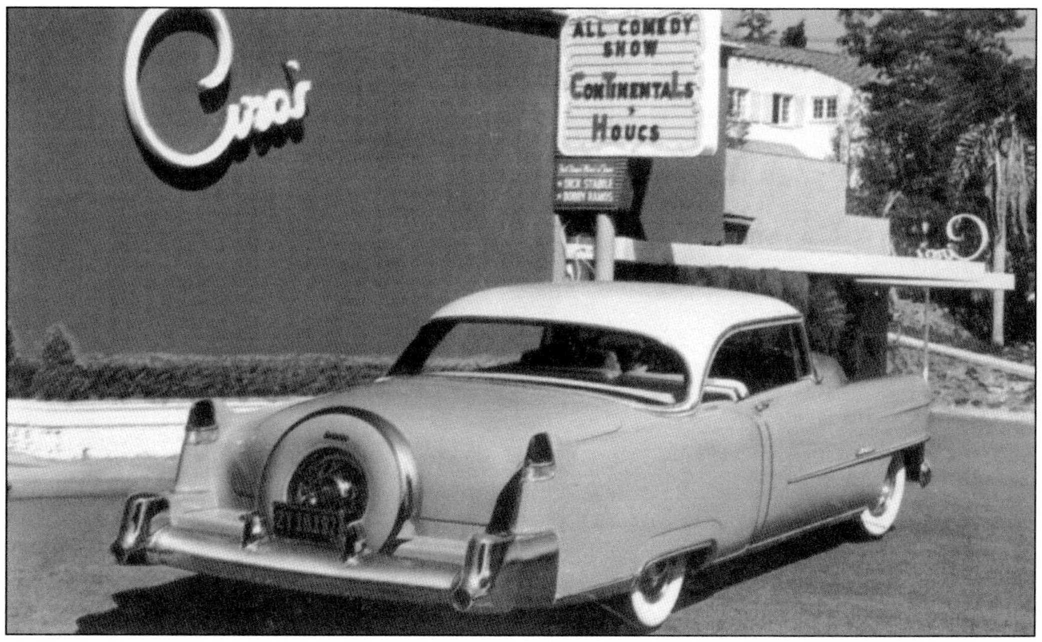

The photograph at right provides an image of a promotional stunt used by Ciro's owner Herman Hover to create interest and publicity for the acrobatic show performing at the nightclub. The picture shows an acrobatic performer from the Carsony Brothers doing a one-handed handstand, using a cane, on top of the Ciro's marquee. Joni James, also mentioned on the marquee, was a traditional pop singer who made more than 25 albums and sold over 100 million records. The image below shows a tourist taking a picture of Ciro's nightclub. Tourists came from all over the world to Ciro's to try and get a glimpse of their favorite stars. The marquee is advertising singer Rose Marie, who was known for her great comedic timing as Sally Rogers on *The Dick Van Dyke Show.* Comedian Lenny Kent was also a featured performer on the marquee.

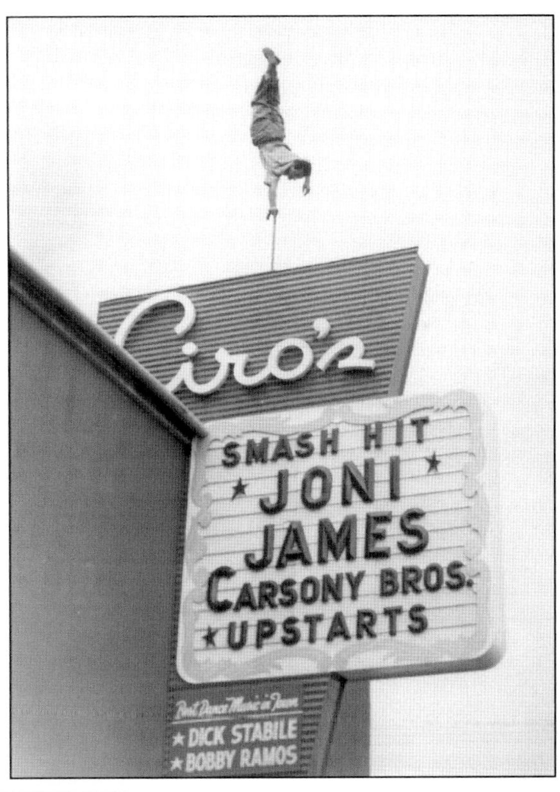

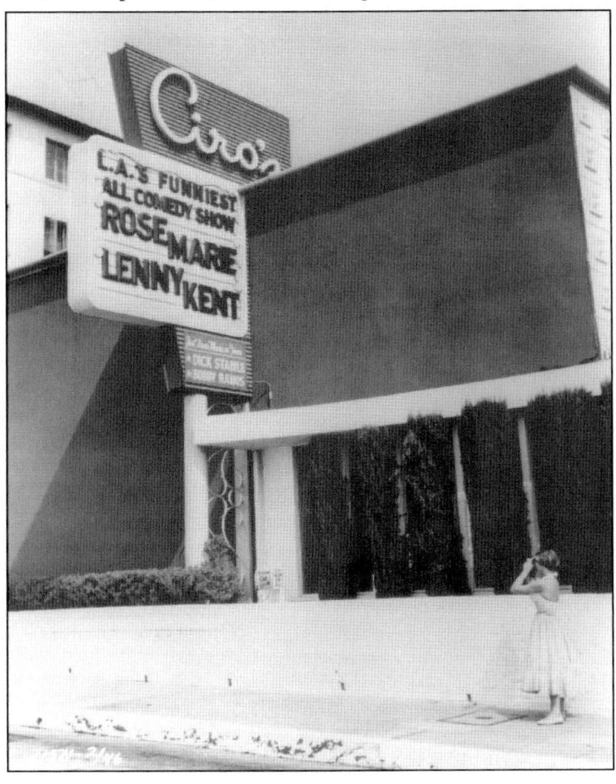

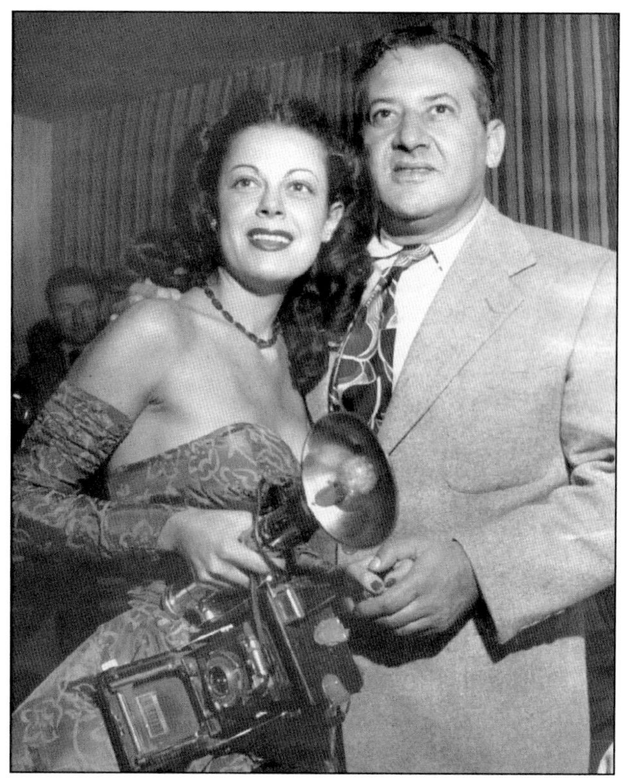

Nancy Caporal was a talented photographer who was one of the most popular camera girls on the Sunset Strip, working at famous clubs like the Trocadero, Cocoanut Grove, and Ciro's. Ciro's amiable owner Herman Hover treated both guests and staff well. Hover booked and created talented headliners. He gave Dean Martin and Jerry Lewis their start, for which they were always grateful. When their salary reached $100,000 a week, they agreed to a steep pay cut to perform at Ciro's for $7,000.

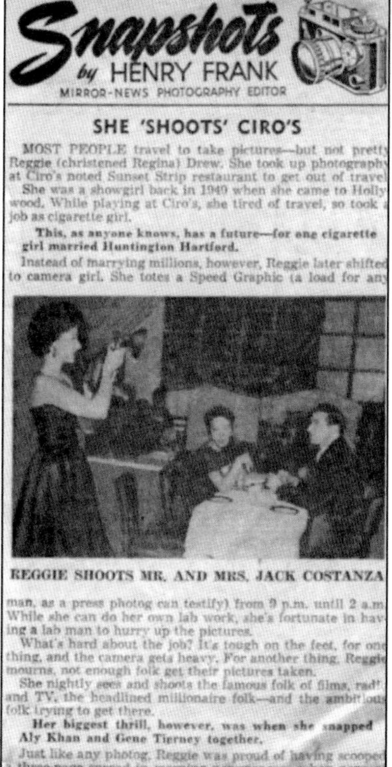

Snapshots by HENRY FRANK
MIRROR-NEWS PHOTOGRAPHY EDITOR

SHE 'SHOOTS' CIRO'S

MOST PEOPLE travel to take pictures—but not pretty Reggie (christened Regina) Drew. She took up photography at Ciro's noted Sunset Strip restaurant to get out of travel.

She was a showgirl back in 1949 when she came to Hollywood. While playing at Ciro's, she tired of travel, so took a job as cigarette girl.

This, as anyone knows, has a future—for one cigarette girl married Huntington Hartford.

Instead of marrying millions, however, Reggie later shifted to camera girl. She totes a Speed Graphic (a load for any

REGGIE SHOOTS MR. AND MRS. JACK COSTANZA

man, as a press photog can testify) from 9 p.m. until 2 a.m. While she can do her own lab work, she's fortunate in having a lab man to hurry up the pictures.

What's hard about the job? It's tough on the feet, for one thing, and the camera gets heavy. For another thing, Reggie mourns, not enough folk get their pictures taken.

She nightly sees and shoots the famous folk of films, radio and TV, the headlined millionaire folk—and the ambitious folk trying to get there.

Her biggest thrill, however, was when she snapped Aly Khan and Gene Tierney together.

Just like any photog, Reggie was proud of having scooped a three-page spread in morning newspapers—when none of the other photogs had any pictures printed.

This short article in the afternoon tabloid newspaper *Los Angeles Mirror* highlights lovely Ciro's photographer and the coauthor of this book, Reggie Drew. In the early 1950s, she was using a heavy camera called a Speed Graphic, which she would tote around from 9:00 p.m. until closing at 2:00 a.m. The photographs would be developed in a darkroom on-site and sold to customers before they left.

Hors D'Oeuvres

CRABMEAT COCKTAIL	1.30
FRUIT COCKTAIL	.95
LOBSTER COCKTAIL	1.30
SHRIMP COCKTAIL	1.25
SEAFOOD A LA RUSSE	1.25
AVOCADO	1.25
CRAB LEG ON ICE	1.80
GRAPEFRUIT JUICE	.65
TOMATO JUICE	.50
MELONS IN SEASON	.90
ASSORTED HORS D'OEUVRES	2.00
SMOKED NOVA SCOTIA SALMON	1.75
STUFFED CELERY	1.25
JUMBO RIPE OLIVES	.60
CHOPPED CHICKEN LIVER	1.10
BISMARCK HERRING, SOUR CREAM	1.10
SARDINES COTE D'AZUR	1.45
PROSCUITO WITH MELON	1.75
HEARTS OF CELERY	.60
BELUGA CAVIAR	5.00

Soups

COLD VICHYSSOISE	.65
GREEN TURTLE AU SHERRY	.75
CREAM OF TOMATO	.65
ONION SOUP	.65
CONSOMME DOUBLE	.65
BOULA BOULA AU GRATIN	.90

Fish

SHRIMP CURRY	2.95
BROOK TROUT SAUTE ALMONDINE	2.90
FILET SOLE SAUTE, MUENIERE	2.50
LOBSTER THERMIDOR	3.00
LOBSTER NEWBURG	2.95

Entrees

MIGNONETTE OF BEEF CIRO'S	3.65
ROAST PRIME RIB OF BEEF	3.35
FILET MIGNON	5.80
NEW YORK SIRLOIN STEAK	5.95
CHATEAU BRIAND BERNAISE FOR TWO	11.00
FRENCH LAMB CHOPS	3.00
STEAK MINUTE SAUTE	3.25
HALF SPRING CHICKEN GRILLE	2.90
BONED ROYAL SQUAB CASSEROLE FERMIERE	3.75
LONG ISLAND DUCKLING BIGARRADE	3.45
LE COQ AU VIN BOURGUIGNONE	3.45
VEAL SCALOPPINI SAUTE VATEL	2.90

SAUCES: BORDELAISE .65 BEARNAISE .65 MUSHROOM .75

Potatoes

FRENCH FRIED	.65
BAKED IDAHO	.65
MASHED	.60
AU GRATIN	
HASHED BROWN	
LYONNAISE	

Vegetables

FRESH ASPARAGUS HOLLANDAISE	1.00
BROCCOLI HOLLANDAISE	1.00
NEW PEAS	.65
STRING BEANS	
ZUCCHINI FLORENTINE	
FRESH STEWED TOMATO	
CREAMED OR PLAIN SPINACH	

Salads

LETTUCE	.75
MIXED GREEN	.75
ROMAINE	.80
CHIFFONADE	.85
AVOCADO	1.25
SEA FOOD	
SLICED TOMATOES	
CAESAR	
CHICKEN	

ROQUEFORT DRESSING .50

Desserts

FRENCH PASTRY	.65
PARFAIT	1.00
PEAR HELENE	1.00
PEACH FLAMBEE	1.75
FRESH STRAWBERRY PARFAIT	1.00
CREPE SUZETTES	2.20
PROFITEROLLES AU CHOCOLATE	1.00
CHERRIES JUBILEE	1.75
BAKED ALASKA (FOR 2)	
FRUIT COMPOTE	
CHEESE CAKE	
MERINGUE GLACEE	
SPUMONI CIRO'S	
PEACH MELBA	
ICE CREAM	

Cheese

AMERICAN	.55
SWISS	.65
CAMEMBERT	
ROQUEFORT	

COFFEE .30 TEA .30 MILK .30 ICED TEA .35 ICED COFFEE .35

SEE WINE BACK OF MENU

French cuisine by chef Rene Milesi was featured at Ciro's. A full course meal at Ciro's cost between $3.75 and $5, and most drinks were $1. Guests who had special food preferences include the following: Errol Flynn (octopus), Diana Lynn (fried chicken), Rory Calhoun (rare prime rib), Lana Turner (seafood), Lizabeth Scott (pheasant), and Peter Lawford (calf's liver and bacon). Sonja Henie was known to make coffee with her personal formula of salt and eggshells; Jimmy Durante was known to prepare veal scallopini; and Keenan Wynn would sometimes prepare a whole meal.

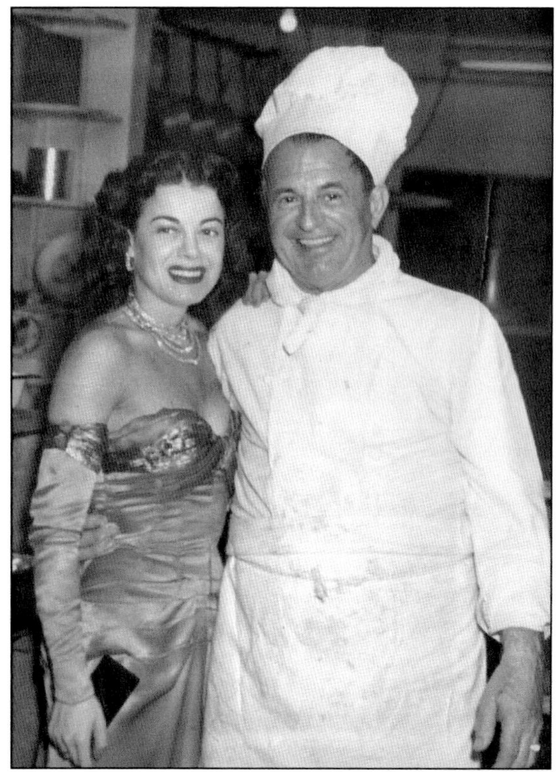

French chef Rene Milesi is pictured with head photographer Nancy Caporal. Each year, the master chef would go to France and Switzerland to learn any new developments in fine cooking and get ideas from cabaret shows in Europe. Head maître d' John "Johnny" Oldrate went to Europe along with the chef, in order to make wine purchases. They would go for three to four weeks at a time.

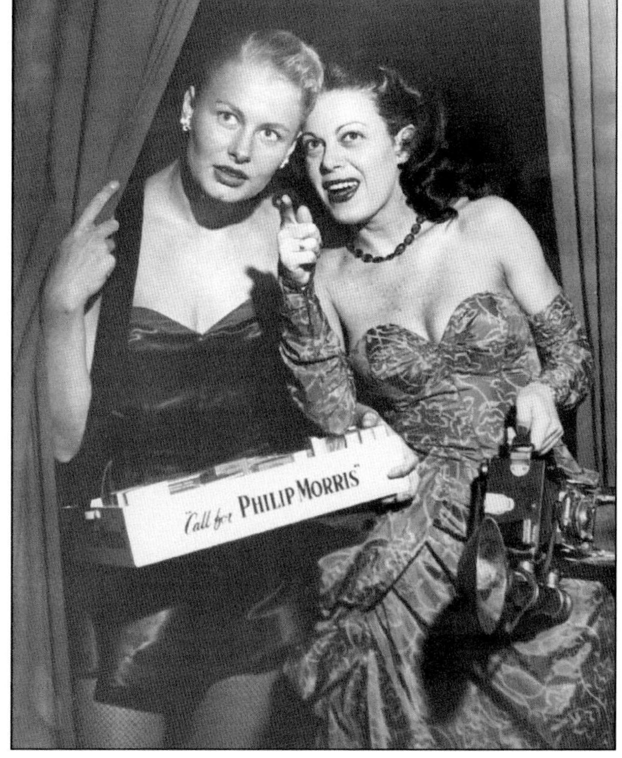

Cigarette girl Margaret "Margie" Barstow and head photographer Nancy Caporal are seen onstage, peering out of the curtain to take a better look at who had just arrived. In mid-August 1951, Hover asked if there was a doctor in the house. Fortunately, there was, as Margie unexpectedly gave birth to their daughter, Rex, in the upstairs lounge at Ciro's. The show continued downstairs.

Ciro's Capers was a monthly magazine published by Ciro's management, which highlighted famous people seen at the club and who they were seen with, actors who received new big contracts, and which studio rented out the Ciro-ette room for lavish parties. Copies were given to actors, local newspaper columnists at the *Hollywood Reporter*, *Variety* magazine staff, studio heads, agents, managers, politicians, those in the public eye, and simply those with a lot of money.

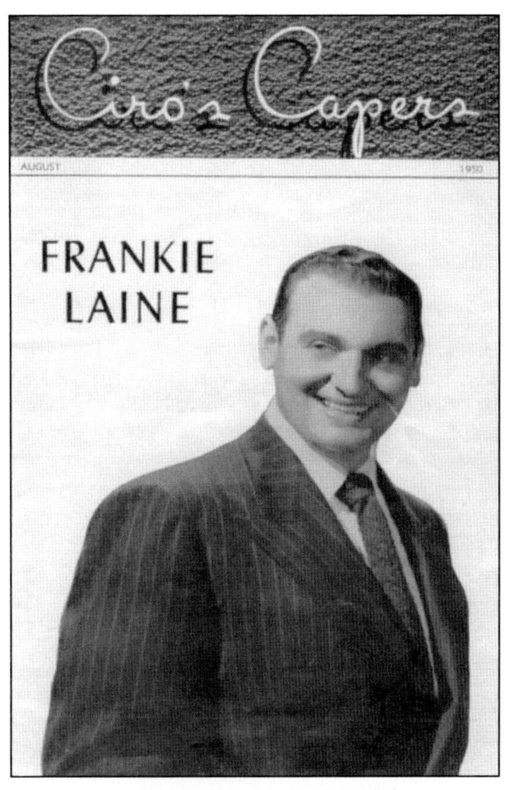

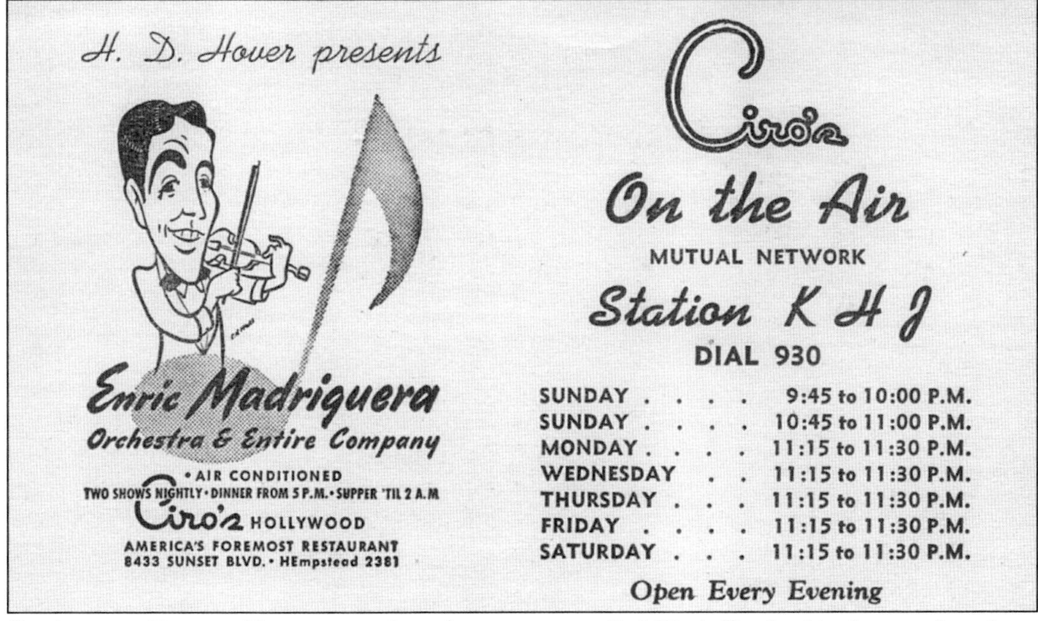

Ciro's owner Herman Hover created a radio program, called *Ciro's On the Air*, that was broadcast from Ciro's lobby and featured orchestra music from the nightclub. Postcards like the one above advertised the radio broadcast. There were eight remote networks broadcast directly from Ciro's each week that were heard over the American Broadcasting Company network. In the Los Angeles area, the outlet was KECA, 790 on the dial.

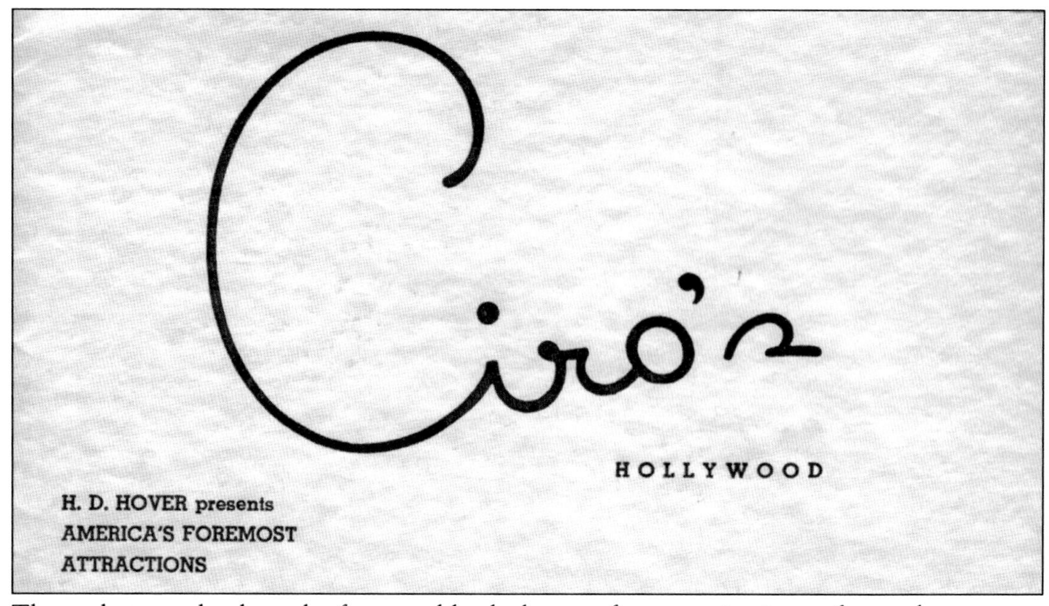

These photographs show the front and back sleeves of a souvenir picture frame that patrons would receive with the purchase of their picture. Friendly head photographer Nancy Caporal took souvenir pictures of customers and kept them on file, as requests for additional copies were often made. The back of the frame included various performers, information on how to purchase additional copies, the date, and the cost for additional pictures to be mailed, which was $1.50 (including tax and mailing fees).

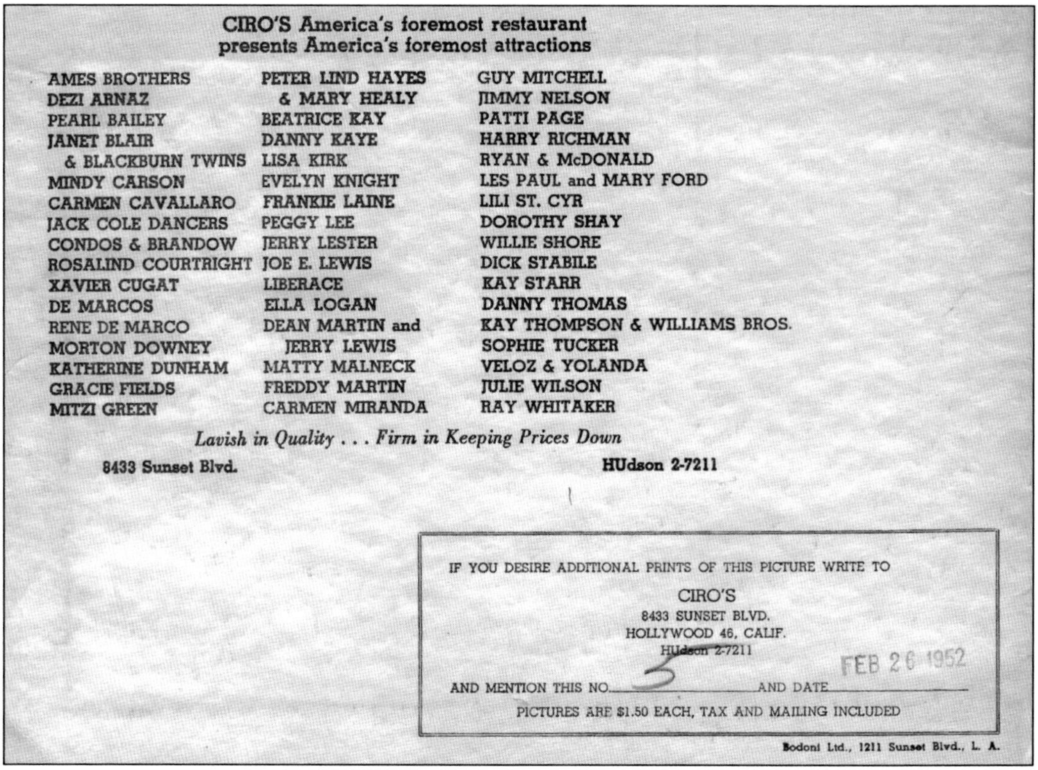

CIRO'S America's foremost restaurant
presents America's foremost attractions

AMES BROTHERS
DEZI ARNAZ
PEARL BAILEY
JANET BLAIR
& BLACKBURN TWINS
MINDY CARSON
CARMEN CAVALLARO
JACK COLE DANCERS
CONDOS & BRANDOW
ROSALIND COURTRIGHT
XAVIER CUGAT
DE MARCOS
RENE DE MARCO
MORTON DOWNEY
KATHERINE DUNHAM
GRACIE FIELDS
MITZI GREEN

PETER LIND HAYES
& MARY HEALY
BEATRICE KAY
DANNY KAYE
LISA KIRK
EVELYN KNIGHT
FRANKIE LAINE
PEGGY LEE
JERRY LESTER
JOE E. LEWIS
LIBERACE
ELLA LOGAN
DEAN MARTIN and
JERRY LEWIS
MATTY MALNECK
FREDDY MARTIN
CARMEN MIRANDA

GUY MITCHELL
JIMMY NELSON
PATTI PAGE
HARRY RICHMAN
RYAN & McDONALD
LES PAUL and MARY FORD
LILI ST. CYR
DOROTHY SHAY
WILLIE SHORE
DICK STABILE
KAY STARR
DANNY THOMAS
KAY THOMPSON & WILLIAMS BROS.
SOPHIE TUCKER
VELOZ & YOLANDA
JULIE WILSON
RAY WHITAKER

Lavish in Quality . . . Firm in Keeping Prices Down

8433 Sunset Blvd. **HUdson 2-7211**

IF YOU DESIRE ADDITIONAL PRINTS OF THIS PICTURE WRITE TO

CIRO'S
8433 SUNSET BLVD.
HOLLYWOOD 46, CALIF.
~~HUdson 2-7211~~

AND MENTION THIS NO. 5 AND DATE FEB 26 1952

PICTURES ARE $1.50 EACH, TAX AND MAILING INCLUDED

Bodoni Ltd., 1211 Sunset Blvd., L. A.

Hover created an atmosphere for his patrons where they could feel comfortable with special orders and special requests. The hatcheck stands at Ciro's had their share of checked animals. Marie Wilson left her little poodle for the attendants to watch, Yvonne De Carlo had the hatcheck girls watch her pet monkey, and one evening, someone checked a pet cheetah. The concession girls courteously looked after these animals while their owners enjoyed the evening.

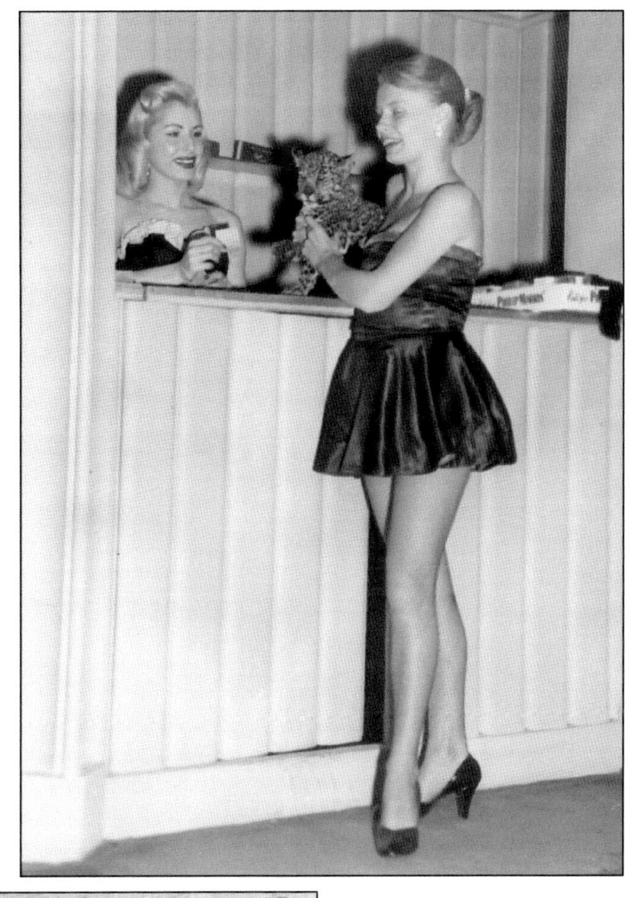

VILLAGE VIGNETTE—A well-heeled playboy at the Kings on New Year's Eve asked the pretty, blonde hatcheck girl, Reggie Drew, what was the largest tip she ever got. She told him 20 bucks…"I want you to remember me as the man who gave you your biggest tip,' 'he said. "Here's $25."…As he walked away, he had an afterthought. "By the way," he asked, "who gave you the $20 tip?" "I'll never forget that," she said. "It was you, sir!"

Although not mentioned by name, the best tipper ever encountered by Reggie Drew, according to this short article, was singer Billy Daniels. One New Year's Eve, Daniels asked Drew what was the best tip she ever received. She replied $20. He proceeded to give her $25. Before leaving, as an afterthought, he asked who gave her the $20 tip. Drew smiled and replied, "It was you, sir!"

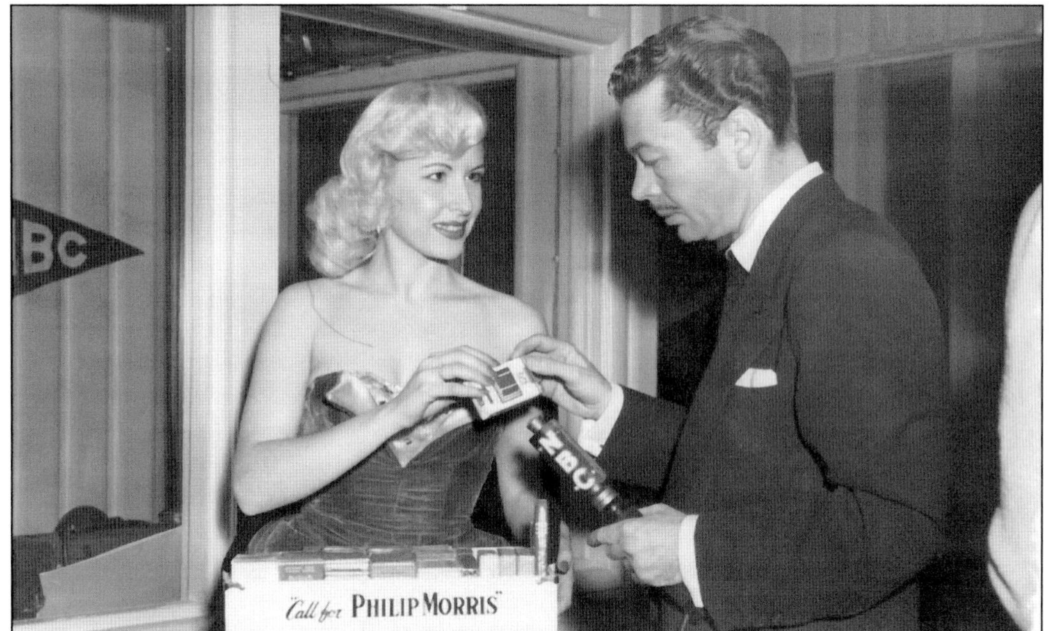

In this image, cigarette girl and concession owner Reggie Drew sells cigarettes to Ciro's NBC television show host Phil Coates. The show aired from upstairs in the Ciro-ette room, which could be also be rented out for sales meetings, cocktail parties, and private dinners. At the suggestion of Peter Lawford and Jackie Cooper, the Ciro-ette room became a club for stars when they preferred to relax in a private atmosphere instead of seeing a show. The room offered a small violin orchestra, a television, and magazines.

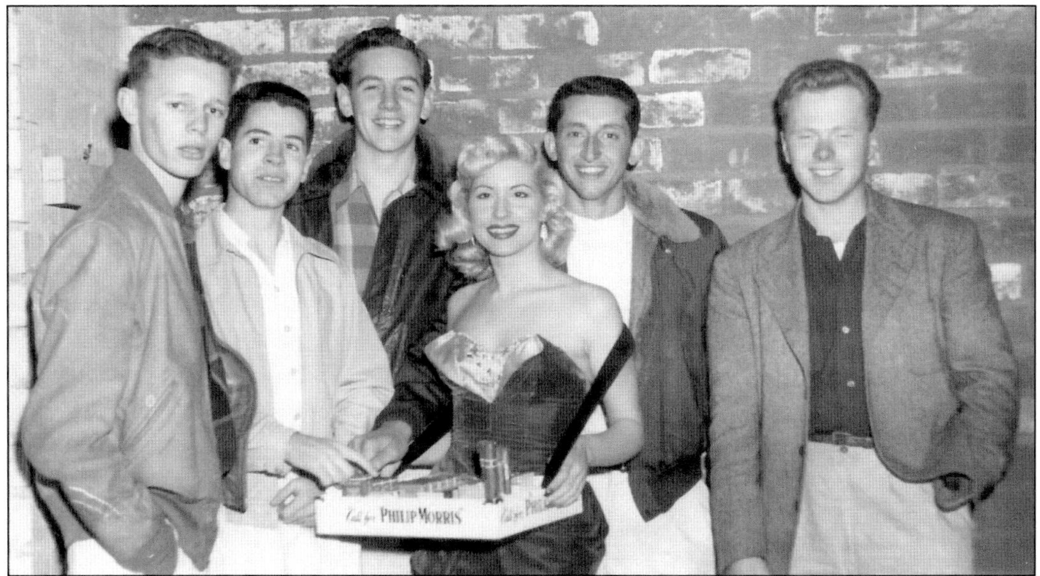

Guests would often want to take pictures with the pretty cigarette girls in their skimpy outfits and fishnet stockings. Sometimes, passes were made at the beautiful staff. Reggie Drew, seen here, was once offered jewels by the shah of Iran and his brother in exchange for sex; she declined the offer. One of the former cigarette girls, Marjorie Steele, married A&P heir Huntington Hartford. Drew was the next cigarette girl hired after Marjorie left.

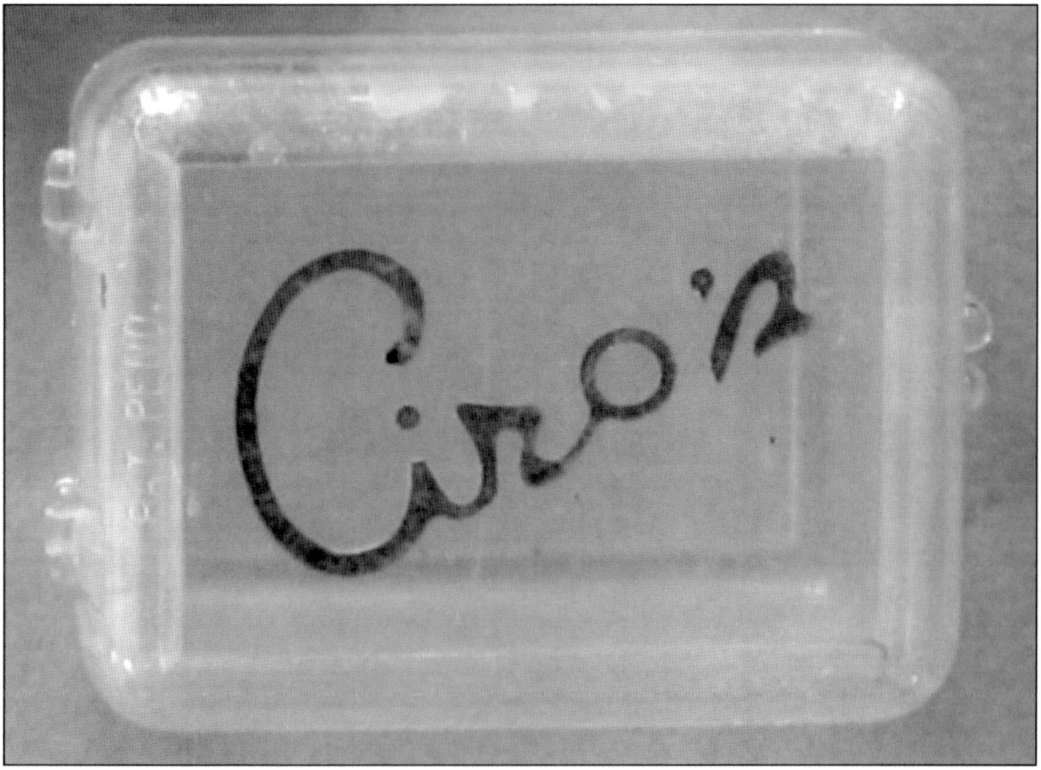

To stay looking their best, patrons could purchase items possibly forgotten, such as lipstick, perfume, or a tie. The photograph above is a sample of a compact case that held lipstick, which was sold at Ciro's. Hover created a mail-order business as a result of requests from fans wishing to purchase Ciro's items. He sold jewelry, perfume, postcards, menus, and more. A box of fancy Ciro's matches, as seen below, cost 50¢ and a bottle of perfume cost $30. Customers could purchase cigarettes for 50¢ and would often give $1, leaving the remaining 50¢ as a tip. The powder room attendant, Hazel Therard, knew CPR and first aid; she was also a dressmaker who kept scissors, needles, and thread handy if someone needed a quick stitch. She had a full case of makeup and perfume for patrons to use. A 25¢ tip was a proper tip at that time.

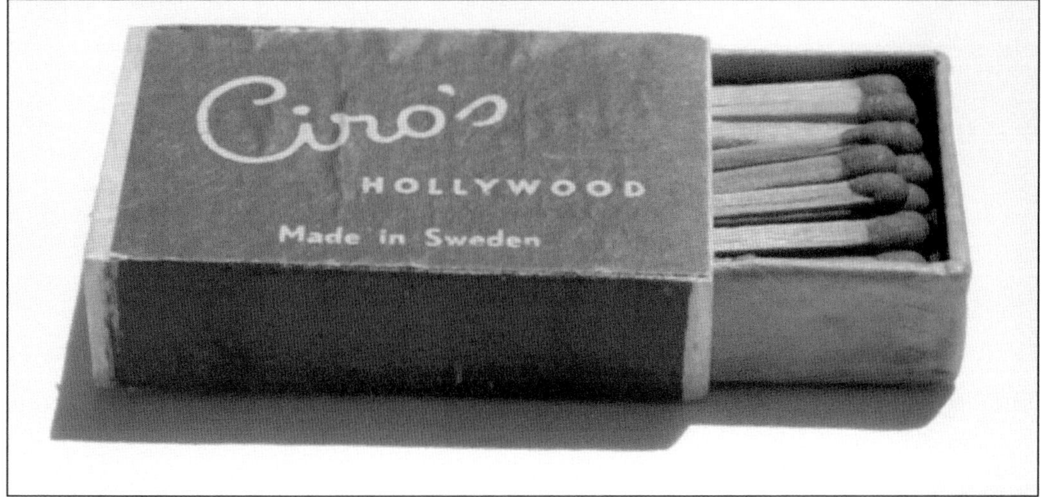

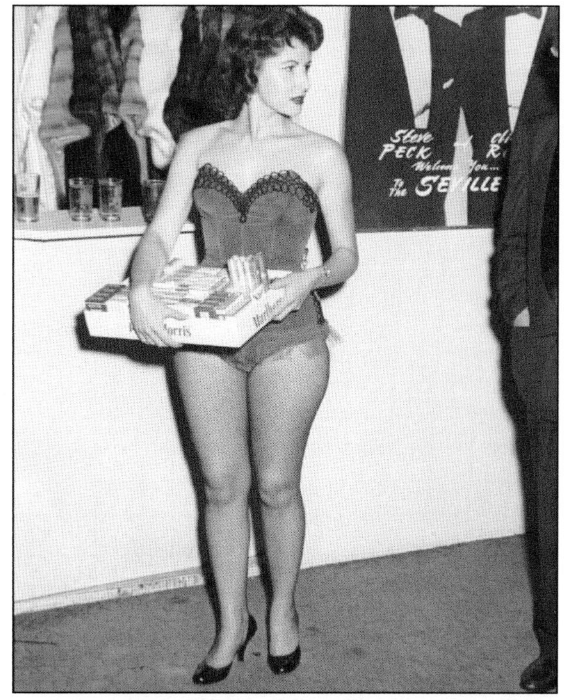

From 1949 to 1957, Reggie Drew worked at Ciro's in various capacities, including as a cigarette girl, concession stand owner, and photographer. She modeled and appeared on television commercials and is the coauthor of this book. The cigarette girls at Ciro's were beautiful and were often models or aspiring actresses. Being a cigarette girl or hatcheck girl was exciting, as these beautiful women were able to interact in proximity to the most well-known, powerful, and famous people in the world. In addition to an hourly wage, tips were the common way members of the staff made a living. Most of the celebrities and other patrons were respectful and did not treat the staff like hired help.

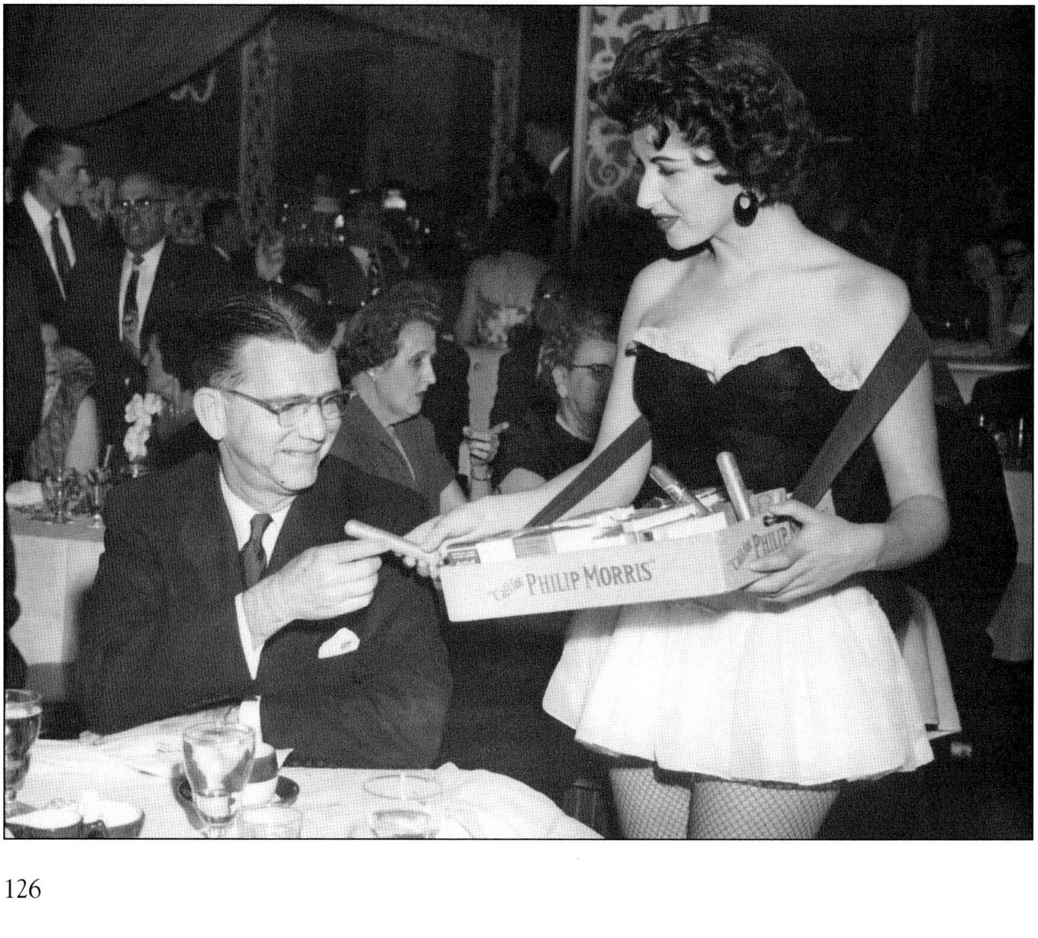

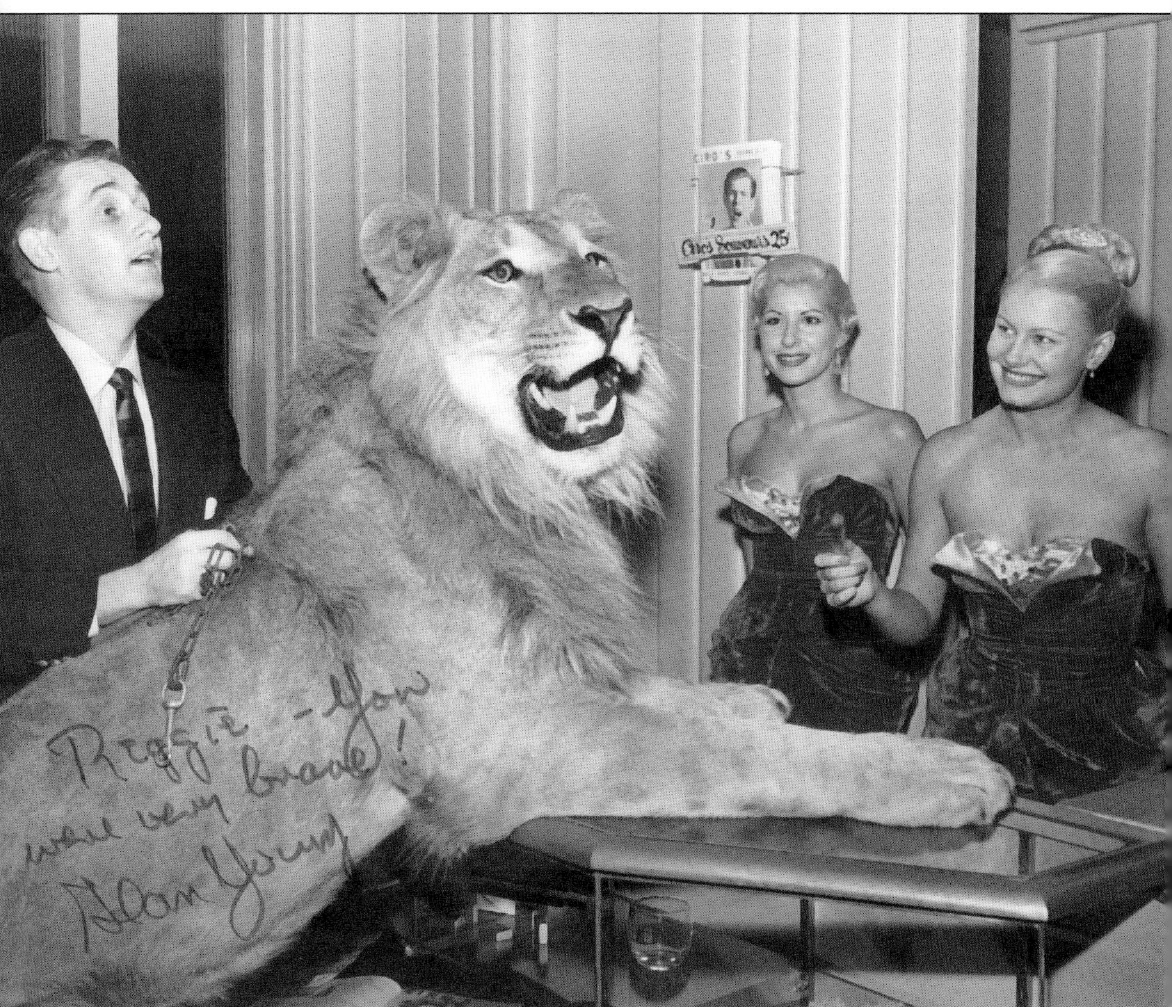

In 1952, as a promotional stunt, RKO Pictures sent actor Alan Young along with Jackie the Lion into Ciro's for dinner and an interview with Paul Coates. RKO was promoting the new movie *Androcles and the Lion*. Pictured here are two brave cigarette girls, Reggie and Marjorie, engaging with the big cat. Young was the star of the movie but is probably best known as Wilbur Post in the hit television series *Mister Ed*.